Music in Jewish Thought

ALSO COMPILED BY
JONATHAN L. FRIEDMANN

*The Value of Sacred Music: An Anthology of
Essential Writings, 1801–1918* (McFarland, 2009)

Music in Jewish Thought

Selected Writings, 1890–1920

COMPILED BY
JONATHAN L. FRIEDMANN

McFarland & Company, Inc., Publishers
Jefferson, North Carolina, and London

LIBRARY OF CONGRESS CATALOGUING-IN-PUBLICATION DATA

Music in Jewish thought : selected writings, 1890–1920 / compiled by Jonathan L. Friedmann.
    p.   cm.
    Includes bibliographical references and index.

    ISBN 978-0-7864-4439-7
    softcover : 50# alkaline paper

    1. Jews — Music — History and criticism.   2. Synagogue music — History and criticism.   3. Jewish musicians.   I. Friedmann, Jonathan L., 1980–
ML3776.M86   2009
780.89'924 — dc22   2009024869

British Library cataloguing data are available

©2009 Jonathan L. Friedmann. All rights reserved

No part of this book may be reproduced or transmitted in any form or by any means, electronic or mechanical, including photocopying or recording, or by any information storage and retrieval system, without permission in writing from the publisher.

Cover images ©2009 Shutterstock

Manufactured in the United States of America

McFarland & Company, Inc., Publishers
  Box 611, Jefferson, North Carolina 28640
    www.mcfarlandpub.com

Table of Contents

Preface 1
Introduction: Sulzer, Idelsohn, and the Revival of Jewish Music 7

PART I: JEWISH SACRED MUSIC 25

  1. The Music of the Jews (1898)
    Sam L. Jacobson 29

  2. Synagogal Music (1906)
    Francis L. Cohen 34

  3. Jewish Music (1917)
    Francis L. Cohen 52

  4. Music of the Synagog (1915)
    Jacob Singer 59

  5. Hebrew Music (1919)
    Lewis M. Isaacs 66

  6. The Music of the Synagogue (1917)
    David de Sola Pool 69

PART II: STUDIES IN JEWISH MUSIC 77

  7. The Music of the Psalms (1894)
    Naphtali Herz Imber 81

  8. The Music of the Ghetto (1898)
    Naphtali Herz Imber 96

  9. Jewish Singers (1910)
    Mendel Silber 106

  10. Composers and Players (1910)
     Mendel Silber 109

11. The Russian Jewish Folk-Song (1917)
    Kurt Schindler 112
12. Hazzanim and Hazzanut (1920)
    Pinchos Jassinowsky 122

PART III: REVIVING JEWISH MUSIC 131

13. Solomon Sulzer: Reminiscences of Vienna (1890)
    Benjamin Franklin Peixotto 135
14. The Life of Salomon Sulzer (1903)
    Adolph Guttman 138
15. Music of the Synagogue (1895)
    Gustav Karpeles 147
16. Secular Currents in the Synagogal Chant in America (1918)
    Joseph Reider 153
17. A Revival of Jewish Music (1919)
    Joseph Reider 163
18. The Future of Jewish Music (1919)
    Jerome H. Bayer 179
19. Music in the Religious School (1919)
    Louis Grossman 186

Sources of Selections 191
Bibliography 193
Index 199

Preface

AT A MEETING OF THE JEWISH Music Forum in 1943, Curt Sachs, Joseph Yasser, and Eric Werner participated in an open discussion about the possibility of defining Jewish music. Taking into consideration issues of religious identity, cultural heritage, ethnic traditions, and Jewish unity, these scholars sought to establish a way of identifying a distinctly Jewish form of musical expression. Yasser, a music theoretician, began by explaining the general purpose of the session: "Scholarly discussions are not held to reach definite and unchangeable conclusions.... Their primary purpose is to stimulate thinking in a certain direction, to broaden horizons, and to remove prejudices and misconceptions."[1] Curt Sachs, a musicologist, approached the topic from a historical perspective, dividing Jewish music into three major epochs — biblical, ghetto (Diaspora), and emancipated (modern) — without attempting to locate common musical elements. Musicologist Eric Werner articulated a functional definition of Jewish music, acknowledging its great diversity and many foreign influences:

> It is irrelevant whether the ancient melodies of the Jews are lost or not. We know that some of them still exist. Yet this preservation has no influence upon the fact that all Jewish groups possess their own songs. It matters little that many folksongs are of non–Jewish origin. This, as we know, is true of all European and much of Asiatic folksong. The decisive fact is that the songs which are generally classified as typically Jewish are being sung at present by Jews exclusively. Even when borrowed, these songs are often reshaped in a really creative way and fused with original elements into an organic reality.[2]

This conversation was stimulated by an emerging recognition that Jewish music is not monolithic. Rather, as one scholar later acknowledged, "the distinctive qualities of Jewish music — such as they may be — remain highly subjective and to an extent elusive."[3] Prior to the mid–twentieth century, the dominant position among scholars was that certain national features were present in all forms of Jewish music, regardless of how geographically or stylistically diverse, and that it was the researcher's job to locate these unifying musical characteristics. Just as Jewish history was viewed as a continuous flow from biblical to modern times, the music of the Jews was thought to contain certain features — subtle or otherwise — that reached back into antiquity.

For nineteenth- and early twentieth-century Jews, coming to terms with life outside of the ghetto and encountering modern scientific and nationalistic views, the idea of a common Jewish musical heritage had obvious appeal. For one thing, it was widely held that all forms of art embodied a "national spirit" which reflected the cultural ideals and distinctiveness of a particular nation. The Germans had German music, the Russians had Russian music, and so the Jews, a nation dispersed among other nations, had unique music of their own. Also, as music during this period became increasingly important in academic and popular circles, with the emergence of musicology, the growing number of composers who incorporated national folk music, and other factors, Jewish scholars recognized the value of presenting Jewish music research to the rest of the world — especially as most Jews sought to uphold their cultural uniqueness even as they participated in general society.

Abraham Z. Idelsohn (1882–1938) was perhaps the most forceful advocate of this position. Idelsohn's areas of expertise were many. He was "a historical musicologist, an ethnomusicologist, a linguist, a scholar of Hebrew poetry, and a liturgist; he was a cantor, a school-master and a composer, a playwright and a storyteller."[4] Almost single handedly, Idelsohn established the field of Jewish music research, publishing his enormous *Thesaurus of Hebrew Oriental Melodies* (1914–1932), still the most comprehensive anthology of Jewish music, and his book *Jewish Music in its Historical Development* (1929), which remains the best historical survey of the various Jewish musical traditions.[5] Like others who have studied Jewish music, Idelsohn was struck by its diversity. He documented the music of hundreds of Jewish communities, noting the differences between them, and the pervasiveness of non–Jewish elements in their songs. Yet, at the same time, he insisted that common, ancient features are found in all Jewish music. As Idelsohn explained:

> Jewish music is the song of Judaism through the lips of the Jew. It is the tonal expression of Jewish life and development over a period of more than two thousand years. To place that song into its ancient and original setting, we must seek the beginning of the people itself. In so doing, we see that just as the Jew, being of Semitic stock, is part of the Oriental world, so Jewish music — coming to life in the Near East — is, generally speaking, of one piece with the music of the Orient. It takes its trend of development through the Semitic race, and retains its

Semitic-Oriental characteristics in spite of non–Semitic — Altaic and European — influences.[6]

While this goal to isolate a common layer in the world's Jewish music can now be viewed as naïve or even futile, Idelsohn's research reflected a general movement in nineteenth- and early twentieth-century Jewish studies, which sought to establish the historical and cultural continuity of the Jewish people. And, while Idelsohn's overzealous attempts in this regard are well known, he was not the only one to apply a nationalistic approach to Jewish music research.

Indeed, there were several studies on Jewish music published *before* Idelsohn established the field of Jewish musicology. Ranging from brief historical surveys and biographies to case studies and critiques of synagogue song, these writings, though lacking for the most part Idelsohn's sophistication and comparative expertise, constitute the first efforts in the historical-scientific study of Jewish music. The essays collected in this book were culled from these formative studies. More specifically, they were published between the death of cantor-composer Salomon Sulzer in 1890 and Idelsohn's ascension as the world's foremost scholar of Jewish music in the early 1920s.[7]

Sulzer was a Viennese cantor-composer who worked to purify the music of the synagogue, both by cleansing foreign accretions and popular styles from synagogue chant and by adding Western harmony and technique to the music of the service. He was the first figure to successfully introduce modern musical practices into synagogue worship, and his efforts to revive and present traditional melodies and modes brought dignity and elegance to a service long considered disorderly and unsophisticated by Christian observers and modernizing Jews alike. Sulzer aimed to elevate the status of Jewish music as an art form and to hold it up as a symbol of national pride. And, just as Idelsohn's work combined loyalty to the Jewish people with modern methods of musical research, Sulzer's stated goal was to restore grandeur and beauty to Jewish sacred music and to introduce modern Western aesthetics into the synagogues of Europe. As Sulzer wrote, "Jewish liturgy must satisfy the musical demands while remaining Jewish; and it should not be necessary to sacrifice the Jewish characteristics to artistic forms."[8]

The essays in this book express similarly this dual goal of preserving Jewish culture and applying modern methods to the evaluation of Jewish music and its history. These writings are representative of the intellectual ethos of their time, understanding Jewish music as an essentially unified phenomenon — despite its regional and historical diversity — and seeking to uncover the inherent "spirit" contained in all Jewish music. In this way, they embody the ultimate concern of both Sulzer and Idelsohn: to bring up to date the study and performance of Jewish music, while at the same time preserving elements thought to be ancient and uniquely Jewish.

Over the years, these writings have received little attention from scholars of Jewish music. This is, of course, not surprising given the fact that they were originally published between the celebrated careers of the Sulzer and Idelsohn, both of whom are considered "fathers" of their fields — Sulzer of modern synagogue music and Idelsohn of Jewish musicology. Yet, it will benefit present-day readers to review these early studies of Jewish music, if only to gain a more complete understanding of the worldview from which the works of Sulzer and Idelsohn emerged.

This does not, however, mean to suggest that these writings are without any value of their own. On the contrary, this book affords contemporary readers an opportunity to discover in these essays the many ideas and viewpoints still vital for the deeper understanding of Jewish music. Moreover, they should be appreciated as important studies in the development of Jewish music research, as well as the broader discipline of Jewish cultural studies. Written by eminent rabbis, poets, musicians, literary critics and biblical scholars, they appraise justly the significance of music in Jewish life and provide insight into the long and fruitful relationship of music and prayer in Jewish worship.

I am grateful to the libraries of Stanford University, Harvard University, the University of Michigan, and the University of California, Los Angeles, for preserving and making available these important writings. I would also like to thank cantor William Sharlin for providing me with additional material essential for this book. Without his guidance, inspiration, and friendship, this endeavor would not have been possible.

Notes

1. From the recorded report of the April 12, 1943, meeting of the Jewish Music Forum, quoted in Irene Heskes, *Passport to Jewish Music: Its History, Traditions, and Culture* (New York: Tara, 1994), pp. 25–26.
2. Ibid., p. 26.
3. Ibid., p. 25.
4. Eliyahu Schleifer, "Idelsohn's Scholarly and Literary Publications: An Annotated Bibliography," in *The Abraham Zvi Idelsohn Memorial Volume*, eds. Israel Adler, Bathja Bayer, and Eliyahu Schleifer (Jerusalem: Magnes, 1986), p. 59.
5. There have been, however, many calls for an updated text. See, for instance, Albert Weisser, "The Need for a New History of Jewish Music: A Preliminary Study," *Journal of Synagogue Music*, vol. 2, no. 2 (1969): 3–14.

6. Abraham Z. Idelsohn, *Jewish Music in Its Historical Development* (New York: Holt, Rinehart, and Winston, 1929), p. 24.

7. Idelsohn's musicological career began in Palestine, where he organized the Institute of Jewish Music in 1910 and the Jewish Music School in 1919. In 1921, he traveled to Europe to make his musical research known, and in 1924 became professor of music and liturgy at the Hebrew Union College in Cincinnati.

8. Salomon Sulzer, *Denkschrift* (Vienna, 1876).

Introduction: Sulzer, Idelsohn, and the Revival of Jewish Music

By THE END OF THE NINETEENTH CENTURY, Jewish emancipation had spread across most of Europe. Discriminatory laws were abolished, equal rights granted, and restrictive ghetto walls removed, allowing Jews, for the first time since the middle ages, to take part freely in European society. Many emancipated Jews were drawn to political and social movements and pledged their loyalty to the Enlightenment ideals of reason and progress. Soon, the authority of the rabbis, who served as civil judges in ghetto communities, was replaced by the rule of national governments, and a Jewish population that had, as a result of segregation and internal stability, been essentially homogenous was faced with three distinct possibilities: assimilation, retrenchment, or modernization.

The first option, assimilation, meant the abandonment of one's Jewish identity and a calculated effort to blend into gentile culture. Retrenchment, on the other hand, entailed a rejection of general society and a forceful clinging to the ways of the past. Reform Judaism emerged from the third option, modernization, as it sought to refashion the Jewish religion in accordance with the times — like Christianity had done — cleansing it of superstition and outmoded elements. Rather than abandoning Jewish affiliation completely, or preserving steadfastly the religion of the ghetto, reformers proposed a modified Judaism that would be acceptable to modern Jews and their Christian neighbors.

Perhaps most important to Christian onlookers were Reform changes to the synagogue service. Careful to maintain the "essence" of Jewish liturgical practice, while at the same time molding religious rituals to reflect European norms, early nineteenth-century German reformers created a synagogue experience guided by a self-conscious desire to achieve "beauty and relevance."[1] In accordance with the ideals of modernity and Western aesthetics, prayers deemed obsolete were expunged from the liturgy, vernacular prayers were added, weekly sermons were instituted, and services were accompanied by choral and organ music.

Outside of the synagogue, *Wissenschaft des Judentums*, the Science of Judaism, became a dominant approach of Jewish scholars. Like the Reform movement, the Science of Judaism emerged as a way to modernize Jewish scholarship with the tools of the time, particularly in the area of textual criticism, while still upholding an emotional tie to Jewish heritage.[2] Almost without exception, scholars of this movement were themselves Jews, and though they applied modern research methods to the study of Judaism, they were nevertheless preoccupied — consciously or not — with upholding a sense of Judaic self-recognition. As a result, the Science of Judaism was, to a great extent, motivated by a threefold agenda: Jewish intellectual renascence, cultural creativity, and spiritual revival.[3]

The closely allied movements of Jewish Reform and the Science of Judaism produced, among other things, an elevated interest in Jewish music. In the Reform synagogue of Vienna, Salomon Sulzer (1804–1890), celebrated cantor and composer, sifted through existing synagogue music, isolating what he believed to be authentic and organic Jewish material from illegitimate and "tasteless" embellishments, and combined time-honored Ashkenazi melodies and modes with the rules and conventions of Western harmony. In the realm of academia, Abraham Z. Idelsohn (1882–1938) sought to demonstrate, through recordings, transcriptions, and analysis, that Jewish folk music worldwide, while exhibiting great diversity, shared a common musical foundation reaching to ancient times.[4] Like Sulzer, Idelsohn was determined to discover and present "purified" Jewish music — music that reflected a unified Jewish character.

For their efforts, Sulzer and Idelsohn are considered "fathers" of their fields: Sulzer of modern synagogue music, and Idelsohn of Jewish music research. And, like most founders of intellectual and artistic movements, few of their convictions have evaded criticism. This is particularly true as both men were caught up in the belief of their time, that through the modern study of Judaism, universal Jewish characteristics would be revealed, thereby giving Jews a distinct cultural identity, even as they shed the trappings of traditional life and entered the general culture as full citizens. This quest for the universal "Jewish Spirit," though unrealistic in light of the great geographic and cultural diversity of the Jews, was especially pronounced in the area of Jewish music, which had been (and still is) Judaism's primary mode of artistic expression. Still, it can be argued that, without this desire to find what is truly Jewish in Jewish music — a mission spurred on by the *Haskalah* (Jewish Enlightenment) and all but abandoned in present-day research of Jewish music — neither Sulzer nor Idelsohn would have engaged in their groundbreaking endeavors, and both the experience of synagogue song and our understanding of Jewish music would have suffered immeasurably.

Without doubt, Sulzer and Idelsohn remain pivotal figures in modern Jewish history. For students of Jewish music, it is virtually impossible to avoid at least mention of their work and influence. Less well known, however, are the writings on Jewish music produced between Sulzer's death in 1890 and Idelsohn's rise to international prominence in the early 1920s. These transitional studies, filled with the romance and idealism of their age, are representative of the intellectual context from which Idelsohn's studies developed. And, inasmuch as Idelsohn is widely acknowledged as the founder of the field, these writings — though for the most part lacking Idelsohn's comparative and analytical expertise — should be viewed as early efforts in the critical study of Jewish music. These essays were stimulated and nourished by the *Haskalah*, and remain intrinsically valuable — if largely outdated — contributions to the development of the field of Jewish musicology.

At the same time, an intellectual context for the chapters that follow may be gleaned from a more thorough review of the careers of Sulzer and Idelsohn. It is thus the purpose of this introduction to provide further insight into the lives and significance of Sulzer and Idelsohn, and, in so doing, establish a historical lens through which to read this anthology.

Salomon Sulzer

Joseph Manizer, a German-born music critic, wrote glowingly of Salomon Sulzer's musical service: "To whatever religion one may happen to belong, I declare that it is impossible to bear witness without emotion, and even not to be actually edified by the conduct of the service which is so simple, so noble, so elevated, and purified from all vain display by a reform in accordance with the times in which we live."[5] Similarly moved by Sulzer's sacred music, Franz Liszt overcame his own anti–Semitism to write: "Rarely have we been so deeply stirred, so affected that our own spirit rendered unresistingly to sympathy and devotion as on that evening when, in the light of a thousand candles like stars on a far horizon, a strange chorus of muffled, hollow voices resounded about us."[6]

Sulzer's appeal to non–Jewish audiences was due in large part to his command of European art music and exquisite vocal abilities. Among other things, Sulzer was a famous interpreter of Franz Schubert, and moved the composer deeply when he sang his *Lied* "Der Wanderer."[7] In gratitude, Schubert contributed a setting of Psalm 92 to the first edition of Sulzer's landmark collection of synagogue song, *Schir Zion* (1839).

Prior to the nineteenth century, cantors were rarely schooled in classical singing, music theory, or choral conducting, and even the ability to read music was not a prerequisite for the job. The majority of cantors learned their craft by attending synagogue services, or by studying with a senior cantor (typically a father or uncle).[8] Sulzer, however, embodied the post–Emancipation preference for attaining both Judaic and worldly knowledge. He engaged in general music studies in Germany and Vienna, studying under Joseph Fischhoff, J. Weigl, and Ignaz von Seyfried. In 1826, he began his forty-year career as cantor of Vienna's Seitenstettengasse Temple, where he became, in the words of cantor William Sharlin, "the singular prime mover of musical modernization who single-handedly, out of the sheer power of his religious personality, transformed the chaotic musical taste of a flourishing reform process into a singular entity — inspired by the vision and beauty of holiness in which tradition, art, and the spirit came together."[9]

Following his contemporaries in other Jewish fields, who wished above all to loosen the shackles that ghetto life had clamped on Jewish practice and ideology, Sulzer introduced a musical service that was both proudly Jewish and thoroughly Western. It was in this way, however, that he departed from the approach of the early radical reformers, who had stripped the synagogue service of virtually all things overtly traditional, including musical norms. Sulzer had profound reverence for Jewish musical tradition, and did not wish to rid the synagogue of Jewish elements. Rather, he worked to purge the service of the unnecessary and, he argued, spiritually damaging influences of popular tunes and musical styles of the day, while at the same time incorporating what he saw as the aesthetic improvements of the gentile world, such as choral music, Western harmony, and general orderliness. As Sulzer wrote, "I made it my duty to give maximal consideration to those tunes which have come down from antiquity and to restore their archaic flavor in its original purity, cleansed from later flourishes of dubious and tasteless character."[10]

With this balanced approach, Sulzer contrasted in particular with Israel Jacobson (1768–1828), a wealthy Jewish merchant who pioneered the reformation of synagogue ritual. In 1801, Jacobson established the first Reform Temple in Europe, on the campus of a boys' school in Seesen, Germany. Anxious to present Judaism in a positive light, and equally eager to let go of identifiably Jewish religious elements, Jacobson provided the Temple with a bell, which, following Christian practice, announced the time of prayer. He likewise introduced German hymns set to the music of Christian chorales, and abolished the traditional chanting of the Bible and liturgy. Instead, Jacobson read prayers and Scripture without melodic chant, mirroring the practice of Protestant churches, and eliminated the position of the cantor. He also gave a weekly sermon, wore a clerical gown, and instituted the confirmation of girls and boys — all practices borrowed from Christian Europe.[11]

Jacobson's model of radical Reform was adopted in many European synagogues. As a result, there was widespread abrogation of traditional liturgical chant, and a marked preference for formal hymns, typically written by Christian composers in the German church style. It should be noted, however, that while the encroachment of church music into the synagogue was guided in part by rabbis endeavoring to create a Europeanized Jewish identity, this phenomenon was also spurred on by Jewish youth who, to a great extent, considered Christian-style worship an attractive alternative to "outmoded" Jewish rituals. In large numbers, young Jews drifted away from their heritage, and became increasingly immersed in the larger Christian environment. As a result, rabbis considered it good policy to embrace Christian musical forms, along with other customs of church worship, in order to bring these young men and women back into the synagogue.[12]

But, as Idelsohn wrote, "Judaism in Germany was too strong, too deep-rooted, Jewish sentiment too full of vitality and of desires for life, the Semitic-Oriental elements in the Jew still too virile to succumb to the ultra-reform movement, to submit to the Europeanization and Germanization of the Jewish soul."[13] Before long, radical Reform aroused a profound desire for moderation in Germany and elsewhere in Europe. After all, though it was widely believed that aspects of Judaism were no longer applicable in modern times, it was also maintained that Judaism was a constantly evolving religion, and that its lasting truths could be dressed up in the garb of modernity without losing completely their Jewish essence.

Sulzer championed this position. In fact, it was his influence that led Isaac Noah Mannheimer (1793–1865), preacher and leader of Vienna's Jewish community, to initiate a moderate reform.[14] Along with Sulzer, Mannheimer, who began as a radical reformer, noticed the divisive effect rapid and unhindered ritual changes were having on his community. Together, these men established a model of Judaism known as the "Vienna Rite," which, in contrast to radical Reform theology and practice, retained prayers for Zion and Jerusalem, insisted upon Hebrew as the language of prayer, did not incorporate the organ, and upheld the ritual and cultural value of circumcision. In 1940, Mannheimer introduced his "unity prayerbook," which made concessions to both the orthodox and liberal parties, and Sulzer published the first volume of his *Schir Zion*,[15] intended to restore traditional melodies and a dignified character to a service he found "occupied with disorderliness."[16] With this new model, Sulzer and Mannheimer brought relative stability to Jewish life in Vienna and other European cities. As musicologist Eric Werner explained in his tribute, "Salomon Sulzer, Statesman and Pioneer":

> Aside from his great and generally known merits as singer and composer, Sulzer rendered invaluable service to the internal unification of the Jews of the Austro-Hungarian empire. After the emancipation of the Jews in the North and West of Europe, a factionalism had arisen in these regions which split the internal Jewish unity. It was the object of Rabbi Isaac Noah Mannheimer of Vienna to prevent such schisms in the community under his jurisdiction and thereby to constitute an example.... He needed the binding force of a synagogue-music which would pursue the same objective with similar methods. Sulzer was the man to do this job.[17]

Most significantly from a musical standpoint, Sulzer recognized the role *nusach ha-tefillah* (traditional modal chant) played in synagogue life, and respected the cultural value of time-honored liturgical melodies. As a result, the cantor's passages in his choral works remained largely faithful to the traditional Ashkenazi modes, though they were cleansed of operatic excesses that characterized the cantorial practice of the eighteenth century.[18] At the same time, Sulzer understood the spiritual efficacy of more "evolved" Western music, and, drawing upon both his religious and modern musical education, composed music that combined Jewish musical heritage with advanced choral technique. In this way, Suzler can be viewed as both a preserver and innovator. As Sulzer himself explained:

> [In] the first place, it behooves us to fight the opinion that the regeneration of the service can be materialized only by an entire break with the past, by abolishing all traditional and inherited, historically-evolved liturgy. To limit the entire service to a German hymn before and after the sermon, to give a certificate of divorce to tradition, was the intention of those who instigated the ill-fated reform in Hamburg and Berlin.... But to me it appeared that the confusion of the Synagogue service resulted from the need of only a restoration which should remain on historical ground; and that we might find out the original noble forms to which

we should anchor, developing them in artistic style. The old generation should recognize the familiar and endeared element, while the young generation should be educated to the appreciation of it. Jewish liturgy must satisfy the musical demands while remaining Jewish; and it should not be necessary to sacrifice the Jewish characteristics to artistic forms. The principle was "to unite the heart of the fathers with that of the children, and to win ambitious youth for the sentiments of the old generation."[19]

With this, Sulzer established order and decorum in the music of divine service, and created a musical style that exemplified the aims of nineteenth-century Jewish modernists. Nevertheless, while Sulzer's primary aim was to preserve traditional Jewish music and dress it in modern harmony, many listeners — both past and present — have labeled his compositions too much like Beethoven or Schubert. And, according to one scholar, many congregants who were moved by Sulzer's rich and sweet voice admitted that his music seemed "strange to their ears" and was "totally linked to the style of the church."[20]

To be sure, Sulzer did not object to the Protestant style. After all, his *Schir Zion* includes works by such Christian composers as Seyfried, Schubert, and Fischhoff; and, as synagogue composer Abraham W. Binder (1895–1966) noted regarding Sulzer's own music, "At times it was Jewish, and at times Protestant."[21] Viewed categorically, the first volume of *Schir Zion* is comprised of eighty-six works by Sulzer, thirty-six preexistent melodies arranged by Sulzer, and thirty-seven works by other composers.[22] This combination of original and "renovated" traditional melodies, along with compositions by prominent non–Jewish composers, suggests that Sulzer was equally comfortable with his Jewish and European identities.

This dual persona did not, however, always find successful musical expression. Sulzer's primary musical weakness, according to Binder, was his dependency on Western harmonization, even when his compositions were based on the synagogue modes. When confronted with a *melos* that was Eastern in character, Sulzer tried to harmonize it with the Western tonic-dominant system, and thus "destroyed the character of the piece."[23] This is apparent, for instance, in his setting of *Avinu Malkenu* (*Schir Zion*, vol. 2, #462). Likewise, Sulzer sometimes changed the *nusach* (traditional modal chant) from the characteristically Jewish minor to major, a stylistic choice reflecting the preference of his day. "The purpose of the early Reform," Binder wrote, "was to eliminate Oriental *melos* and everything that sounded 'too Jewish.' The soul of the synagogue went out with this change. It was for this reason that people who know the musical tradition of the synagogue have called [Sulzer's] music 'un–Jewish.'"[24]

Moreover, while Sulzer wrote many exquisite cantorial recitatives, utilizing "purified" Jewish melodies and motifs, his choral responses were often set in a purely Western style, creating an incongruous effect. In fact, the Protestant style dominates the majority Sulzer's choral pieces, making his goal to restore the "archaic flavor" and "original purity" of Jewish music seem limited to his solo passages. Furthermore, it has been revealed that, in a memorandum written in 1876, Sulzer recommended the introduction of an organ, the use of German hymns, and the abolition of biblical cantillation in the service, liturgical changes that followed those of the radical German reformers, but were in opposition to the moderate reform he introduced with Mannheimer decades earlier. For this reason, it has been argued, "Sulzer offered his community only a compromise between his own musical compositions and prevailing practice."[25]

Still, it is important to view Sulzer's musical agenda in its proper historical context. As Werner asked those quick to dismiss Sulzer's music, "Was not Spinoza influenced by Descartes, Maimonides by the Arabic philosophers, Heine by Goethe? Even our very tradition-minded composers today [the 1950s], do they reflect the style of gentile masters such as Bartok or Hindemith?"[26] Werner held Sulzer up as an example for all synagogue composers, writing that he "mastered the musical technique of his time, but he also applied this very technique to our tradition.... Moreover, his was a sincere reverence for our tradition, provided it was genuine. He began the enormous process of sifting the false from the legitimate, the cheap imitation from the organically grown original. This is still the main task of the responsible Jewish musician."[27]

Binder, too, though critical of many of Sulzer's compositional choices, was careful to view him as a man of his time: "Whatever our criticism of Salomon Sulzer may be today, he must be viewed historically. He was the product of a particular period which demanded change, and he gave it his imprint. It took courage and talent to accomplish the changes he instituted." And, much like Werner, Binder viewed Sulzer as a role model for other synagogue musicians. "He left to cantors of all times an example to emulate. His complete dedication to his profession, the sanctity and dignity which he brought to it, made everyone in and out of the synagogue respect him and his office."[28]

For many present-day cantors, Sulzer does remain a powerful symbol of the profession. However, as Werner observed in 1954—150 years after Sulzer's birth—while most American cantors profess to revere Sulzer, "Only a few rather mediocre choral compositions of his are regularly sung in all congregations."[29] Today, Sulzer's music has drifted even further into obscurity. Most American synagogues have adopted congregational singing, limiting the use of a choir to the High Holy Days, and the only pieces by Sulzer still used regularly are those easily sung by the congregation. Almost without exception, these functional short pieces are waltzes (for example, *Sh'ma Yisrael, Ki Mitziyon, Hodo Al Eretz*), displaying the influence of Johann Strauss, who lived in Vienna at the same time as Sulzer, and almost all of them function as accompaniment to choreographic departures during the service, such as the removal of the Torah from the ark. Reflecting on the continued use of these selections, Sharlin wrote, "It is of considerable irony that all of these melodies (modified in part) though of surely lesser musical import for Sulzer, have been kept alive until today in almost all branches of our synagogues, while the massive, more 'serious' substance of his liturgical works are rarely to be heard."[30]

Abraham Z. Idelsohn

Latvian-born musicologist Abraham Z. Idelsohn (1882–1938) championed the nineteenth-century conviction that all poetry and music embodies a pure and inherent national spirit. Factors such as acculturation and sociological shifts, crucial to the development of all tradition and folklore, are virtually absent from Idelsohn's work, and his conception of Jewish history was similarly naïve. Indeed, despite his fruitful encounters with various Jewish communities from around the world, his understanding of Judaism remained monolithic and non-pluralistic — a fact that suggests his ideological convictions were perhaps stronger than his ethnographic skills. Yet, it was this quest for the essential spirit of Jewish music that drove Idelsohn to collect his ten-volume *Thesaurus of Hebrew Oriental Melodies* (1914–1933), a monumental work that, in Werner's appraisal, "constitutes an almost comprehensive collection of Jewish folklore, reasonably — not systematically — ordered, fairly reliably transcribed, and, at least in part, well analyzed and interpreted."[31]

Much like Sulzer, Idelsohn maintained that there are uniquely Jewish qualities to be found in the music of the Jews; but while Sulzer's mission to purify Jewish music of inorganic intrusions was limited to Ashkenazi synagogue song, Idelsohn sought to uncover unifying elements contained in the music of all Jewish communities, no matter how disparate. Thus, for instance, even as Idelsohn reported that the roughly three hundred synagogues he visited in Jerusalem "were conducted according to the customs of the respective countries, and their traditional song varied greatly from one another," he argued that this musical diversity was due mainly to the encroachment of non–Jewish music, and that "the Jewish elements are found in all traditions, and only these are of interest to the scholars."[32]

In this way, Idelsohn embodies what ethnomusicologist Kay Kaufman Shelemay calls the "central paradox" in the understanding of Jewish music. "While Idelsohn perceived and acknowledged diversity as the reality in Jewish music practice," Shelemay writes, "he spent his entire career seeking to document commonalities that he believed existed within divergent musical traditions."[33] Unable to distance himself from an emotional attachment to Jewish culture and history, Idelsohn, like most Jewish scholars trained in the nineteenth-century Science of Judaism, allowed his romantic vision of the Jewish world to color his analysis of its musical output. Importantly, too, while Idelsohn's nostalgic outlook informed his high opinion of Jewish folksong, it also fueled his criticism of Jewish-born composers who contributed to the larger musical world, such as Mendelssohn, Mahler, and Schoenberg. As Idelsohn wrote: "The Jewish song is a folk art, created by the people. It has no art song, and no individual composers. Composers of Jewish origin have in their creations nothing of Jewish spirit; they are renegades or assimilants, and detest all Jewish cultural values. The few composers who remained with the fold have mostly corrupted the Jewish tradition with their attempts to modernize it, and have added very little toward genuine Jewish song."[34]

Idelsohn began his study of Jewish music in Libau, Latvia, where he sang as a chorister for the local cantor, Abraham Mordecai Rabinowitz, and became acquainted with the music of European synagogue and classical composers. Idelsohn continued his general music education at the Stern Conservatory in Berlin and the Leipzig Academy, and in 1903 accepted a position as cantor and *shokhet* (ritual slaughterer) in Regensburg, Bavaria. The following year he moved to Johannesburg, South Africa, where he served as cantor, and in 1906 settled in Jerusalem, where he was engaged as cantor and music teacher at the Hebrew Teachers Seminary. "About this time," Idelsohn explained, "the idea dawned upon me to devote my strength to the research of the Jewish song. This idea ruled my life to such an extent, that I could find no rest."[35]

Idelsohn was immediately and profoundly struck by the diversity of the Jewish communities living in Palestine, and embarked on an ambitious project to record their musical traditions. To this end, he was awarded a research grant from the Academy of Science in Vienna, and in 1914 published the first volume of his *Thesaurus of Hebrew Oriental Melodies*, focusing on the

Yemenite community in Palestine. Idelsohn was especially interested in this community, believing that, because of its historical seclusion, Yemenite Jewry preserved linguistic and musical traditions that were relatively uninterrupted by outside influences and internal change. Over the next twenty years, this project expanded to include the music of Babylonian, Persian, Bukharian, Oriental Sephardic, Moroccan, German, Eastern European, and Hassidic Jewish communities in Palestine and the Diaspora.

The 1920s saw Idelsohn rise to international notoriety. In 1921, he traveled to Europe to present his musical research, and the following year gave lectures in the United States. In 1924, he was invited to catalogue the Eduard Birnbaum collection at the Hebrew Union College in Cincinnati. Like Ideslohn, cantor Birnbaum (1855–1920) combined scholastic inclinations with exceptional musical ability, and dedicated his life to both liturgical service and musicological endeavors. Over the course of forty-five years, Birnbaum accumulated a vast collection of eighteenth and nineteenth-century European synagogue music, including copies he made from Sulzer's handwritten manuscripts, all of which was secured by the Hebrew Union College in 1923.[36]

It is worth mentioning that, as a young man, Idelsohn went to Koenigsberg to meet cantor Birnbaum; but, as Idelsohn later wrote, their brief relationship was less than fruitful: "At the time I knew nothing of Birnbaum's work, all I knew was that he was the successor to the famous Weintraub. I found him steeped in German music, his voice insignificant, his *hazzanut* (cantorial art) unappealing and not Jewish. I visited him only a few times; he never instructed me and never showed me his collecton."[37] It was only after working with the collection in Cincinnati that Idelsohn gained tremendous respect for Birnbaum. In a long out-of-print essay, "Song and Singers of the Synagogue in the Eighteenth Century," Idelsohn professed his admiration for Birnbaum's unprecedented accomplishments as scholar and collector, and expounded upon the significance of his collection. The insights this essay reveals, both into Birnbaum's efforts and Idelsohn's passionate interest in Jewish music research, deserve quoting at length:

> They (the singers and cantors) share the same lot as most of the Jewish poets of the Synagogue, in regard to the data of their life-record; but, while the poets frequently incorporated their names in acrostics, the musicians had no such tool, and therefore their names were forgotten while their songs delighted the souls of thousands and thousands. It is only sheer accident that their creations were preserved in writing and (still more extraordinary!) in their own handwriting. There remains yet to be acquired a considerable quantity of fairly rich material in the valuable manuscripts of those Jewish singers and musicians who first started using European means to express their musical thoughts.

Indeed it demanded great energy and patience and endurance and devotion on the part of that person who would gather those remainders of yellow music sheets of the eighteenth century, poorly written, scattered throughout the world in obscure corners, with the rubbish of dusty archives of the old communities in Central Europe, or in the hands of the descendents of old *hazzanic* families who had not the slightest idea of their historical value. And such a person — indeed a personality — the Synagogue song found in the late Eduard Birnbaum (1855–1920), cantor of Koenigsberg Germany — a man who devoted forty-five years of his life, until his death, to that tedious task — a man who collected single-handed more material than an entire institution with a staff of employees would have gathered. Due to this unique devotion to and love for his ideal, *The History of Jewish Music*, the Jewish people is now in possession of a collection of its songs. And due to the bibliographical foresight of Mr. A. Oko, librarian of the Hebrew Union College Library, who sensed the far-reaching import of the unique collection, we are able to become acquainted with the distinctive Jewish song of the eighteenth century."[38]

Shortly after Idelsohn began cataloguing Birnbaum's material, the school hired him as professor of music and liturgy. During his time in Cincinnati, Idelsohn published the last five volumes of his *Thesaurus*, as well as other studies, including *Jewish Music in Its Historical Development* (1929) and *Jewish Liturgy and Its Development* (1932). Deteriorating health forced Idelsohn's early retirement in 1934, a fact he sorely lamented: "In 1929 I was taken sick with coronary-vessel disease, and was laid up for six months. But in 1931 I had a paralytic stroke on my left side. This repeated several times, so that I could not teach any more, nor write, nor move about, nor read much. I can do nothing, but waste my time in reflection."[39]

As mentioned, Idelsohn was trained in nineteenth-century historical musicology, and had a generalist approach to Jewish music research, insisting that, while regionally and stylistically diverse, all Jewish music contained an essential continuity, both in spirit and musical characteristics. To be sure, this conviction did not end with Idelsohn — a fact not surprising given his great influence in the field of Jewish musicology. For example, in 1970, Hungarian-American composer Alfred Sendrey wrote that, "just as most of the religious and secular institutions of the Hebrews were of foreign origin, adjusted to suit their own national needs, so their music, though greatly influenced by that of the environment, preserved obvious traits."[40]

Such assumptions have produced the widespread myth that "all [Jewish] musical traditions are reducible to one 'Platonic' *Ur*-tradition, to an ontological *prima essentia*, from which they all emerged in the course of time."[41] Indeed, this line of thinking is still dominant outside of the academy.[42] In the last few decades, however, the majority of Jewish music scholars have arrived at a very different conclusion: the great diversity of Jewish music suggests that there is no definably "Jewish music," but rather "music of the Jews."[43] As Israel Adler, a preeminent Jewish musicologist, explains:

> [T]he further we pursue our methodological endeavors to provide a reliable basis of documentation and primary sources for our field of studies, and the closer we come to recognizing the ever-increasing complexity of the mosaic emerging from the musical source material related to the dozens of Jewish ethnic traditions, East and West, the less we feel assured that overall statements concerning the synthetic nature of characteristics of Jewish music can ever be attempted in the framework of scientific investigation. The attempt to identify internal elements, such as characteristic scales or intervals, as pertaining to the musical language of an archaic Jewish *Urmelos*, has indeed always been tempting, but it seems to exceed the humble possibilities and limited domain of scholarly investigation in our field of study.[44]

Jewish music did not develop in a vacuum. For millennia, Jewish communities have existed in Diaspora, interacting with diverse peoples and environments, and, inevitably, developing varied styles of music. In most regions of the Diaspora, the music of the Jews is tied closely to that of their non–Jewish neighbors. So, even if, centuries ago, Jewish communities tried to preserve ancient Jewish musical elements — perhaps linked to the Jerusalem Temple — they have over time been obscured beyond recognition. As one scholar observed, "The mirage of Jewish music evaporates as you gaze at it, replaced by the vision of a group of Jews singing whatever they like, from any local source."[45]

Furthermore, though it is widely accepted that the oral tradition is better preserved at the periphery of a given culture than at its center,[46] the music of such remote communities did not evade completely the forces of change. This is true of Diaspora communities that had little contact with their non–Jewish neighbors and remained isolated from later Western musical developments, such as the Jews of Yemen and Babylonia (Iraq). Some scholars, including Idelsohn,[47] have assumed that these Diaspora communities, because of their antiquity and historic isolation, remained faithful to the practice of the Temple, and preserved a relatively unadulterated and uniquely Jewish musical heritage. It is almost certain, however, that the oral transmission of this music, while carefully passed on, did not escape alteration. Some pitches were likely changed from generation to generation, either intentionally or as the result of improper memory. And, it is unrealistic to presume that Iraqi and Yemenite Jews were totally unaffected by the music of neighboring Muslim communities, even if they had little direct interaction. As one scholar writes, in addition to the sound of the local *muezzin* calling Muslims to prayer, "Occasional lullabies, work songs, or children's rhymes must also have penetrated the Jewish community and subconsciously altered the holy traditions."[48]

Still, the great value of Ideloshn's research cannot be denied. Though his attempts to locate a common and unifying strain within the music of the Jews, going as far back as the Second Temple and before, may today seem somewhat absurd, it was this passion for locating a common musical language that drove Idelsohn to amass his enormous *Thesaurus of Hebrew Oriental Melodies*, still considered the most important anthology of Jewish chants and songs.[49] He was the first serious musicologist to document the living world of non–European Jews, and to transcribe the melodies of these diverse communities. With the *Thesaurus* and other works, Idelsohn introduced a sophisticated and far-reaching approach to the study of Jewish music, and, in so doing, established the field of Jewish musicology.

The Content of This Book

The essays in this volume represent both a historical and intellectual bridge between Sulzer and Idelsohn. Published between Sulzer's death in 1890 and Idelsohn's rise to fame in the 1920s, the writings in this anthology embody in many ways the same cultural and intellectual forces that motivated these giants. Some express a desire to both improve the music of the synagogue and prove the universal import of Jewish music to the Christian world—a mission first championed by Sulzer. And, like Idelsohn's studies, these essays were the product of a larger post–Emancipation movement to give attention to Jewish cultural history. While certainly of lesser significance than the major works of Sulzer and Idelsohn, these writings demonstrate the lasting impact of Sulzer's effort to renovate synagogue song, and the burgeoning research in Jewish music from which Idelsohn's studies emerged.

Some generalizations can be drawn from the overview of Sulzer and Iselsohn that shed light on the essays in this collection. Both men pioneered the application of modern methods to Jewish music, Sulzer with the introduction of Western harmony and technique into the synagogue and Idelsohn with his fieldwork and historical analyses. They also understood the profound role music plays in the demarcation of Jewish identity, especially as the Jews sought equal status in a Christian society that took great pride in its own rich musical heritage. Likewise, both Sulzer and Idelsohn believed that "pure" Jewish music, stripped of inorganic and inartistic accretions, would serve as evidence for the historical continuity of the Jewish people, and that such music should be restored as part of an effort to ensure Jewish survival and unity in an era of widespread assimilation and fragmentation.

Such positions and motivations are evident in the writings that comprise this volume. Part I, "Jewish Sacred Music," offers six chapters on the development and use of music in Jewish ritual from the biblical period to the first two decades of the twentieth century. Part II, "Studies in Jewish Music," presents scholarship into more specific areas, including the Book of Psalms, songs of the Hasidim, Jewish contributions to general music, Russian-Jewish folksongs, and the songs and function of Ashkenazi *hazzanim* (cantors). Part III, "Reviving Jewish Music," is comprised of two short biographies of Salomon Sulzer, a tribute to composer Louis Lewandowski, and four essays articulating the need for Jewish music stripped of overtly Christian and secular influences in the synagogue, religious school, and Jewish home.

To be sure, some of the arguments presented in these chapters are no longer widely accepted. There are historical omissions and misinformation, sweeping generalizations, and other outdated elements that would not appear in more contemporary studies. Still, these essays are among the first to view Jewish music through a modern historical-scientific lens, and should be viewed as valuable contributions to the evolution of Jewish musicology.

Notes

1. Norman Solomon, *Judaism: A Very Short Introduction* (New York: Oxford University Press, 1996), p. 101.

2. Kay Kaufman Shelemay, "Mythologies and Realities in the Study of Jewish Music," in *Enchanting Powers: Music in the World's Religions*, ed. Lawrence E. Sullivan (Cambridge, MA: Harvard University Press, 1997), p. 301; Lawrence A. Hoffman, *The Canonization of the Synagogue Service* (Notre Dame, IN: University of Notre Dame Press, 1979), p. 1.

3. Irene Heskes, *Passport to Jewish Music: Its History, Traditions, and Culture* (New York: Tara, 1994), p. 23.

4. Shelemay, p. 300.

5. Joseph Manizer, *Esquisses Musicales* (Paris, 1838), quoted in Geoffrey Goldberg, "Jewish Liturgical Music in the Wake of Nineteenth-Century Reform," in *Sacred Sound and Social Change: Liturgical Music in Jewish and Christian Experience*, eds. Lawrence A. Hoffman and Janet R. Walton (Notre Dame, IN: University of Notre Dame Press, 1997), p. 62.

6. Franz Liszt, *The Gipsy in Music*, trans. Edwin Evans (London: William Reeves, 1926), p. 52.

7. Macy Nulman, *Concise Encyclopedia of Jewish Music* (New York: McGraw-Hill, 1975), p. 197.

8. Marsha Bryan Edelman, *Discovering Jewish Music* (Philadelphia: Jewish Publication Society, 2003), p. 57.

9. William Sharlin, "Congregational Singing Past and Present: Continuity and Fragmentation," *CCAR Journal: A Reform Jewish Quarterly* (Spring 1994): 36.

10. Salomon Sulzer, Preface to *Schir Zion* (1840); quoted in Irene Heskes, ed., *Studies in Jewish Music: Collected Writings of A. W. Binder* (New York: Bloch, 1971), p. 284.

11. Abraham Z. Idelsohn, *Jewish Music in Its Historical Development* (New York: Holt, Rinehart, and Winston, 1929), p. 236.

12. Ibid., pp. 242–243.

13. Ibid., p. 246.

14. Goldberg, p. 62.

15. Volume one of *Schir Zion* bears no specific date of publication, but its printing is generally believed to have occurred between 1838 and 1840.

16. Salomon Sulzer, preface to *Schir Zion*, ed., Eric Werner (New York: Bloch, 1954).

17. Eric Werner, *From Generation to Generation: Studies on Jewish Musical Tradition* (New York: American Conference of Cantors, 1967), pp. 158–159.

18. Edleman, p. 58.

19. Salomon Sulzer, *Denkschrift* (Vienna, 1876).

20 Leo Landman, *The Cantor: An Historical Perspective* (New York: Yeshiva University, 1972), p. 72.

21. Abraham W. Binder, "Salomon Sulzer's Legacy to the Cantorate," in *Studies in Jewish Music: Collected Writings of A. W. Binder*, ed. Irene Heskes (New York: Bloch, 1971), p. 287.

22. Abraham Lubin, "Salomon Sulzer's *Schir Zion*, Volume One: A Survey of Its Contributors and Its Contents," *Musica Judaica*, vol. 8, no. 1 (1985–86): 29.

23. Binder, p. 287.

24. Ibid., p. 286.

25. Ernst Daniel Goldschmidt and Akiva Zimmerman, "Solomon Sulzer," *Encyclopedia Judaica*, 2007, vol. 19, pp. 308–309.

26. Werner, *From Generation to Generation*, p. 160.

27. Ibid.

28. Binder, p. 288.

29. Werner, *From Generation to Generation*, p. 157.

30. Sharlin, p. 37.

31. Werner, *From Generation to Generation*, pp. 166–167.

32. Abraham Z. Idelsohn, "My Life: A Sketch," *Jewish Music Journal*, vol. 2, no. 2 (1935): 9.

33. Shelemay, p. 300.

34. Idelsohn, "My Life: A Sketch," p. 9.

35. Ibid., p. 8.

36. Heskes, *Passport to Jewish Music*, pp. 6–7.

37. Idelsohn, "My Life: A Sketch," p. 8.

38. Abraham Z. Idelsohn, "Songs and Singers of the Synagogue in the Eighteenth Century," *Hebrew Union College Annual* (1925): 398; quoted in "Manuscripts of Jewish Music in the Eduard Birnbaum Collection." *Hebrew Union College Annual* (1944): 397.

39. Idelsohn, "My Life: A Sketch," p. 11.

40. Alfred Sendrey, *The Music of the Jews in the Diaspora* (New York: Thomas Yoseloff, 1970), p. 420.

41. Eric Werner, "The Role of Tradition in the Music of the Synagogue," *Judaism*, vol. 13, no. 2 (1964): 156.

42. Shelemay, p. 302.

43. Edelman, p. 10.

44. Israel Adler, "Problems in the Study of Jewish Music," in *Proceedings of World Congress on Jewish Music, Jerusalem 1978*, ed. Judith Cohen (Tel Aviv: Institute for the Translation of Hebrew Literature, 1982), p. 16.

45. Mark Slobin, "Learning the Lessons of Studying Jewish Music," *Judaism*, vol. 44, no. 2 (1995): 223.

46. Werner, "The Role of Tradition in the Music of the Synagogue," p. 161.

47. Amnon Shiloah, *Jewish Musical Traditions* (Detroit, MI: Wayne State University Press, 1995), p. 31.

48. Edelman, p. 9.

49. Eliyahu Schleifer, "Jewish Liturgical Music from the Bible to Hasidism," in *Sacred Sound and Social Change: Liturgical Music in Jewish and Christian Experience*, eds. Lawrence A. Hoffman and Janet R. Walton (Notre Dame, IN: University of Notre Dame Press, 1997), p. 13.

PART I
JEWISH SACRED MUSIC

Introduction

IDELSOHN NOTED THAT "Jewish prayer has ever been rendered in music."[1] This statement should come as no surprise, given the spiritual value ascribed to music in the Bible and rabbinic literature. As Pope Benedict XVI notes, "The importance of music in biblical religion is shown very simply by the fact that the verb 'to sing' (with related words such as 'song,' and so forth) is one of the most commonly used words in the [Hebrew] Bible," occurring 309 times.[2] Likewise, various rabbinic quotations convey a high regard for prayer-song: "Where there is song, there shall be prayer,"[3] "The angels only sing on high when Israel sings below,"[4] and "What is service with joy? Song"[5]—just to cite a few.

Scholars have long been intrigued by this close relationship of music and prayer in Jewish ritual. During the late nineteenth and early twentieth century, several essays were published describing this age-old connection. For the most part, these were overviews, avoiding details of musical diversity and style in order to present a sweeping history of Jewish music. Mapping the development of Jewish song from the days of the Jerusalem Temple to the present, most scholars of this period wished to demonstrate an essential continuity of Jewish music. This agenda was part of a larger movement to establish a common cultural heritage of the Jewish people. By and large, these writers were convinced that all forms of art embodied the "inherent spirit" of a nation, and that the music of the Jews was no exception.

The six essays in Part I convey this attitude to a greater or lesser extent. Beginning with a defense against the claim that Jewish music is a "nonentity," Sam L. Jacobson's (1873–1937) essay, "The Music of the Jews," expresses, among other things, praise for modal liturgical chant and disdain for identifiably foreign musical elements in synagogue song. Originally published in *Music Magazine* in 1898, Jacobson's article is in many ways indebted to cantor-composer Salomon Sulzer (1804–1890), who worked to refine synagogue music and purify it of extraneous material.

Next are two essays by Francis L. Cohen (1862–1934), both written for encyclopedias (*Jewish Encyclopedia* and *Encyclopedia of Religion and Ethics*). Cohen, who was chief minister of the Great Synagogue in Australia, wrote extensively on Jewish music, and was particularly interested in the historical development of synagogue song beginning with the chanting of the Bible in ancient days. Among the many fine points he presents is the theory that, as a result of iconoclasm stemming from the biblical injunction against idolatry, the Jewish people favored the cultivation of music and literature over the visual arts. As Cohen explains, "There remained only for this people the sister arts of poetry and music, in each of which they have contributed much to the treasure-store of civilization."

Like Cohen, Jacob Singer wrote several articles on the subject of Jewish music. Singer was rabbi of Congregation B'nai Jeshurun in Lincoln, Nebraska, from 1912 to 1923, and served on the American Reform movement's Committee on Synagogue Music. His essay "The Music of the Synagog" traces briefly the history of synagogue song from the Bible to the early twentieth century. Importantly, the essay concludes with a widely held conviction of his time: "The distinctiveness of Synagogal music can be secured only by a discriminate use of traditional material, recast in a form suited to the musical requirements of our day."

In an article originally published for *The Encyclopedia Americana*, Louis M. Isaacs (1877–1944) offers a brisk survey of musical references in the Bible and ancient Judaism, rightfully pointing out that, while music is prevalent in the Bible, the text is "bare of any real indication of its form, nature or mechanics"—a fact that continues to challenge biblical scholars today.[6] Isaacs, a native of New York City, worked as both a lawyer and composer, and this lucid essay demonstrates his serious interest in and commitment to Jewish music.

David de Sola Pool's (1885–1970) essay is in some respects a departure from the other writings in this part. Pool served as minister of the Spanish-Portuguese Congregation Shearith Israel in New York, the oldest synagogue in the United States, and wrote numerous books and articles on a variety of Jewish topics. In this essay, which first appeared in *The Menorah Journal* in 1917, Pool does not argue for a unity of Jewish song, but rather admits that it is "almost impossible to generalize about something so varied as Synagogue music." Illustrating this point, he alludes to a comparative study he made of Sephardic melodies sung in London, Manchester, Amsterdam, New York, Montreal, and eight other locations, from which he concluded that even popular congregational melodies exhibit melodic variations from synagogue to synagogue. He also explains how differing environments have exerted influence on the music of the Jews, noting, for example, elements of Moorish music in the songs of the Sephardim, and the distinct German flavor of German synagogue melodies. Still, Pool agrees with his contemporaries that cantors and synagogue composers should avoid the "characterless borrowing" of non-Jewish music for Jewish services, arguing that, "If it is true that the music of Wagner or of Schubert is characteristically German, or if the music of Verdi is expressive of the Italian temperament, such music, brilliant though it may be, is not expressive of the Jewish religious temperament."

Notes

1. Abraham Z. Idelson, *The Ceremonies of Judaism* (Cincinnati: National Association of Temple Brotherhoods, 1930), p. 95.
2. Joseph Ratzinger (Pope Benedict XVI), *The Spirit of Liturgy* (San Francisco: Ignatius, 2000), p. 136.
3. *Devarim Rabba*, 80: 2.
4. *Hullin*, 91b.
5. *Arakin*, 11a.
6. See, for instance, Joachim Braun, *Music in Ancient Israel/Palestine: Musical, Written, and Archaeological Sources*, trans. Douglas W. Stott (Grand Rapids, MI: Wm. B. Eerdmans, 2002).

1. The Music of the Jews (1898)

Sam L. Jacobson

IT IS MAINTAINED BY MANY that "Jewish music" is a nonentity, that the chants and melodies coming to us by tradition are not "Jewish," but merely are, and have been, used by Jews. This is rather a refinement of terms than a matter for serious consideration. There is certainly a class of music that originated with the early Jew — that is founded on modes of peculiar construction, materially differing form others of either ancient or later periods — and that has always been distinctly associated with the religious services of the Jews. Some of the chants and melodies are of comparatively late composition, but being based on the modes in vogue among the Jews of the far distant past, and being used by none other, they belong none the less to the music of the Jews. Investigation has proven the antiquity and sole use by Jews of the traditional chant, and while the traditional melody may not aspire to the same distinction, it has always been the property of the Jews.

The early priesthood studied and practiced music with consummate skill. Bringing the guiding light of religion to the people, teaching being their sphere of industry, they were ever seeking the best means of inculcating the lessons of Judaism; music naturally proved of greatest assistance, being part of the natural language of mankind. Even today pedagogy knows no more potent means of instilling an idea into the youthful mind than by association with music, and it is generally conceded that a text garbed in appropriate music is more readily grasped, assimilated and remembered than is one in the form of a plain statement. Artificial language, or word-language, appeals to the understanding, but music, the universal language of the soul, arouses the emotions, and thence progresses to the activities of the mind. Pursuing this train of reasoning to its logical conclusion, they gave each portion of the synagogal and home services the intonation and accent that most closely echoed the sentiment involved. Subsequently, each verse and each chapter of the Bible, each prayer, each glorification, each benediction, was given an intonation and accent — but always evidencing a class relationship.

These chants gradually became generally familiar, and were transmitted from one individual to another and from one generation to another, until this age possesses them in all the completeness and correctness permissible by, and obtainable through, tradition and painstaking research.

Prof. Dr. Ferdinand Hiller says: "These melodies are to the musician a source of infinite delight. They often appear as the spontaneous outpouring of devout souls, and one is at a loss to understand how such outbursts of melody could have been so faithfully preserved for countless ages without a more substantial and enduring medium than popular tradition. And now, as to their great originality: Our musical thought nowadays is so strictly governed by modern harmony that we could hardly consider a melody without thinking at the same time of its underlying harmonic basis. But here we have before us continual melodies which, on account of their peculiar intervals, cannot be forced into our musical system, and which, in spite of this fact, do not lack a distinctive musical mode as a foundation. Many of these melodies are so touching in expression, others so grand in force, that they affect us powerfully, even though most of us may not be able to decipher their text."

The traditional chant is very different from the traditional melody. The former is the intonation of the liturgy, a sort of cantillation, the latter a hymn; the one is ancient in every particular, abounding in augmented and diminished intervals, unrelated to modern musical schemes and having an indefinite rhythm, the other simple and according to rather modern modes.

Investigators in this field claim that the traditional melody is of German origin and dates back only to the first half of the last century, and merely forms an epoch in the history of the liturgical music of the synagogue. However, these melodies are characteristically Jewish in sentiment, speaking the highest aspirations, the deepest sorrows, ecstatic joys, dire lamentations — and in music sublime and beautiful. The Jewish heart finds expression in Jewish music.

A well-defined system of notation, indicating the chant to be employed, is found in the Hebrew Bible and in some of the Hebrew prayer books, but it is the subject of some controversy. Nevertheless some eminently satisfactory results have been obtained from the different solutions, and it is to be hoped that a positive and impregnable conclusion will obtain. The music of the Jews is veiled in much uncertainty, and although frequently subjected to scholarly research, but faint rays of light of absolute knowledge come to us.

Modes

According to Joseph Singer, chief cantor of the congregation of Vienna, the ritual melodies are based on three modes, originating in a pre–Christian era, namely: those chants or melodies which differ from these modes are either mixtures of these modes, or are of modern origin.

The Revs. Kaiser and Sparger, in commenting upon this, say: "We find that these two modes (1st and 2nd) are undoubtedly of remote antiquity. Measuring their relation to the church modes, we find that mode No. 1 corresponds to the Aeolian, and mode No. 2 to the Mixo-Lydian modes of the Gregorian system.... The probabilities are that the Jews, as well as the Greeks and Arabs, obtained these modes from the same source, namely, from the Egyptians.

"For our mode, No. 3, however, we can find absolutely no record anywhere. This mode, which, like the other two, is based upon strictly scientific principles, does not find its parallel in any of the ancient or modern systems of tonality. And it is this fact which makes it as peculiarly important for the development of the music of the synagogue. It is exclusively Jewish.

"Furthermore, the fact deserves special mention that, while in those of our melodies which are based upon the first two modes, slight deviations from the basis if their tonality may occur, the melodies based upon the third mode are always and everywhere the same, and that even the closest scrutiny will fail to detect the least deviation from the scale C, Db, E, F, G, Ab, Bb, C. It is more than probable, therefore, that the largest part of the cantillations and melodies of the temple were based upon this mode, while the other two were used to but small degree."

Modern Music

Nowadays, in the majority of synagogues, music of all kinds is utilized — sacred songs, secular songs and selections from operas to which are adapted sacred words, Te Deum, glorias, etc., from Episcopal and Catholic church music with modified text, etc., but this is not from necessity. The Jewish music of modern composition is the fruit of centuries of musical thought and musical training. Extraneous influence have not affected the true style, but all that has proven worthy of adoption or imitation is employed: The compositions of Lewandowski, Naumbourg, Sulzer, Kaiser, Goldstein, Davis and others, whose names alone are voucher for musical excellence, are built on the modes, and possess the characteristics of the music invented by the early Jews, and take position among musical gems.

It is true that the harmony in much Jewish music is decidedly meager, but perhaps the explanation may be found, not in presuming the composers incapable or the themes unworthy, but in expediency. Synagogal music is usually written within the capacity of the mediocre choir and organist, in order that all congregations may have attractive services. With many rabbis and their flocks it has long been an earnest endeavor to resume congregational singing, and this has been a vigorous cause of the simplicity, melodic and harmonic, of much of the music. Able and painstaking musicians overcome this objection by supplying the deficiency.

The music employed in the different synagogues partakes of the nature of the respective mode of worship: in the strictly orthodox service the prayers are chanted, the hymns are traditional melodies, the men alone participate in the responses, and no musical instrument is permitted to be sounded (other than the *shofar* on the New Year's Day and once at the close of the Day of Atonement), while in the reform service the reading of the prayers is characterized by all the refinements and subtleties of the elocutionary art at the command of the reader, the hymns are of ancient and modern composition and adaptations of all varieties, and the music is rendered by choirs of mixed voices, accompanied by organ and sometimes other instruments. One southern rabbi, an accomplished musician and composer, and himself an eminent cantor, invariably secures the best services obtainable, and has at times employed a chorus and a large orchestra in connection with his regular choir.

Mention is made in the Bible of the harp, lute, trumpet, cymbals, bells, etc. The position in the service occupied by these instruments cannot be positively stated, for all the traditional chants and melodies have been transmitted in the melody form alone, the harmony now used in connection with them being of recent accomplishment. Some scheme of harmonization and instrumentation, however crude, probably existed, for the souls that could gush forth in such exquisite melodies must have been gifted with the power to amplify them.

Jewish music, too, has seen decadence and regeneration. Popular airs and folksong were used (and are occasionally in this age) a la Salvation Army, but better judgment eventually banished them to whence they came. Some cantors possessing superior vocal powers were not above prostituting their sacred offices to a means of self-aggrandizement, and personal jealousies on this account were not unknown. The result is readily imaginable. At the end of the last century, when instrumental music was not permitted in the synagogue, some cantors had assistants who imitated the voices of orchestral instruments in accompanying the solos of the cantor. But conscientious endeavor on the part of the true musicians of the temple arrested the downward tendency and corrected the perversion.

The music of the Jews is a garden rich in choicest flowers. Much of it has been explored and cultivated, but parts of it are yet undeveloped. The soil is fertile and the harvest promising.

2. Synagogal Music (1906)
Francis L. Cohen

THE DESIRE TO READ THE Scriptures in the manner indicated in Nehemiah 8:8 — "They read form the scroll of the Teaching of God, translating it and giving it sense; so they understood the reading" — has from time immemorial resulted in the use of some sort of musical declamation for the passages uttered aloud in the synagogue. For reasons very similar to those there discussed, the prayers and praises equally with the lessons have always been thus musically declaimed; and this declamation, developing in many lands under the influence of varying tonal surroundings through the long centuries, has gradually become extended into the vocal melody, solo or choral, in which the whole of the traditional services are now presented. The earliest synagogal music was founded upon the same system and method as prevailed in the orchestra of the Temple itself. Joshua ben Hananiah, who had served in the sanctuary as a member of the Levitical choir (Ar. 11b), told how the choristers went in a body to the synagogue from the orchestra by the altar (Suk. 53a), and so participated in both services. As the part of the instruments in the Temple musical ensemble was purely that of accompaniment, and the voices could have given an adequate rendition without accompaniment, the absence of instruments from the synagogue in no way modified the system of the song itself. This presented little that to modern ears would appear worthy the name of melody, being, like the Greek melodies which have been deciphered, entirely of the character of a cantillation — that is, a recitation dependent on the rhythm and sequence of the words of the text instead of on the notes of the tune, and influenced by the syntactical structure of the sentence instead of by the metrical form of the musical phrase. Nor would the style of singing—nasal, shrill, and alternately full of intricate graces and of sudden pressures on emphatic notes—altogether commend itself to Western ears as graceful or harmonious.

The dispersal of the Temple singers and the cessation of the performances of the musicians in the sanctuary influenced but slightly the synagogal cantillation, since the desire of many authorities that song should be abstained from in lasting mourning for fallen Zion, was never generally heeded when it became a question of song in worship. Indeed, from the earlier centuries there had been evident a desire to enhance the importance of the singing in the synagogal ritual. The officiant was required to have a pleasant voice and a clear enunciation (Ta'an. 16a), and the voluntary assistance of good vocalists was regarded as meritorious. Among such Hiyya bar Adda is prominently mentioned. Women were from the first entirely silent in the synagogue (Ber. 24a). The *Shema*, known to all, was chanted in unison; but the "*Amidah*" *(Shemoneh Esreh)* was intoned by the officiant only, the congregation responding loudly in unison, as also when *Kaddish* was read (Sotah 49a; Shab. 119b). The Psalms were chanted originally in a responsive antiphony (Sotah 30b); but soon the antiphony developed into a general unison, as became the case, too, with the other passages gradually added to the ritual.

Later Amplification

Yet it was only with the *piyyutim* that music found scope for development within the walls of the synagogue, as the ritual began to crystallize into definite form, and prayerful verses took the place of didactic and dogmatic texts. The *hazzan* now became primarily the precentor. He sang the *piyyutim* to melodies selected by their writer or by himself, thus introducing fixed melodies into synagogal music. The prayers he continued to recite as he had heard his predecessors recite them; but in moments of inspiration or emotion he would give utterance to a phrase of unusual beauty or power, which, caught up by the congregants, would be repeated and preserved as a worthy expression of the thought underlying the day's service, coming at last into the form of a definite and well-recognized musical sentence, and so forming the substance of a prayer-motive. There was little need to prompt him to greater energy in this direction; from the first it became more necessary to keep his intensity in check.

Ancient Elements

The music may have preserved a few phrases in the reading of Scripture which recalled the song of the Temple; but generally it echoed from the first the tones which the Jew of each age and country heard around him, not merely in the actual borrowing of tunes (of which there is continuous evidence from the days of Ibn Ezra; comp. his commentary on Ps. viii.), but more especially in the prevailing tonality or description of scale on which the music was based. These elements persist side by side, rendering the traditional intonations a mass composed of details differing immensely in age and in style, and only blended by the gradual modification of each by what must be regarded as the old and constant flux of their rendition. The oldest element is the parallelism which runs through all the traditions, according to which chants divergent enough in detail of tune, and systematically so in tonality or scale-structure, are applied to corresponding passages after a similar method. This peculiarity appears to have been recognized as early as the days of Hai Gaon (d. 1038). It has been shown to be very ancient, and possibly to date back to the method of rendition utilized for the Psalms in the Temple ritual. The underlying principle, according to the present writer's formulation, is the specific allotment in Jewish worship of a particular mode or scale-form to each sacred occasion, because of some aesthetic appropriateness felt to underlie the association. In contrast to the meager modal choice of modern melody, which is fettered within the range of two modes, the minor and the major, the synagogal tradition revels in the possession of a number of scale-forms preserved from the remote past, much as are to be perceived in the plain-song of the Catholic, the Byzantine, and the Armenian churches. And it draws its supply not alone from the same sources as these Christian traditions: it finds itself enriched also from the origins from which proceeded, on either hand, the Hungarian-Wallachian Gypsy melody and the music of the Perso-Arab system. In this way the music of the synagogue enshrines elements of the theory and the practice of western Asia, which centered in Babylon, and which have left their effects in all lands between Moorish Spain and Dravidian India.

Modal Feeling

And this modal feeling is not alone the conspicuous characteristic of the *hazzanut*— that traditional style of free vocal recitation of a prose text, in which synagogal music differs so greatly from secular music in the Western world — but it may be traced also in those older tunes which, constructed in modern rhythmic form and thus recognizable by ordinary hearers as melodies in the modern sense.

Another marked element, of later origin but equally wide diffusion, is that style of florid melodious intonation which requires the exercise of vocal agility. It existed, as the cantillation of Scripture shows, even before the recital of the services was entrusted to the *hazzan* as the specialist. It was introduced into Europe in the seventh century, then rapidly developed, and more than aught else led to the complaints against the *hazzanim*. Yet many of the influences to which this intricate vocalization was due lay in the old Jewish tradition as to what was a seemly method of expressing devotion. Similar influences had built up, upon old outlines coming from Asia Minor, the figuration which distinguishes also certain sequences in the Catholic plain-song. But the Church plain-song never developed the rapid and florid ornamentation of the synagogal *hazzanut*, because of the early development of choral participation in the church service. So, too, in the Sephardic, or Southern, use, the pronounced share of the congregation in the recital of the prayers tended to check its excessive employment.

Later Debasement

But among the Northern Jews especially the isolation and the poverty of the worshipers shut them off from the enjoyment in secular life of those successive developments of the contrapuntal art — first in the music of the mass, then in the music of the dignitary's chamber — which culminated in the rich figuration which marks the compositions of the early eighteenth century. In the synagogue, where those worshiped who were banned from such enjoyment, it was the adulation of admiring listeners that too often prompted the officiant to forget the text-matter in the song-manner, and even more to develop the technical intricacy of synagogal music by the utilization also of florid ornamentation in which his hearers, out of touch with any music but the folk-music of their day, were not likely to detect the echoes of contemporary instrumental virtuosity. In the end, the echoes of what a *hazzan* heard of the sensual tastelessness of the "*Zopf*" style, which ruled musical Europe in the eighteenth century, completed that debasement of synagogal music from which the efforts of a century of work by Jews who had acquired a little of the taste of the cultured musician have only recently begun to lift it.

Age of Song Elements

The age of the various elements in synagogal song may be traced from the order in which the passages of the text were first introduced into the liturgy and were in turn regarded as so important as to demand special vocalization. This order closely agrees with that in which the successive tones and styles still preserved for these elements came into use among the Gentile neighbors of the Jews who utilized them. Earliest of all is the cantillation of the Scriptures, in which the traditions of the various rites differ only as much and in the same manner from one another as their particular interpretations according to the text and occasion differ among themselves. This indeed was to be anticipated if the differentiation itself preserves a peculiarity of the music of the Temple. Next comes, from the first ten centuries, and probably taking shape only with the Jewish settlement in western and northern Europe, the cantillation of the *Amidah*, which was the first portion of the liturgy dedicated to a musical rendering, all that preceded it remaining un-chanted. Gradually the song of the precentor commenced at ever-earlier points in the service. By the tenth century the chant commenced at *Baruk She-Amar*, the previous custom having been to commence the singing at *Nishmat*, these conventions being still traceable in practice in the introit signalizing the entry of the junior and of the senior officiant. Hence, in turn, appeared cantillation, prayer-motive, fixed melody, and hymn as forms of synagogal music.

Reminiscences of Gentile Sacred Melody

The contemporaneous musical fashion of the outer world has ever found its echo within the walls of the synagogue, so that in the superstructure added by successive generations of transmitting singers there are always discernible points of comparison, even of contact, with the style and structure of each successive era in the musical history of other religious communions. Attention has frequently been drawn to the resemblances in manner and even in some points of detail between the chants of the *muezzin* and of the reader of the Koran with much of the *hazzanut*, not alone of the Sephardim, who passed so many centuries in Arab lands, but also of the Ashkenazim, equally long located far away in northern Europe. The intonations of the Sephardim even more intimately recall the plain-song of the Mozarabian Christians, which flourished in their proximity until the thirteenth century. Their chants and other set melodies largely consist of very short phrases often repeated, just as Perso-Arab melody so often does; and their congregational airs usually preserve a Morisco or other Peninsular character. The Cantillation reproduces the tonalities and the melodic outlines prevalent in the western world during the first ten centuries of the Diaspora; and the prayer-motives, although their method of employment recalls far more ancient and more Oriental parallels, are equally reminiscent of those characteristic of the eighth to the thirteenth century of the common era. Many of the phrases introduced in the *hazzanut* generally, closely resemble the musical expression of the sequences which developed in the Catholic plain-song after the example set by the school famous as that of Notker Balbulus, at St. Gall, in the early tenth century. The earlier formal melodies still more often are paralleled in the festal intonations of the monastic precentors of the eleventh to the fifteenth century, even as the later synagogal hymns everywhere approximate greatly to the secular music of their day.

Prayer-Motives

Next to the passages of Scripture recited in cantillation, the most ancient and still the most important section of the Jewish liturgy is the sequence of benedictions which is known as the *"Amidah"* (*Shemoneh Esreh*), being the section which in the ritual of the Dispersion more immediately takes the place of the sacrifice offered in the ritual of the Temple on the corresponding occasion. It accordingly attracts the intonation of the passages which precede and follow it into its own musical rendering. Like the lessons, it, too, is cantillated. This free intonation is not, as with the Scriptural texts, designated by any system of accents, but consists of a melodious development of certain themes or motives traditionally associated with the individual service, and therefore termed by the present writer "prayer-motives." These are each differentiated from other prayer-motives much as are the respective forms of the cantillation, the divergence being especially marked in the tonality due to the modal feeling alluded to above. Tonality depends on that particular position of the semitones or smaller intervals between two successive degrees of the scale which causes the difference in color familiar to modern ears in the contrast between major and minor melodies.

Throughout the musical history of the synagogue a particular mode or scale-form has long been traditionally associated with a particular service. It appears in its simplest form in the prayer-motive — which is best defined, to use a musical phrase, as a sort of coda — to which the benediction *Berakhah* closing each paragraph of the prayers is to be chanted. This is associated with a secondary phrase, somewhat after the tendency which led to the framing of the binary form in classical music. The phrases are amplified and developed according to the length, the structure, and, above all, the sentiment of the text of the paragraph, and lead always into the coda in a manner anticipating the form of instrumental music entitled the "rondo," although in no sense an imitation of the modern form. The responses likewise follow the tonality of the prayer-motive.

This intonation is designated by the Hebrew term *niggun* ("tune") when its melody is primarily in view, by the Judeo-German term *steiger* (scale) when its modal peculiarities and tonality are under consideration, and by the Romance word "gust" and the Slavonic *skarbowa* when the taste or style of the rendering especially marks it off from other music. The use of these terms, in addition to such less definite Hebraisms as *ne'imah* ("melody"), shows that the scales and intervals of such prayer-motives have long been recognized (e.g., by Saadia Gaon in the tenth century) and observed to differ characteristically from those of contemporary Gentile music, even if the principles underlying their employment have only quite recently been formulated.

Modal Difference

The modal differences are not always so observable in the Sephardic or Southern tradition. Here the participation of the congregants has tended to a more general uniformity, and has largely reduced the intonation to a chant around the dominant, or fifth degree of the scale, as if it were a derivation from the Ashkenazic daily morning theme, but ending with a descent to the major third, or, less often, to the tonic note. Even where the particular occasion — such as a fast — might call for a change of tonality, the anticipation of the congregational response brings the close of the benediction back to the usual major third. But enough differences remain, especially in the Italian rendering, to show that the principle of parallel rendering with modal difference, fully apparent in their cantillation, underlies the prayer-intonations of the Sephardim also. This principle has marked effects in the Ashkenazic or Northern tradition, where it is as clear in the rendering of the prayers as in that of the Scriptural lessons.

All the tonalities are distinct. They are formulated in the subjoined tabular statement, in which the various traditional motives of the Ashkenazic ritual have been brought to the same pitch of reciting-note in order to facilitate comparison of their modal differences.

Chromatic Intervals

By ancient tradition, from the days when the Jews who passed the Middle Ages in Teutonic lands were still under the same tonal influences as the peoples in southeastern Europe and Asia Minor yet are, chromatic scales (i.e., those showing some successive intervals greater than two semitones) have been preserved. The Sabbath morning and weekday evening motives are especially affected by this survival, which also frequently induces the Polish *hazzanim* to modify similarly the diatonic intervals of the other prayer-motives. The chromatic intervals survive as a relic of the Oriental tendency to divide an ordinary interval of pitch into subintervals, as a result of the intricacy of some of the vocal embroideries in actual employment, which are not infrequently of a character to daunt an ordinary singer. Even among Western cantors, trained amid mensurate music on a contrapuntal basis, there is still a remarkable propensity to introduce the interval of the augmented second, especially between the third and second degrees of any scale in a descending cadence. Quite commonly two augmented seconds will be employed in the octave, as in the frequent form — much loved by Eastern peoples — termed by Bourgault-Ducoudray "the Oriental chromatic."

The "harmonia," or manner in which the prayer-motive will be amplified into *hazzanut*, is measured rather by the custom of the locality and the powers of the officiant than by the importance of the celebration. The precentor will accommodate the motive to the structure of the sentence he is reciting by the judicious use of the reciting-note, varied by melismatic ornament. In the development of the subject he is bound to no definite form, rhythm, manner, or point of detail, but may treat it quite freely according to his personal capacity, inclination, and sentiment, so long only as the conclusion of the passage and the short doxology closing it, if it ends in a benediction, are chanted to the snatch of melody forming the coda, usually distinctly fixed and so furnishing the modal motive. The various sections of the melodious improvisation will thus lead smoothly back to the original subject, and so work up to a symmetrical and clear conclusion. The prayer-motives, being themselves definite in tune and well recognized in tradition, preserve the homogeneity of the service through the innumerable variations induced by impulse or intention, by energy or fatigue, by gladness or depression, and by every other mental and physical sensation of the precentor which can affect his artistic feeling.

Thus the absolute freedom and spontaneity of the development in no wise diminish a general agreement in the renderings favored in congregations far distant from one another — whether the style adopted be broad and restrained, as with the Westerns, or florid and intense, as with the Easterns — among those who follow the Ashkenazic rite. Indeed, few as are the points of contact to be observed between the definite tunes utilized in the tradition of the Ashkenazim and in that of the Sephardim, they are many and obvious between the cantillation of the "*Amidah*" and the ancient benedictions preceding and following the *Shema* in both rites. Grouping of notes, points where ornaments are introduced, phrasing of the text, retardations and pauses, even complete musical sentences, and several such differing in outline and in tonality from any other European music, not infrequently coincide in the two rituals, particularly where the precentor intones one of the less-elaborated services, as those of week-days, or eschews the excessive ornamentation favored by some schools on the special festival days. This agreement, it should be noted, occurs mainly in the ancient parts of the liturgy, which the two rituals inherit in common from before the eighth or the ninth century; and their differences, too, in the intonation of these ancient passages lie mainly in tonality much as their own various forms of cantillating alike the Scriptural lessons and those older sections of the prayers differ more in this respect than otherwise.

After the ninth century, when borrowed airs began to find their way into the synagogue, the old modal material was also utilized to construct tunes for sections of the service to which the cantillatory development of the prayer-motives had not been applied. First of these were the chants for psalms or versicles, for sentences, that is, of similar length and structure and not varying essentially in sentiment. Some were simple, approaching monotone, suited for congregational response; others were influenced by the desire for ornament and variation, and reproduced the binary tendency of the *hazzanut* with a primary and a secondary motive. Those of the first class are either founded on the cantillation or echo the form of Gregorian psalmody with intonation, mediation, and ending; the others, later in origin or in shaping, take on a more definitely tuneful form, and reproduce their structure in settings for the metrical text of *piyyutim*. It is in these chants, and in rather later synagogal form, based on similar material, that the musical figuration not infrequently presents points of contact, on the one hand, with the Gregorian music of the Catholic tradition or, on the other, with the traditional intonations of the Moslems. In the condition in which the chants have been evolved from their traditional form there are obvious traces of later development, reaching, indeed, down to the actual present; but their original shaping and definite acceptance into the synagogal corpus of sacred song took place between the eighth and thirteenth centuries. It was at the latter epoch that the common people, to whose music alone the Jews would consciously have responded, broke loose from the modal restrictions of the theorists, alike of the Church and of the Perso-Arab schools, and all over western Europe anticipated the modal revolution which in formal art-music was delayed until the middle of the seventeenth century.

Later Melodies

Troubadours, trouvères, and minnesingers, as well as jongleurs and minstrels, had by this time laid the foundations of modern melody in their ever-extending use of the diatonic scale; and Jewish melody responded to the impulse. Where synagogal music of later birth maintains a modal difference from the music of the street outside, it is only in the utilization of material dating from before the fateful fifteenth century, when the expulsion from Spain set a seal upon the Peninsular tradition of the Sephardim, and the labors of Jacob ben Moses Mölln of Mayence (1365–1427) and his disciples gave a final redaction to the use of the Ashkenazim; or else where the officiant or his teachers were residents in eastern Europe, under the influence of Slavonic and Gipsy passion in melody, or in Moslem lands, where the short, infinitely repeated phrase in the distinctive Perso-Arab scales still prevails in every-day music. Chief among such later melodies, often reproducing at least the style of older Hebraic intonations, are the settings for a text that vary with the occasion, in response to the fundamental principle of parallel form with modal variation underlying the cantillation and the *hazzanut*. Very characteristic of the whole class in all its features of style and handling are the settings for what may be termed the "introit"—i.e., the passage where the senior precentor takes up the chanting of the morning service at the approach of its more important phases, relieving his junior, who has in simpler form intoned the earlier private prayers and introductory psalms. The music which precedes presents in contrast the settings in the Northern tradition so utilized, in ascending degree of importance on Sabbath, festival, and Penitential Day.

Fixed Melodies: Hymns

But besides the traditional material of such actually Jewish origin and development, there has been preserved in the music of the synagogue a considerable mass of melody directly adapted from the folk-song of Gentile neighbors, or constructed on the general lines of musical development in the outer world. In the latter class falls almost the whole of the choral music of the synagogue, the work of composers who either avowedly shaped their work upon the wider, as contrasted with the purely ecclesiastical, lines of art, or were unconscious of the historic and esthetic value of the traditional material. The borrowed or adopted melodies, on the other hand, were already associated in the outer world with the secular song or dance, and were taken into the synagogue simply from the lack of available melody as the number of Neo-Hebraic hymns rapidly increased. Then their pleasing jingle often, their tender expressiveness sometimes, early led to their retention and perpetuation and to their adoption as the traditional setting of the verses to which they had first been adapted, and often of others as well.

Borrowed Popular Airs

Not all the airs which reproduce external folk-songs, however, were thus actually and directly borrowed; for a goodly number must have been the composition of the *hazzanim*. But even so, they were close imitations of the popular melody of the day; and they lack any Jewish characteristic to bring them into line with the older traditional elements. Abraham ibn Ezra (on Ps. viii.) refers to the introduction of such alien airs in the eleventh century; and according to S. Archevolti in the sixteenth century (*Arugat ha-Bosem*, p. 100), the practice was a general one in the days of Judah ha-Levi (early part of twelfth century). Much controversy raged over this practice; but that it became firmly fixed in synagogal life the number of such adopted melodies referred to in the rubrics of the *Machzorim*, as well as in the pages of the controversialists, conclusively proves. Indeed, Israel Najara, rabbi of Gaza (who died in 1581 and whom Delitzsch calls "the founder of the Jerusalem ritual"), published 650 Hebrew lyrics, especially written to fit the melodies of Arabic, Turkish, Greek, Spanish, and Italian songs selected by himself.

This procedure was not peculiar to the synagogue. Dufay, the most prominent musician of the Gallo-Belgic school about the end of the fourteenth century, had substituted a popular secular melody as the basis of the music of the mass in place of the "cantus firmus" traditional in the Church; and this practice became universal in that school of musicians and their successors. The most favored of these secular airs, "L'Homme Armé," partly appears also in the *Mizmor Shir* of the Sephardic tradition. The synagogal musicians, the *hazzanim*, had already, as has been seen, thus endeavored to bring the music of worship into harmony with every-day life outside the sanctuary; and they closely followed the later amplifications of the practice, such as that of the early Protestant hymns, in which a very slight change in the words of the original German produced an immense one in the meaning, as when H. Isaak's "Innsbruck, I Must Leave Thee" (1440) became "O World, I Soon Must Leave Thee." So, too, in Jewish practice a slight change in sound was held to be warrant enough for the devotional utilization of an air. Thus to the tune of "En Toda la Tramontaña" was written *Shir Todah le-Elohim Tanah*; and to "Muerame mi Alma, ai! Muerame" was written *Meromi 'al Mah 'Am Rab Homah*. In another direction it is found that a slight correspondence in the meaning of the initial words was considered adequate connection, as when the verses *El he-Harim Essa 'Eni* are set to the air of "A las Montañas Mi Alma! a las Montañas Me Iré," or "Mar li Mar Mar Mar" to the Turkish "Krodas Yar, Yar, Yar," where, furthermore, the word "*dost*" (friend) ending each line in the modal, is translated by the Hebrew "*dodi*" in a similar position. Such incongruities, indeed, existed as a hymn commencing *Shem nora*, to the tune of "Señora"; and *Ya'alat ha-mor* to "Perdone di amor." Few of such adaptations were adopted into the liturgy itself, although some are to be traced, as, for instance, the beautiful tune of Abraham Hazzan's to Gerona's fine hymn commencing *Ahot Ketannah*, which was composed on the lines of a popular Levantine song, "The Little Maid."

Imitations

The well-known melody of *Ma'oz Zur* was likewise adapted from a street song, and selected by Luther for his first choral on such lines, as well as by the German Jews for their *Hanukkah* hymn. Among other secular airs of European peoples adapted by Jews to sacred use may be mentioned: "Permetid Bella Amaryllis," "Tres Colores in Una," "Temprano Naçes Almendro," "El Vaquero de la Morayña," "Fasi Abassi Silvana," "Les Trois Rois," "Les Filles de Tarascon," "PorqueNo Me Hablas," "Partistas Amiga," "Pues Vos Me Feristes," "Blümlein auf Breiter Heide," "Dietrich von Bern," "Pavierweiss," "En los Campos di Alvansa," "Un Poggio Tiene la Contessa,"

"Giulianita," "Doliente Estaba Alessandri," and even, in the last century, such melodies for the *Kaddish* as "La Marseillaise" or actually "The Girl I Left Behind Me," or for *Adonai Melek* on New-Year's Day an aria from "Traviata."

Especially has it been in the *zemirot* or domestic table hymns that popular airs have been adapted and transmitted. The father would think rather of the sprightly interest of the air he sang than of its suitability or Jewish character. Thus, for instance, *Shir ha-Ma'alot* (Ps. 121) is widely sung among German Jews to a modification of a melody from "Fra Diavolo." The melodies utilized in the ceremony of the Benediction of the Priests are very frequently such echoes of contemporary popular song. One of the best may be quoted from Japhet's collection of the synagogal melodies of southwest Germany, which are particularly replete with folk-song elements.

Modification in Tradition

But very often a modification has been, in the course of tradition, introduced into the popular melody which has given it a Jewish flavor, and has served to differentiate it both from the secular original and from the Christian version, when, as in the older German melodies is often the case, the air has been utilized also in the hymnody of the Protestant Church. This feature has been alluded to in the case of *Ma'oz Zur*; and it is shown in the melody for *En Kelohenu*, where the addition of a vernacular translation is the excuse for the introduction of a strain of melody in one of the older modal tones of the synagogue, while the Hebrew is sung in the modern scale and style. The effect of the custom is well brought out in the *pizmon* (hymn) *She'eh Ne'esar*, for the Fast of the 17th of Tammuz, where the modification introduced in the cadence greatly enhances the beauty and effect of the air. The fast day and its associations have seemed to the *hazzanim* to call for the expression of emotion to which the wail of the augmented second in the cadence of the Oriental chromatic scale could alone give utterance. This wail is quite absent in the Church tradition, in either form in which it has been perpetuated.

The condition in which the Jews found themselves in the sixteenth, seventeenth, and eighteenth centuries deeply affected their only form of art, their synagogal music. Where the darkness was deepest, like that which presages the dawn, the dignity of the song of the sanctuary was brought lowest. It was an age which summed up all the faults of the past, of *pilpul* in the melody of the sanctuary, of intricacy, astounding ingenuity, and *ad captandum* virtuosity: the manner, not the matter, being ever considered. Emotionalism and novel effects, often of a ludicrous character, interested and even fascinated congregations whose synagogue was their only club, and whose manners at worship were almost those of schoolboys in the playground. The return stream westward from the Jewish districts of Poland had now set in. Young precentors traveled about from congregation to congregation, bringing new melodies, and also fortifying and unifying the old tradition. These wandering minstrels, journeymen of their craft, often brought with them apprentices, a vocal orchestra rather than a choir designated *meshorerim* or song-makers. Their function was that of the youthful Levites who had stood below the platform of the singers in the Temple, to "give flavor to the song" (Ar. 13b). The *hazzan* now forced his voice to excess in a formless chant, full of repetition, all runs and turns and embroideries — bravura like the violin-playing of a Hungarian Gypsy rhapsodist, seeking to reinforce his tones by supporting the jaw behind the ear with his hand after the fashion of the London costermonger, or to get new effects by thrusting his thumb into his throat, an ancient practice known in the Temple (Yoma 38b) and illustrated on the Nineveh slab depicting the capture of Susa. Meanwhile "singer" and "bass" stood at either hand: one a boy with clear treble; the other a man with deep, bourdon tones. By ear alone, improvising rather than following a prearranged harmony, they accompanied the *hazzan*, imitating the bees and the birds, simulating the tones of the flute, the bassoon, or the now obsolete serpent, and giving vent to an impetuous fancy in incoherent though melodious passages. Such a form of concerted synagogal music vigorously survives in Poland and Galicia, and is still to be heard in the ghettos of London and New York.

Beginnings of the Modern Choir

Men who, in advance of their brethren, sought to beautify the sanctuary with high and perfected art, dwelt in Italy at the commencement of the seventeenth century. E. Birnbaum has shown how many Hebrews then and there took part in artistic musical life. In 1622 Solomon de Rossi published at Venice his *Ha-Shirim Asher li-Shelomoh*, being the first trained musician to labor with effect for the regeneration of the song of Zion, or to compose synagogal music on contrapuntal lines. He was thus the father of modern synagogal composers. Led by his keen and active sympathy, the artistically cultured Leon of Modena, himself the possessor of a sweet tenor voice, had already associated with other Italian rabbis in the issue of a pastoral letter (1605) advocating and authorizing the introduction of mensurate and polyphonic music into the synagogue

Influence of Sulzer

But little progress was made until the burst of the Jewish renascence in the early part of the nineteenth century. The Berlin community in 1824 saw the first establishment of the modern synagogal music. The early reformers went perhaps too far in their modernization of the intonations and the choral portion alike; but in due time the recoil corrected the errors of excess. Even Solomon Sulzer, the master of all modern workers in synagogal music, was a little inclined to iconoclasm in his purification and simplification of the traditional intonations. But his *Schir Zion* (Part I. produced in 1840; Part II. in 1865) set a high classical model alike for the old declamation, the old melodies, the traditional responses, and the modern settings of those sections of the service now allotted to the four-part choir. Modeling on the elaborate choral music of the Catholic Vienna of his day, he was yet so imbued with the traditional spirit, and so richly equipped with the traditional material, that he was able to create music which brought the ancient Oriental origins, the echoes of so many and so varied times, places, and manners, and the artistic outcome of the work of the great moderns into a noble homogeneity at once profoundly devotional and subtly dramatic. Maier Kohn in 1839 had already brought out for the Munich congregation the first modern handling of the old traditions; but it was the work of Sulzer which first penetrated the consciousness of Jewry and awoke the new harp of Judah. In 1843 H. Goldberg of Brunswick followed with a new effort, of great value in a fresh direction, in founding modern Jewish congregational singing, and showing how the synagogal music might attain to a refined and pure method even where the organization of a full-trained choir was impossible. The work was carried on by H. Weintraub in 1859, whose skill and judgment restored the traditional florid intonation to the importance it was well-nigh losing in face of the choral development. Moritz Deutsch of Breslau projected about the same time a companion to the seminary in the form of an institute for the training of cantors. His wide acquaintance with the old intonations and his extreme accuracy render his "Vorbeterschule" (1871) of particular value.

A monumental exposition of the *hazzan*'s art, uniting the old intensity with modern cultivated taste, was forthcoming in 1878 in the "*Ba'al Tefillah*, *oder der Praktische Vorbeter*" (revised ed. Frankfort-on-the-Main, 1883) of Abraham Baer of Gothenburg, in which he set forth the vocal expression of the entire Jewish liturgy according to the Ashkenazic use; blending Polish and German variants of the *hazzanut* with material for all passages not already consecrated by tradition. It is a collection of high historical as well as practical value.

Many, and often able, as have been the workers who have carried on in German lands the labor inaugurated by Sulzer, none was more eminent than Louis Lewandowski. His fine presentation of traditional melody in his "*Kol Rinnah u-Tefillah*" (Berlin, 1870, 1883) was associated with valuable congregational material; and his "*Todah we-Zimrah*" (Vol. I, 1876; Vol. II, 1883) completed a noble choral presentment of the synagogal liturgy. This master did perhaps more than any other of the past generation to bring the modern renascence of synagogal music home to the ordinary congregant. His skilful utilization of traditional material in organ accompaniments is especially prized.

Transcribers and Composers

Early work had been done in England, though not with the laborious thoroughness of the Germans. Isaac Nathan had written in 1815 and 1823 on synagogal music and had first presented "Hebrew Melodies" to the world. D. A. de Sola, in 1857, was first to utilize the hint of L. Dukes (in "Orient, Lit." x.) that synagogal music was a field to be cultivated from the historic standpoint. Together with E. Aguilar he set down the traditional airs of the Sephardim, with their rich element of Moresque and Spanish melody. In France S. Naumbourg produced in 1847 and again in 1863 his "*Zemirot Yisrael*," enshrining the simple but fascinating tradition of northern France and the Rheinland, leaving Provence and the Biscayan regions to more recent investigators (Crémieu, etc.). Naumbourg's work was at once valuable for the new material (upon which Meyerbeer and Halévy cooperated, as did Schubert and others of less note in Sulzer's) and for his labors in the field of the musical history of the older traditional melody. His influence secured for Paris an eclectic choir-book prepared by E. David, and so constructed as to form a musical companion to the prayer-book in the hands of choristers. This work prompted later the preparation by Cohen and Mosely in London (1887) of a handbook of synagogue music for congregants also, in which for the first time synagogal musicians appeared as editors only and not as composers. In 1899 the London handbook, revised by Cohen and Davis, on improved lines, sought to cover with wide choice the whole region of synagogal choral song in the "Voice of Prayer and Praise," invariably associating congregational responses with the traditional intonation of the *hazzanut*, and paying due regard to the tonic sol-fa notation taught in British elementary schools. A valuable presentment of the Italian traditional versions was published by F. Consolo in his "Libro dei Canti d'Israele" (Florence, 1892). Some melodies of the Turkish rite have been recorded, as also some of the South-Russian tradition. The field of the African and Asiatic uses remains untouched beyond their Scriptural cantillations.

Instrumental Music

Instrumental music is quite a modern feature in synagogal worship. Owing to the rabbinical "fence" which prohibited the use of an instrument on Sabbath and festivals because of the probability that it would require tuning or other preparation, it is still avoided by conservative congregations on those days. Much controversy has raged about this point in Jewish as in other communities. The earlier hesitation of the Church to adopt the organ because it was "a Jewish instrument" has been reproduced in the assumption of many Jews that it was specifically a Christian one. It is still banned by rigid adherents to old ways; but in ordinary conservative congregations it is unhesitatingly employed at weddings and other services on weekdays.

An organ has been long a feature of the Alt-neu Schul at Prague. A new one was built there by a Jewish donor in 1716. Other instruments were more freely introduced in the past than was the organ. In the twelfth century Pethahiah of Regensburg saw them in use in Bagdad on the intermediate days of festivals. It was long ago deemed indispensable for players to be present at a Jewish marriage; and MaHaRIL (Jacob Mölln ha-Levi) is recorded to have led a wedding party outside the jurisdiction of magistrates who forbade their employment, before solemnizing the marriage. An orchestra or military band has frequently participated in the synagogue service. In 1837 the band of the Royal Horse Guards played during the dedication service of the New Synagogue, Great St. Helen's, London. More recently the orchestra has accompanied the singers in the prayers and praises also. The instrumental accompaniment is one of the finest features in the work of more recent synagogal musicians such as M. G. Löwenstamm (Munich, 1882).

Present Conditions

Of the present state of synagogal music it may be said that medieval conditions still reign in the majority of synagogues. Moorish and Levantine congregations and the smaller ones of Russia, Poland, Galicia, Rumania, and even Great Britain and America, still exhibit the musical defects of the eighteenth century. But in the larger synagogues of those countries, as in central and western Europe generally, while the *hazzan* still retains his important functions, the traditional intonations have been simplified and purified through acquaintance with the classical style of the concert-room, and he is more a precentor than a solo vocalist. The four-part choir is usually composed of boys and men, more rarely of women and men, and is with more frequency relegated to a gallery as it comes rather under the direction of a technically trained musician as choir-master than of the *hazzan* as general musical director. The choir almost everywhere now sings well-designed, harmoniously and expressively written, and adequately dignified music, the responses being more and more based on the traditional intonations. Psalms, versicles, and anthem-like pieces closely imitate the devotional music of Gentile neighbors; but the composers also frequently evince a desire to give utterance to a Jewish sentiment in the tones handed down from the past. In many of the synagogues of the United States there is no choir in the European sense, its place being taken by a single or a double mixed quartet of selected singers, in which, strangely enough, Gentiles are permitted to be the majority of those appointed to lead Jewish worship. Yet even here the tendency is now evident to combine the fullest modern artistic resources with the essentially traditional material consecrated by ancient custom of which Lewandowski was the foremost exponent.

3. Jewish Music (1917)
Francis L. Cohen

ART IS THE MEANS BY WHICH man seeks to interpret the aspiration of the mind to the senses. The Jews appear in history already barred off by their rigid iconoclasm from the expression of feeling through the pietile and plastic arts, nor had they settled habitation or surplus resources long enough to find such expression through the allied art of architecture. There remained only for these people the sister arts of poetry and music, in each of which they have contributed much to the treasure-store of civilization. But, little as Hebrew poetry has diverged from the original field of its art — the expression of religious emotion — even less has Jewish music, the forms and styles of which had crystallized before the Jews came under the influence of modern musical development. This development reaches back only a few centuries; and the Jews have touched it only since their release from the Ghettos.

It is possible that Jewish music at first displayed little original characteristics; being merely a provincial variety of the general art which spread, as the survivals show, from the Hellenic region to Dravidian India. It is evident from such allusions as those of Psalm 137 that the Jewish musicians had a reputation beyond their own borders. The traditions of the First Temple were revived in the Second, if on a more modest scale. It is from the Hasmonean and Herodian epochs that we derive the Talmudic traditions of Temple music. The *shofar*, the rude bugle of ram's horn, sounded in conjunction with the straight silver trumpets as a signal for the Temple routine as well as in the intervals (*selah*) of the Psalm with the daily sacrifice, is obviously the same instrument as is still sounded by the Jews on the Day of Memorial each September. Under the cymbal-beat (which took the place of the later chironomy and the modern baton) of Ben Arsa, the last conductor, a small orchestra, resembling modern combinations more than anything else in antiquity, accompanied the Levitical singers, in the unison, with an occasional much-repeated melodic figure on the larger harps. The only thing approaching instrumental solo music, besides the blasts of the trumpets and horns, was a wailing flute melody, played twelve days a year before the altar. The last leader and trainer of the Temple choir was Hogras, whose described technical procedure confirms what analogy indicates, that the singing was nasal, shrill, and full alternately of intricate graces and of sudden pressures on emphatic notes, to an extent which would deprive it of melodious significance for a Western ear.

Yet this was the primal source of the music of the Diaspora, for, as R. Joshua ben Hananiah, himself a Levite and a chorister, afterwards told, the choristers went in a body on certain occasions from the altar to the synagogue within the Temple precincts, and sang in both services. The Synagogue took over from the Temple the silence of the women worshipers, the unison of boys and men in the singing, and its character as a cantillation rather than a melody — features still differentiating the worship-music of the Jew from that of his Western Christian neighbor. The dispersal of the Temple musicians made little difference, since it had been deliberately arranged that the voices could give adequate rendition without instruments. Though in the earlier centuries of the Diaspora many endeavors were made to check the Jewish tendency to songful utterance, no attention was paid to this aesthetic principle where worship was in question. In those early centuries a desire is already evident to enhance the importance of song in worship. The officiant was required to have a clear enunciation and a pleasant voice, and the voluntary assistance of good vocalists in leading the chanting is repeatedly recorded with high approval. In prayer proper, *Amen* and similar responses were all that congregations added, and this was in a loud exclamation, without regard to tune or time. But the praises were, on the contrary, deliberately sung, at first in the responsive antiphony, to a chant possessing easily-remembered melodic features, and afterwards more and more in general unison; and the same rendition was followed as other passages beyond the Psalms and the earliest hymns were added to the ritual.

The intonations of the officiant known as the *koreh* ("reader"), *sheliach tzibbur* ("emissary of the congregation"), and later as the *hazzan* ("overseer," originally rather a warden or beadle), were not tuneful in the modern sense. Among the Jews the desire to read the Scripture publicly in the manner described in Nehemiah 8:8 had early resulted in all the proceedings in synagogue and school alike being carried on in a form of musical declamation. Early Jewish music, like much of their ritual music still, was cantillation, vocal movements depending not upon the rhyme or sequence of the sounds chanted, but upon the rhythm and sequence of the syllables to which they are chanted. In consequence, characteristically Jewish music, however melodious it may appear when sung with a text, loses its melodic meaning when played upon an instrument.

The first portion of this antique cantillation to take definite shape was the intonation traditionally utilized for the reading of the Scriptural lessons. This was due to the early acceptance of the diacritical signs attached to the Biblical text as the Masoretic accentuation. A master of the third century deprecates the ingratitude towards the Giver of their voice as "read [the Scripture] without tunefulness and repeat [the Mishna] without chanting" (B. Tal. *Megillah* 32a). Even the Mishna itself had diacritical points added for the chant later on; and a manuscript so pointed was available in the fifteenth century. The Talmud and the Codes are still studied in the academies of Jewry with a sing-song intonation, which is found considerably to assist in the prosaic comprehension of the unpointed text. Some such prosody or accent (both, of course, meaning "singing to speech") was found necessary by all the ancients before the introduction of punctuation; and, precisely as with the plain-song of the Church, private *memorias technicas* developed in the synagogue into a set system of accentuation and of musical interpretation of the accents.

The musical interpretation of the three "poetical" books (Job, Psalms, Proverbs) has been lost since the fourteenth century, the congregational recital of the Psalms having eventually turned the frequent repetition of an identical verse-accentuation into a fixed melody steadily recurring. But the "prose" Scriptures (the remaining books) were recited by an individual; and here the accents are still followed in each case. From a very early period a musical principle has flourished in Jewish music, no doubt, derived from the Babylonian art, as it still survives in the *raga* of India. This is the specific association of some model melodic phrase, some particular mode or scale-form especially, with each mental attitude or an occasion associated with such sympathy. Not only is this principle in action in the interpretation of Biblical accents, the same signs being sung on a similar melodic outline though in a different key or mode according to the occasion, but also determines the "prayer-motives" (as the writer terms the outlines of melody developed in chanting the devotions), which differ in tonality rather than in tune. All this is so reminiscent of the musical theory and practice of East Asia, in Greek mode, Perso-Arab scale, and Indian raga, that the writer would trace it back to the Temple, and see in the "headings" of the Psalms, not bold shots of the Masoretes at a meaning, but geographical names (as in the Greek system, instruments tuned on which were actually in use in the Temple) of the respective scales in which the chief musician was to lead the rise and fall of intonation. The rise and fall was still found designated by the teacher's finger when Petahiah of Regensburg visited Baghdad synagogues in the twelfth century, and it has been quite recently noticed among Yemen Jews.

The Hebrew accents, like the *neums* of the Church plain-song, appear to have been originally rough diagrams of the movement of the teacher's finger. A trope (brief melodic phrase) is chanted on the tone-syllable marked by the accent, and the general reciting-note carries on to the next accentuated syllable. Here and there tropes are strongly reminiscent of similar phrases used in church or mosque, but in all the traditional uses this feature is prominent, that the outline of the trope varies not, whether according to the book being read or the service at which it is read, while the tonality, the mode or scale-form employed, does not vary.

The same modal feeling appears in the *hazzanut*, or intonation of the prayers by the officiant. Here, not only the well-known modes of the Church plain-song usually called Gregorian are utilized, but also others surviving only in the Byzantine and Armenian Churches, as well as the Hungarian-Wallachian gypsy melody and the Perso-Arab system. Another very characteristic difference is the style of florid melodious improvisation which embroiders the outline traditional motive with elaborated vocal agility. The outline motives themselves, like the cantillation of Scripture, may have taken shape about the commencement of the medieval period. But the intricate vocalization, which well-nigh fatally overlaid Jewish music later on, developed in recent centuries among the Jews of Northern Europe, isolated in their Ghettos from the artistic awakening of the Western world. Only the last generation has seen the great work of reformation executed by the scholarly men, learned in modern music as in traditional Hebrew lore, who made the introduction of choral numbers into the Jewish services possible. And the tasteless, excessively florid style is not yet extinct; it flourishes among the Jews of Eastern Europe even when they migrate to Britain or America; and it is this vocal gymnastic which finds a large sale as "Hebrew" gramophone records, and so is presented to the general world as the typical Jewish music.

The manner in which the traditional "motive" (usually the concluding phrase of the prayer leading into a benediction with congregational response) is amplified into *hazzanut* depends on the custom of the locality and the powers of the officiant, who accommodates the traditional strain to the structure of each sentence by embroidering it with melismatic ornament as the text suggests an emphasis warranting departure from the continuous reciting-style. No two transcriptions of this most characteristic Jewish music will therefore coincide in anything beyond tonality and broad outline of melody, becoming at last identical only in the fixed closing phrase of the passage. In the cantillation of Scriptures, on the contrary, the earliest transcription printed (in J. Reuchlin, *De Accentibus*, Hagenen, 1518, book III, *ad fin*), when divested of quaint harmonization and reversal avowedly added by the transcriber, is found identical with the latest now in use in the synagogues.

At the same time, it is evident that the contemporaneous musical fashion of the outer world has been constantly finding its echo within Jewry. The adoption of the neo–Hebraic poetry in hymns for Jewish worship from the earliest medieval days provided material for the imitation by Jews, or often direct utilization, of the folk-song of their European neighbors. From the ninth century these borrowed airs began to find their way into the synagogue, where they are still preserved, often with a Jewish flavor added in transmission. Such transmission has been, until quite recently, entirely oral. First came the chants for versicles, often strikingly similar to Gregorian intonations; then more definitely tuneful short melodies, quite a number of which were adopted by the Jews in Spain before 1492 and are still deservedly treasured among their descendants. Tunes of the Minnesinger period came into Jewish music with the increasing neo–Hebraic hymns of the later Middle Ages. In the eleventh century in Spain, and in the fifteenth in Germany, allusion is made to the wideness of the practice of singing Jewish hymns, in synagogue and at home, to the throne of secular folk-songs, even as was similarly done for the music of the Mass. Among the Spanish Jews the Hebrew text chosen often reproduced the opening words of the secular song to the same tune, as when the air of "Señora" was sung to the hymn commencing *Shem Nora* ("Name Sublime"). This resembles the change of the German drinking song, "Innsbruck! I must leave thee," into the hymn, "World! I soon must leave thee." Indeed, the very first secular song of the many which Luther adopted for the tune of a chorale had already been so utilized by the German Jews for their still most popular hymn. A considerable number of the tunes occasionally used for domestic hymns have the name of the original song recorded. Those used in synagogue are of greater antiquity or, if of recent composition, usually by Jews trained in modern music.

From the sixteenth century on, and to a certain extent still, until the Jewish immigrants into emancipated lands become acclimated, the stream westward of escape from the obscurantist conditions of Eastern Europe has colored Jewish music with tints which differentiate it greatly from that of modern world at large. Aspirants for positions as *hazzan*, or precentor, traveled about from congregation to congregation, bringing new melodies, synagogal or domestic, and fortifying and unifying the older traditional material. They even resuscitated ancient Temple features, the accompaniment of the tenor by lads' voices in unison, while the bass hummed a figured reinforcement below, the tenor adding runs and turns and grace-notes lavishly, supporting his jaw with his hand behind his ear like a London costermonger, or getting striking effects by inserting his thumb in his mouth, as did Hogras in the Temple (B. Tal. *Yoma* 38b) or the singers on the Nineveh slab depicting the capture of Susa.

The first musician, in the modern sense, who worked in Jewish music was Salomon de Rossi, one of a school of Jewish masters who succeeded each other at the court of Mantua from 1542 to 1628. Leo of Modena induced other Italian Rabbis to join in a pastoral advocating the introduction of mensurate polyphonic music into the synagogues. But little progress was made elsewhere until the Jewish Renaissance burst in Germany in the early nineteenth century. The progress since made has been rapid, and the Jew now officially utilizes all the wealth of scientific vocal music that his neighbor uses. But not instrumental: the organ has been made the test between "orthodox" and "reform"; and the instrument that was once objected to in the early Church as a form of "Judaizing" is now considered by traditionalist Jews to introduce a "Christianizing" tone into their own worship. Not even in Scotland has the "kist o' whustles" been so wrangled about. Not that instrumental music is itself objected to; at Jewish weddings it has for ages been deemed indispensable, and ingenious stratagems are recorded in the Middle Ages to secure it in the face of prejudice and persecution. The objection is to the use of any instrument needing tuning on the Sabbath, and to the introduction into Jewish worship of tones specially associated with the ritual of another creed.

Around the marriage ceremonies and the family table gathers the vast repertory of tuneful hymns and tender intonations which outside the synagogue ritual constitute Jewish music.

Transcriptions of the cantillations by grammarians have been many, from Reuchin onwards. Writers of instrumental music have transcribed many a tender Jewish air, strains having even been selected as subjects for orchestral writings. The greatest popularity to music presumably Jewish, though actually only a small extent so, was given by Byron's *Hebrew Melodies* (1815), written for application to such airs in imitation of Moore's immensely successful *Irish Melodies*. In every country of Europe and in America collections of Jewish music, traditional and original, have appeared from the pens of precentors and choirmasters. The greatest of these precentors was Solomon Sulzer (Vienna, 1804–1890), and of these choirmasters Louis Lewandowski (Berlin, 1823–1894). De Sola, Hast, and Mombach, of London, Naumbourg of Paris, Consolo of Florence, also deserve mention; and especially A. Baer of Gothenburg, whose presentation of traditional Jewish intonations (Frankfort, 1878 and 1883) is monumental.

4. Music of the Synagog (1915)

Jacob Singer

"Heaven contains sacred spheres revealed only through melody and song."— Zohar

The musical traditions of the synagog are closely allied to the unique experiences of the Jewish people. To trace the origin and growth of these songforms, one must note the parallel development of music among the peoples with whom the Jews came into contact. While little information is derived from literary sources regarding the music of antiquity, nevertheless, for our investigation, both Biblical and contemporaneous allusions to music demonstrate its importance in the life of ancient Israel. Comparative studies of subsequent literature throw additional light upon the development of the later forms, and a knowledge of the folksongs of Europe and the Orient renders further help in clarifying this strange medley of song derived from many ages and peoples, so that it gradually assumes an historical sequence and continuity.

Music in the Bible

Bible students are aware of the numerous allusions to music in connection with private and public, secular and sacred, events in the life of ancient Israel. "Israel must have been a people of unusual musical temperament, whose daily nourishment was song and sound" (Cornill in *Monist*, Apr., 1909). This seems to have been generally recognized, so that the place of the Jew in modern music is regarded by one writer as "a survival of the old faculty" (Krehbiel in *American Hebrew*, May 27, 1891). More significant is the close kinship found in prophecy and in public worship. The etymology of the words "prophet" and "music" throws light upon the origins of both forms of emotional experience. The root of *nabi*, prophet, means "to bubble up," "pour forth," suggesting the flow of words under excitement or inspiration. The root of the Greek word *mousa* also refers to inspiration, and is connected with *mantis*, prophet, and "mania."

While little provision is made for music in the ritual of pre-exilic times, the early forms must have been strongly influenced by David (Am. 6:5), which doubtless affected the sacred music of later times. The instruments enumerated include the stringed, the wind and the percussive groups. After the Babylonian exile music assumes a greater importance in the ritual of the Temple (Ezek. 2:65; Neh. 7:2, 6; 10:40). From the literary structure of some of the Psalms we infer that they must have been intoned antiphonally, and our conjecture is strengthened by descriptions of the ancient song recorded in our literature. The now unintelligible headings of the Psalms are doubtless musical rubrics and belong to the old levitical nomenclature. The singing was relegated to a trained chorus, augmented by a boys' choir and accompanied by stringed and percussive instruments (Erubin, 2:6). The omission of the signal-instrument, the *shofar*, is significant, since these are capable of sounding the overtones only, as in the case of the modern army bugle. Apparently, the music of old was based upon a definite tonality, so that these signal-instruments could not participate because of their tonal limitations. In the Hellenistic period, the Greek theory of music modified the secular, and perhaps also the sacred, music of the Jews. While the Psalms were intoned responsively, either by two choruses or by a leader and a chorus, the congregations joined in singing "Amen," "Hallelujah," and "His kindness endureth for ever" (Neh. 5:13; I Cor. 14:16). The earliest form must have been a kind of "speech-song" or declamation based upon a definite "mode." The participants in the Temple choir received special training for five years (Hul. 24a), and the number of the instruments was fixed, so as to assure the proper ensemble of tone-color and volume (Er. 10a).

Synagogal Music

That the synagog fell heir to the Temple song is indicated in the record which informs us that the Temple singers went in a body from the Temple to the Synagog, and therefore participated in the services of both (Succah, 53a). We may reasonably assume that the Scriptural cantillation — the melodic phrases which are almost universal among Jews to our day in reading some of the oldest prayers — contains survivals of the ancient song. That more has not been preserved is accounted for by the political misfortunes of the Jews, and the consequent gloom cast over their lives and reflected in the religious codes which banned instrumental music from sacred and secular life. Dispersed among hostile peoples, the Jews ceased to sing "the songs of the Lord in a strange land." Instrumental music was eliminated from Jewish worship, and only the *chalil*, the instrument of mourning, was used in Talmudic times. The *shofar* or ram's horn is the only survival of ancient signal instruments. Fragments of the oldest modes have come down to us in our cantillations and chants, and in the ecclesiastical modes of both the Eastern and Western Churches.

Traditional Variants and Musical Forms

There are three distinct traditions of musical forms preserved by the Jews, and these are contained in the North-European (Ashkenazic), and South-European (Sephardic), and the Oriental, rituals, respectively. Melodically, the three are quite distinct, but similarities in tonality or "mode" appear in a number of instances. Of the European rituals, the northern is more unique and contains a larger number of archaic elements. Historically the southern communities enjoyed a greater freedom of association with their neighbors, with the result that Moorish and South-European melodies have greatly altered the character of their musical traditions. The Jews of central and northern Europe, on the other hand, were subjected to a more rigorous social and cultural isolation; hence, to satisfy their religio-aesthetic needs, they were compelled to develop the meager musical fragments preserved in their ritual. The same phenomenon appears, even in our own day, in the comparatively isolated life of East-European Ghettos, where the folksongs contain many phrases and tonalities taken directly from the Synagogal chants. Traces of traditional Jewish music appear in the works of Rubinstein, Goldmark and other Jewish composers.

Of musical forms, the cantillation is first, and is used for reading the various selections from the Bible — a practice which goes back to Temple usage. Here one finds a selection of "modes" and melodic phrases which reveals a fine sense for the aesthetic appropriateness of each, prompted both by the text and by the occasion. The cantillation of the Pentateuchal portions, in "mode," range and melodic style, is conversational or almost narrative in character. A sadder strain appears in the Prophetical portions, manifested in a change of "mode," as well as in melodic phrase, so as to express faithfully the content of the portions, reflecting also the trying times prior to the Maccabean revolt (165 B.C.), when Prophetical readings were introduced into public worship. The concluding prayers, which contain the promise of a future restoration, assume a cheerful and triumphant character. We note a similar change in "mode" in the cantillation of the book of Esther (2:5, 6), where reference is made to the captivity, and accordingly the happy "Esther" strain gives way to the melancholy cantillation associated with the book of Lamentations. The musical phrases are indicated by *neginoth*, which resemble the "neumes" both in character and function. The musical equivalents for Job, Proverbs and Psalms have not been retained by the European communities.

Other musical forms appear in the "prayer-motives," which consist of improvisations based upon a definite "mode." This type was especially cultivated by the *hazzanim* or precentors, who appear as leaders in Jewish worship from the end of the Roman period down to our own time. The "fixed melody" grew out of this school, and those phrases that made a special appeal were retained and transmitted among adjacent communities. The hymns are quite modern, as indicated by their rhythmic character and their almost universal use of diatonic scale. A number are directly traceable to the folksongs of Europe, and the practice of using secular tunes goes back to ancient usage. Still, in modern melodies of the Synagog, one meets augmented seconds and other modal peculiarities which impart to these songs an undeniably archaic character.

The great bulk of Synagogal music is a medieval product, and in many respects it may be regarded as an arrested development. This is not surprising when we consider the historical conditions under which this song took its rise. That any art-impulse should have been retained by the Jews points to their marvelous vitality and to their intense love for this sacred song. The older elements are registered in the cantillations and the "prayer-motives," and the approximate age of each can be determined by a theoretical analysis of each form and by comparative studies in church and in folksongs of Europe and the Orient (particularly the Perso-Arab melodies). We find traces of the old pentatonic scale of the non-diatonic modes that were rejected by the Western Church. The common elements of Church and Synagogal music are due to a common origin rather than to direct borrowing, and the historical antagonism between the two institutions confirms this contention. A common source will also account for parallels noted in the chant used for reading the Koran. The "modes" found in Synagogal music are these: "the immutable genus" (with both conjoint and disjoint tetrachords), the Mixolydian (seventh century), the Aeolian (ninth), the Ionian (thirteenth), the pentatonic, the Hypodorian, the Dorian, the Phrygian, and the "mixed genus" (C, Db, E, F, G, Ab, C — a chromatic tetrachord followed by the first species). Similar modes appear in the Catholic, Byzantine, and Armenian Churches. Later specimens reflect Hungarian-Wallachian Gypsy melody and the music of the Perso-Arab system. Whether we are to regard this "mixed mode" as from an "original and independent source," as some hold, or merely as a survival of an Oriental tendency to subdivide the intervals in each scale, is difficult to determine. It is noteworthy, however, that this unique scale does not occur in the Scriptural cantillation of the European rituals, the admittedly oldest parts of the service. This "Oriental chromatic" does appear, however, in the cantillation of the Baghdad ritual. In the European tradition we find it in the "prayer-motives" of the service of the Penitential season, although it is used in other parts of the Sabbath and Holy Day services.

Payyetanim

Between the ninth and the sixteenth centuries the prayer book of the Synagogue was enriched by the words of the *payyetanim* or religious bards. The need for musical settings for the increasing number of hymns was largely supplied by the folk song developed by the Troubadours and the Minnesingers. These melodies, however, in no sense displaced the older material. Many of our finest specimens of *hazzanut* ritual chant emanate from this period; the most popular is the *Kol Nidrei*, which has been given a place in musical literature by Max Bruch's setting, and the opening theme of the ancient melody also appears in Beethoven's C-sharp major Quartet, op. 131, "adagio quasi un poco andante." The *Abodah*, intoned on the Day of Atonement to the words used by the High Priest of old (Yoma, 3:8), is stronger in its portrayal of grief and richer in historical reminiscence. It is the "Martyr's Song" *par excellence.*

The "hymns" form the latest type of Synagogal music, and are derived from comparatively recent times. Occasionally a fragment of the older "modes" serves to give it distinctness. Some are directly borrowed from or patterned after European folksongs. One of these has found its way into the Church (the tune "Leoni").

Decadence

The sixteenth century shows a gradual shifting of Jews to Slavic lands, with the result that their music became modified by their new habitat. Gradually the Polish school of precentors gained ascendancy, and, after the persecutions of the seventeenth century, a number found their way into Western countries and thereby enlarged their sphere of influence. Owing to the cultural status of those Slavic lands, a marked decline sets in, and the traditional melody suffers accordingly. Here we note the inartistic embellishments and the "melismatic" runs that obscure the simpler melodies of old. Despite the protests recorded in rabbinical writings, these vagaries and forced imitations of instrumental effects further deteriorated the music of the Synagog.

Regeneration

With the dawn of a new day, a change for the better became inevitable. The political emancipation of the Jews after the Napoleonic wars enabled them to participate in the intellectual and aesthetic life their neighbors; hence, the need for reform made itself felt. Italy, as the home of the Renaissance, presents the first attempt to modernize the music of the Synagog. In the sixteenth century a number of Jews took part in the musical development of their day, of whom Solomon de Rossi may be considered an exponent. His collection of liturgical compositions show the influence of Palestrina's works. Although de Rossi received the moral support of the Jewish leaders of his day, his efforts nevertheless affected his immediate community alone. It is only in the beginning of the nineteenth century that definite steps were taken to revise the traditional music and make it comport with musical standards. Sulzer may be regarded as the protagonist of this movement, and his example was ably followed by Lewandowski, Naumbourg, Deutsch, and others.

Modern Status

The regeneration of Synagogal music has been but partly successful, and its future progress will encounter unavoidable difficulties. Much that has been done calls for critical revision, and those who have undertaken this work have not always striven to realize clearly defined aims. The rapid transition from the old to the new order of things has resulted in a loss if material that had intrinsic worth. The problems confronting composers of Synagogal music must not be minimized. If one attempts to retain the old "modes" and yet to couple them with harmonizations based upon our diatonic scale, such efforts will result in hopeless confusion. Writers of Synagogal music must realize that there are Synagogal "modes" just as there are Gregorian modes. A retention of the old form is prompted by religious as well as aesthetic considerations; for a sacred art depends for its effectiveness upon historical associations, and these cannot be eliminated without impairing its very aim. It is obviously impossible to retain musical curios in the modern Synagog, since the purpose of public worship is attained in the development and not in the antiquarian character of the music. The works of the masters of sacred music are accorded a sympathetic hearing in the modern Synagog, but these must not displace the ancient forms which grew out of the soul-life of Israel's experiences, and which therefore quicken the holiest impulses in the hearts of Jews today. The distinctiveness of Synagogal music can be secured only by a discriminate use of traditional material, recast in a form suited to the musical requirements of the day.

5. Hebrew Music (1919)
Lewis M. Isaacs

FROM THE MANY BIBLE references to music, the inference necessarily arises that it filled a large part in the life of the ancient Hebrews. It is spoken of not only in the service of religion, where it might naturally have been looked for, but also on the battlefield, at the harvest feasts and in the home. Elisha prophesies under its inspiration. The victory at the Red Sea, the return of Saul and David after the battle with the Philistines, all-important national events are celebrated in song. The details of the Temple music, the names, divisions and functions of the singers and instrumental performers are referred to at length. David utilized no less than 4,000 singers in the service, of whom 288 were "skillful" — i.e., virtuosi. Josephus, describing the preparations for the dedication of the Temple, speaks of a band and chorus of 200,000 trumpets, 40,000 string instruments and 200,000 singers; and, even if these figures are liberally discounted, the number must have been imposing.

Yet, in spite of all that modern research has accomplished in reconstructing the vital facts of Jewish history, very little definite information exists on the subject of Hebrew music. This, in itself, is a strong indication that music was but slightly developed by the Jews. Even among the Greeks, most advanced of the ancient peoples in all that concerned the arts, it had practically no independent existence, but was bound up with poetry and dancing and entirely subservient to their demands. The Greeks spent much effort over the scientific aspects of music and its aesthetic considerations and their speculations on the subject are preserved in fairly elaborate form; but there is no trace of music among the Hebrews; not even any suggestion bearing on its use is to be found in the widely varied laws of the Pentateuch. The Bible is bare of any real indication of its form, nature or mechanics. All reasonings on the subject are necessarily a priori.

In any discussion of ancient music it must be borne in mind that a different thing is meant than that which the word connotes in its present-day signification. Music, as an art, has the three dimensions of rhythm, melody and harmony; while at the dawn of civilization it was, as one writer has well put it, a "flatland" of two dimensions only, rhythm and melody. So far as scholars have been able to discover, harmony is an entirely modern development. The terminology of the Bible is a stumbling block to the path of students on the subject, who cannot even identify some of the musical instruments named. There are, for example, several Hebrew names which may mean harp, an instrument undoubtedly in use by them, *kinnor, nebel, asor,* all translated in the English version of the Psalms as "psaltery." The *ugab*, an invention credited to Jubal, is variously called "organ" and "pipe." The one instrument preserved to this day is the *shofar*, a curved trumpet, made of the ram's horn, which is still heard in the synagogue on important holy days. It is the *shofar* which sounded amid the smoke and thunder of Mount Sinai when the Commandments were given to Moses and to its blast the walls of Jericho fell. While the exact facts are lacking, it is established that the Hebrews had instruments in the three modern categories of string, wind and percussion instruments. Save as there may have been interludes between the choral singing and the chanting of the prophets, there seems to have been no independent instrumental music; but it almost invariably accompanied the voice and the dance. Hebrew song was probably a unison chant or song-speech, more or less melodious, but entirely subordinate to the text in rhythm and accent. From the form of much of the verse, it seems to have been, at times, antiphonal. Undoubtedly it was crude and noisy and probably without definite pitch, judged by Occidental standards. Even modern Oriental music sounds so to Western ears.

In his method of intoning prayers, the Orthodox Jew of today follows the tradition which has been handed down probably from the remote days of the Temple; but this chanting has very little in common with music. It is, in a sense, rhythmical, but the rhythm is that of the words. It has sequence and variations of tone, but they are based on the syntactical structure of the sentences, not the musical exigencies of melody. When, at times, this chanting approaches music in formal semblance, it is an accident due to textual or syntactical impulse. It is always plausible, that the plain song of the early Catholic service, which, in the course of the first thousand years of the Christian era, developed into a rounded and organized body of chants, appropriate to every branch of religious worship, is the direct descendant of the ritual chant of the synagogue. At all events, the latter could not have been without its influence upon the early members of the Christian clergy.

Although there is no music now extant traceable to the Hebrews of the Bible days, a body of music of some size and distinct character has grown up during the past few centuries, which, by long association with the ritual and the home-life of the Jews of all countries, has achieved the right to the title of Hebrew music. Differences may be noted between the music of the Sephardic or Spanish-Portuguese Jews and that of the Ashkenazim or Jews of northern Europe, explainable, in part, however, by differences in environment. Probably the oldest of Jewish melodies now in use is the famous *Kol Nidre*, sung on the eve of the Day of Atonement. It has been popularized through Max Bruch's rather free improvisation. The Chanukah hymn, *Mo'oz Tsur*, the *Oz Yoshir*, sometimes asserted to be Miriam's song of triumph, the *Shir Hama-a-los*, accompanying the grace after meals, the *Addir Hu*, and several other of the Passover songs and the *En Kelohenu*, are known throughout the entire Jewish world. These, and a number of others, with the original texts, were brought together a few years ago in a Hebrew hymnal by Mrs. Solomon Schechter and Lewis M. Isaacs. A real though recent addition to distinctive Jewish music is the Zionist song *Hatikvah*, which is, however, spiritually and atmospherically old.

No account of Hebrew music would be complete without mention of Solomon Sulzer, the foremost name among Jewish cantors. Born in Austria in 1804, he devoted his marked musical talent to the service of the synagogue. In a whole-hearted endeavor to reconstruct the music of the Jerusalemic days — a task which his enthusiasm refused to admit was impossible — he introduced reforms in the ritualistic chanting, which, while sacrificing little of the traditional atmosphere, vastly improved its musical value. He arranged and composed a large number of responses and settings of psalms and prayers, the best of which are contained in a collection called *Shir Zion*, which have made for themselves a permanent place in the Jewish world.

6. The Music of the Synagogue (1917)
DAVID DE SOLA POOL

IT IS ALMOST IMPOSSIBLE TO generalize about something so varied as Synagogue music. For Synagogue music is of every age and every place. Comparatively little of it has been recorded in written form. The music of the Synagogue in such important and characteristic communities as those of North Africa, Greece, Turkey, Egypt, Aleppo, Baghdad, and places still further East, has been neither recorded nor studied, so that almost the whole of the material available for scientific study belongs to only three broad groups: the Russian, or Eastern European; the German, or Central and Northern European; and the Sephardic or Southern European. Even here, records in written form date only from about the middle of the nineteenth century, and accordingly, we are not surprised to find a boundless flexibility and variability in the transmission of traditional themes and melodies. As a rule, congregational melodies have suffered less change through the centuries than have melodies which were sung by the *hazzan* alone. These latter were subjected to the idiosyncrasies of taste, the temptation of the high or low range of voice and the extemporizing inspiration of the individual singer. From a slight comparative study I have made of Sephardic melodies as sung in London, Manchester, Ramsgate, The Hague, Amsterdam, Hamburg, Paris, Florence, Janina, New York, Montreal, Philadelphia and the West Indies, I have found that not only have the traditional melodies as sung by the cantors been transformed with the utmost diversification, but also that traditional congregational melodies vary even within the same city. For instance, in the City of London, in the North of London and in the West of London, we hear the same melody variously sung, such is the variation to which Synagogue music even with a group is susceptible.

The Primitive Chants

There are, however, a few generalized conclusions which may be made in brief survey. We may say that, as a general rule, the oldest musical portions of the Synagogue service are not the melodies but the chants which the Bible and the basic prayers of the liturgy are intoned. The masoretic accents accompanying the Hebrew text in the Bible have more than grammatical and syntactical values; they are also the musical notation indicating the chants for the Pentateuch, for the Prophets and for the other Biblical books. The predominant thought or sentiment associated with the occasion of the reading or with the sense of the section read originally determined the nature of the chant. The springtime happiness of the Song of Songs called forth an entirely different mode of cantillation from that awakened by the tragic anguish of the Book of Lamentations. The solemn nature of the penitential days stirred the reader of the Law to a different chant from that in which he read the Law on other days of the year. Similarly with the prayers; the emotional inspiration of each day determined the tonal nature of the recitative. This happened the more readily, because, to a considerable extent, the same prayers are read throughout the year, and with a fixed ritual the dominant mood of a particular holy day could be expressed and interpreted only through change in the chant.

The Wide Range of the Synagogue Melodies

The calendar of Biblical readings is practically the same the world over, with a resultant underlying unity in the interpretive character of the musical recitatives associated with the Bible. But the poetical parts of the liturgy differ widely in the various rituals. Since it is these lyrical passages which have lent themselves most readily to melodic treatment, the diversity of their musical development is paralleled only by the diversity of ritual through the extension of our Golus. We therefore have to deal with a wide range of material; as soon as we leave the primitive chants and turn our attention to melodies.

Thus we find nothing in common between the melodic structure of the characteristic hymns of the Spanish Jews and those of the Russian Jews. The historic reason for this is not far to seek. To the best of our knowledge there have been no dominating Scarlatis, Palestrinas, Bachs or Handels of the Synagogue. The melodies of the Synagogue hymns were usually composed either by the poet who wrote the words of the hymns, or by *hazzanim*. In either case the melody originated under the local musical influences of the particular land of its composition. Therefore we find that many of the melodies of the Sephardim have a strongly marked Moorish or Arabesque character, pointing back to an origin more than five centuries ago when the Sephardic communities still lived in the Iberian Peninsula. Melodies of the German Jews often show pronounced German influence; the melodies of the Italian Synagogue show marked Italian influence; the melodies of the Jews of the Orient reflect Turkish and Syrian musical standards; many melodies of the Hassidim show Gypsy influence, and the melodies of the Eastern European Jews often show Slavonic and even Tartar influences.

The Older Melodies and Their Origins

Sometimes melodies were taken into the Synagogue from the outside world, and many of our best known melodies may ultimately have, and in some cases demonstrably have, a non–Jewish origin. But these borrowings, once they had entered the synagogue, were apt to be Judaized by their new environment through chromatic variation and characteristically Jewish melismatic ornamentation. The leading Rabbis in every generation frowned down on the borrowing of secular and profane melodies, thus limiting the amount of borrowing and keeping the music of the Synagogue relatively pure in its original Jewishness of inspiration.

The oldest melodies, whether original or borrowed, have lost most of their primitive character in transmission and transplantation. But they have preserved enough individuality to allow of certain generalizations being made about them. Many are composed within a strikingly limited range of notes. Others had and even have no fixed time, the rhythm being changed elastically within the melody, to accommodate the words of the hymn. Many are in modes which are neither major nor minor, but which are classified according to their chromatic variation and augmented and diminished intervals, under such archaeologically formidable names as Mixolydian, Hypodorian, etc. Many of the older melodies, particularly those that have arisen outside of Europe, use thirds of tones; but these thirds of tone have been smoothed out into comparatively colorless semitones under the influence of modern European standards. All the other melodies were originally innocent of anything like the expanded polyphony of modern harmony, and in the latter day attempt to harmonize and regulate these melodies, much of their primitive character has been irretrievably lost.

The Modernizing of Synagogue Melodies

The modernizing of these ancient melodies necessarily followed the breaking down of the Ghetto walls. Within the Ghetto, Jewish music acquired to the greatest degree that intensification which became characteristic of all forms of Jewish life as a result of the immuring and narrowing of Jewish activity in the Ghetto. The Jew in the Ghetto could not as a rule express himself through the arts, since sculpture and painting were almost tabooed, and there was no opportunity for architecture. But he was free to roam through the fields of melody to his heart's content, and music, which has been called the poor man's Parnassus, became exuberant beyond the confines of modern aesthetic canons of musical art. This very exuberance gave to the Synagogue music of the Ghetto a power, a plaintive appeal and passionate outcry that are matchless, and that could have been evoked only by the hopeless, purposeless, but exquisite sufferings of the Golus. When this dynamic Ghetto Synagogue music emerged into the world, it was pruned of fervid outpourings, harmonized for choral purposes, and reduced to conventional forms. This simplification took place under the influence of the musical standards of the non–Jewish environment, and under the pressure of adaptation to the harmonic requirement and the inflexible temperament of the organ which came into the Synagogue from the Christian church. This change meant the sacrifice of much that had given to Synagogue music in the Ghetto its emotional Jewish character. Yet, since Jewish music is local in its character and appeal, the Jews of Germany find in this modernized Synagogue music the conventional expression of the Jewish feelings, just as the Jews of Russia and Poland associate their emotional religious feelings with the music known to them in their synagogues from their childhood, and the Sephardic Jews find the satisfaction of their emotional religious needs in chanting the familiar words of prayer to the well-loved melodies of their Synagogue.

The question is constantly asked, "Which is the oldest of our Synagogue melodies?" It is not possible to give any authoritative answer to this question. But *Az Yashir Moshe* (D. A. de Sola, *The Ancient Melodies of the Spanish and*

Portuguese Jews, p. 9) has been traditionally believed to be the oldest melody of the Synagogue. We find serious statements to the effect that to this identical melody the triumphant paean of redemption was sung at the Red Sea by Moses and Miriam over three thousand years ago. The most that we can say for this tradition is that if it has never been proved to be correct, it has at least never been disproved. It must be left to individual musicianly judgment and skepticism or faith, to decide whether this simple melody may justly claim such illustrious lineage. The melody is composed to two somewhat contrasting phrases, both of which are simplicity itself. Another famous Sephardic melody is one of those to which *Hallel* is sung (D. A. de Sola, *Ibid.*, No. 42, p. 39). When in the *New York Tribune* of September 26, 1915, I traced back its age as demonstrably earlier than 1750, Mr. H. E. Krehbiel rebuked me for my needless caution. He asserted that "it is unquestionably an old, possibly an extremely old, Hebrew melody"—a statement that agrees with my own opinion. But although not much is known of its ancestry, I can give authentic information about its descendant, for its child is no less famous a melody than the one to which *Hatikva* is sung. To my certain knowledge, the Rev. Mr. Perlzweig, *hazzan* of the Finsbury Park Synagogue, in London, adapted the traditional Sephardic melody to *Hatikva*. The relation of the two melodies is so close as to be obvious to even the least musical of us.

The Haunting Beauty of Kol Nidrei

The most famous of the Russo-German Jewish melodies is *Kol Nidrei*, which has become widely known outside the Jewish community through its transcription by Max Bruch. The *Kol Nidrei* melody goes back to dim antiquity in its origin. But we are unable to date its composition, although phrases similar to some of its most striking passages can be found in old non–Jewish music. Owing to its association with the most solemn service of the Jewish year as well as to its haunting beauty as a melody, it has become perhaps the best loved of all Synagogue airs. The version as given by Max Bruch contains elements which do not belong to the *Kol Nidrei*, particularly one contrasting theme of light, folksong character, which has been taken form the Passover service, and somewhat irrelevantly added to the Atonement melody.

Kol Nidrei on the concert platform is not the same and cannot mean the same as *Kol Nidrei* in the Synagogue. The moment music leaves the Synagogue, and is made into material for a concert or a phonograph record, it suffers degradation. Its profane musical value may perchance be fully appreciated in a concert hall. But we irretrievably lose its emotional associations, its national expressiveness and its personal spiritual values which make it a priceless heritage in the Synagogue.

A comparison of *Kol Nidrei* with the two Sephardic melodies *Az Yashir Moshe* and *Hatikva* will immediately bring out one characteristic difference between Sephardic music and German or Russian Jewish music. The Sephardic service is sung for the most part by the congregation, and the melodies are therefore, as a rule, simple in construction and limited in range. But among the Ashkenazim, the cantor is the real leader of the service, and consequently, elaborate and florid music of wide range, in which the cantor's vocal powers have free play, marks much if not all of the liturgical music of northern Europe.

The Objections to Borrowed Music

In every generation we have been tempted to introduce into the Synagogue non–Jewish music. But although from days of old, we Jews have sought to "sing unto the Lord a new song," we have no justification for appropriating the music of our neighbors. If it be true that the sacred music of Bach and Handel expresses the emotions of Protestant Christianity, supremely beautiful though this music may be, it is out of place in a Synagogue. If it true that music of Wagner and Schubert is characteristically German, or that the music of Verdi is expressive of the Italian temperament, such music, brilliant though it may be, is not expressive of the Jewish religious temperament. Jewish cantors of today are learning to avoid the characterless borrowing of the religious souls of their neighbors that was so common in the era of Emancipation and Reform, and are either harking back to traditional themes or are bringing into the Synagogue new melodies of their own composition. Many of these modern compositions do not impress us as being characteristically Jewish. But perhaps the cause of this is due to something more than the fact that these modern anthems are composed for the comparatively un–Jewish service of a reformed temple. We cannot sing the songs of the Lord in a strange land.

"By the rivers of Babylon,
There we sat down, yea, we wept,
When we remembered Zion.

Upon the willows in the midst thereof
We hanged our harp.
For they that led us captive
Asked of us words of song
And our tormentors asked of us mirth:
'Sing us one of the songs of Zion.'
How shall we sing the Lord's song
In a strange land?"

But in our own land shall we not find anew a music that shall be intrinsically, originally and creatively Jewish, born out of the regenerated Jewish life in Palestine?

PART II
STUDIES IN JEWISH MUSIC

Introduction

JEWISH MUSIC IS, IN THE WORDS of musicologist Ruth Rubin, "as diverse and variegated as the Jews themselves. There are the songs of the Oriental Jews — Yemenite, Sephardic, Persian, Daghestanian, Babylonian, Moroccan; the Ladino songs of the Spaniolic Jews with their large collection of liturgical melodies; the Yiddish folk songs and Hassidic tunes (with or without words) of the Eastern European Jews."[1] Religious and secular songs are found throughout the world's Jewish communities, differing one from another depending on the region, city, or even synagogue in which they are found.

In this section, we move from the general to the particular, encountering six early studies in specific areas of Jewish music. While these essays are, for the most part, modest in scope and sophistication, they do exhibit clearly the nationalistic spirit of the time, and the once vital search for "authentic" Jewish melodies.

This section begins with two selections by Naphtali Herz Imber (1858–1909), a Jewish poet from Galicia most famous for writing *Hatikvah*, the Zionist and later Israeli national anthem. As a poet, Imber was most interested in the relationship of words and music, and the first of his two essays, "The Music of the Psalms," praises the musical qualities implicit in the Book of Psalms:

> In them one finds the deep heartbreaking tones of a Beethoven, as well as the smooth, light, laughing, comic song of an Offenbach; the silent, sweet whisper of love's longing, as well as the wild galloping Hallelujahs suggestive of Wagner's

Walküre. In the Psalms is contained the music of the past, present and the future. What wonder, then, that their publisher and editor, King David, lives, and will live, in the grateful memories of the lovers of the best music!

In "The Music of the Ghetto," Imber explores the nature and function of Hasidic songs. Hasidic (pious) Judaism is, essentially, a revivalist movement that began in Eastern Europe during the last third of the eighteenth century, which utilizes earlier traditions of mystic *Kabbalah* and medieval pietism as the foundation of a religious praxis centered on joy and ecstatic devotion. Imber found the Hasidim to be "the most good-hearted fellows I ever came across on God's green earth," and presents in this essay, to the best of his ability, an ethnographic study of Hasidic life, and the prominent role music plays within it.

Mendel Silber (1882–1970) departs from the topic of Jewish music, per se, to explore the contribution of Jewish singers, musicians, and composers to the larger world of Western music. Silber was a rabbi and a medical doctor, and served as dean and professor of psychology at the University of New Mexico before becoming rabbi of Congregation Gates of Prayer in New Orleans. It was perhaps his involvement in both secular and sacred pursuits that led Silber to write his book *Jewish Achievement* (1910), in which he examines the influence of prominent Jews in general society, ranging from agriculturalists and soldiers, to authors and bankers. "Jewish Singers" and "Composers and Players," the two essays presented, were originally published in that book. Among other things, Silber argues that the Jews are, as a people, naturally inclined to sing, drawing a connection between the prominence of Jewish-born singers on the opera stage and biblical accounts of the Levitical choir: "It would indeed appear strange, were we not to find excellent singers among the people that had already in earliest times cultivated the art to a degree that made it possible for four thousand singers to be employed in the Temple service."

Next is a paper by Kurt Schindler (1882–1935), "The Russian Jewish Folk-Song," which was first delivered at a concert of Jewish music performed at the Horace Mann Auditorium in New York on May 14, 1917. Schindler, a German-born composer and conductor who came to the United States in 1905, had a particular interest in the folk music of the world. This study grew out of his encounter with Russian Jews in New York, who, in his words, "convinced me of the priceless worth of these possessions of the Jewish race." The essay begins with an examination of four categories of Russian Jewish folksongs — songs of lament, love and parting, dance and wedding, and humor — and follows with the question, "Is there a Jewish folk music entirely distinctive from the music of other nations?" To this, Schindler claims — however erroneously — that, while the Jews have "a specific genius for assimilation and amalgamation," and though the rhythms employed in European Jewish folk music vary from region to region, "the melody — the soul of music — remains the same."

Pinchos Jassinowsky's (1886–1954) essay, "Hazzanim and Hazzanut," concludes this part. Jassinowsky was an accomplished *hazzan* (cantor), composer, poet and teacher. He was born in the Kiev region (the town of Romanovka), and made a career for himself in the United States as a service leader and concert performer. Jassinowsky was one of many exceptionally skilled cantors of the golden age of *Hazzanut*, lasting from the late nineteenth century to the 1940s. During this time, waves of Jewish immigrants from Eastern Europe came to America, and brought with them a love of intricate, emotional, florid, and often-virtuosic synagogue singing, which combined Ashkenazi prayer modes, motifs from biblical cantillation, traditional melodies, Hasidic tunes, and local musical elements from European host cultures. In this selection, Jassinowsky gives an account of the development of *hazzanut* (cantorial art), which he traces to Jews exiled to Babylonia after the destruction of Jerusalem's First Temple in 586 B.C.E. Seeking to establish a historical continuity of cantorial singing from ancient times to the present, while focusing largely on the emotional qualities of this music, Jassinowsky argues that, to a great extent, "the chants of the synagogue service have been of more powerful effect upon the souls of the listeners than the prayers themselves," and that the "prayers that are sung are part of the cantorial art of earlier days, and now our regular liturgical expression."

Note

1. Ruth Rubin, *A Treasury of Jewish Folksong* (New York: Schocken, 1950), p. 11.

7. The Music of the Psalms (1894)

Naphtali Herz Imber

IF THE BEAVER WAS THE MENTOR of primitive humanity in architecture, teaching Mr. Adam how to construct a home á la model outlined by the four-legged little professor, a construction known by the name of "pale building," then the nightingale was the first professor in nature's college of music, teaching primitive man how to sing and to render his supplication to the Unseen in unspeakable expressions, in the thrill of Music. The primitive man, who was at that time a tenant in nature's big palace, the primitive forest, dwelt as the neighbor of the birds. There in nature's music hall he had noticed that every morning when father Sol opened his golden window in the east, a cheerful thrill went through the air, and the little birds were cheering and greeting the rising sun with music in the air. That salutation, the primitive man thought, was a pleasant attribute to Him, whom he, the primitive man, in his simplicity worshiped as God, Creator, the Sun. He also began to cheer the rising sun, the revealing God, in that way of singing which he was being taught by Madam Nightingale. Here we see how music was the first to inspire the stupid brains of man to look on high, pointing him to a higher and nobler life. The sun was worshiped as God, and the first inspiring, divine thought of mankind was music. Music is the mother of religion, and the grandmother of civilization. It is curious to note how that prehistoric relic of musical evolution is entombed in the language of the ancients, in the Chaldean, and Hebrew tongue. Bird is in both languages *Zipor*, while the term for morning is *Zepar*; so that morning and bird are identical according to the conception of the prehistoric man, and here we find the keynote to the above outline in musical evolution. We also find in heraldic emblems the account of how music was taught to man. The birds, from the little swallow to the mother eagle, were taken up as protectors by the various tribes of humanity's family. When the *goat* was worshiped as a deity they applied to him the term *Zepar*, the name of both the birds and morning. When the ox was worshiped they called him *Shir*, which also means a song. Music was the divine revealer long ere God chose to reveal himself otherwise. Music runs like a thread through all the ages and the dispensations, as a connecting link between God and man. A religion without music has ever been no religion, and the Chaldeans, who were star-worshipers in the third dispensation, thought of the singing stars as gentlemen Adam thought of the singing birds. Job says, "the morning stars are singing, and the sons of God jollify." Job was a Chaldean, and probably a star-worshiper, who through supplication was converted to Jehovah's cult.

Primitive Hebrew Music

The Hebrew term for music is *Shir*, in Arabic *Shair*; it means also *line, wall* and *sight*. All these three originate from one conception, *even*, which is the most marked in music, in rhythmic array of sentences, stanzas, and the gradual raising of the voice. Indeed music marshaled the nations on the road of marching civilization, officered the soldiers in the battle array, and gradually lifted mankind up on the progressive way of life. A primitive lawgiver needed not to be armed with occult power in order to bring the people into submission; a singing bird nestling in his breast was the best testimony of his divine inspiration. And a singer was the lawgiver. On that ground, Moses, being a stutterer, was afraid that the Hebrews might not listen to him. Mohammed's success can be ascribed to his poetical book, the Koran, which is written in the rhythmic line of Arabic poems. The sentences in it are called *sura*, denoting long lines. The primitive rhythmic rule was very simple, more calculated as to the number of words than to the harmony of sounds; hence the brevity of the sentences. The Bible is written and composed on the same principle of music; and even classic Arabic and Hebrew, no matter of what subject they treat, are written and must be read in a musical strain. If a philosopher wants to impress an oriental with his philosophy, he must see to it that his arguments appeal to the ear, rather than to the common sense of the listener. The Five Books of Moses are written in a poetical scale, but only a few chapters deserve the name of poetical touch. These are, the dialogue of Lemech with his wives, the parting blessing of the patriarch Jacob, the song of Moses, and his farewell address. This latter, or last, chapter is the gem of primitive Hebrew poems; in which the lines are arranged metrically, corresponding each to the other, in a harmonious, melodic, sound, needing no instrument to execute it. The meter of these stanzas is arranged in such a regular line, that we are tempted to believe that they already had written or unwritten musical laws. But the fact is, that musical notes and regulations were brought into effect under King David, and were made laws under the composers, Asaph, Heman and the Sons of Korach. The Bible, or the Five Books of Moses have musical notes besides their reading punctuations. On the Sabbath and on holy days the portion for the week is read in the synagogue, and the "reading" has a special musical tenor, according to the musical notes. It is more of a peculiar accent of a peculiar nation than a musical aspect, as the same tenor sounds from Genesis to the end of the last verse of the last chapter of the Five Books, with the exception of the few poetical pieces in them. Again, the portion of the prophets which is read after that of the Pentateuch has a marked national air, and a peculiar musical touch worthy to give it a place of in a celebrated concert.

The Temple as a Musical College

The Hebrews, to the time of the first century A.D., had no religion, as we understand the term religion — that which links us to the spiritual life. That link is a missing one in the Mosaic cult, and the so-called ancient Hebrew religion was nothing but a mere social, civic array of laws. It may at first look appear strange, how a whole nation without a cheerful outlook into eternity, could exist without a religion in the midst of an idealistic pagandom. But considering it carefully, we will find that the ancient Hebrews had the most noble religion, the religion of music. Indeed, only the wordless, the unspeakable, but rich-in-expression, tongue of music is able to answer the riddles of life in such a consoling and satisfactory manner. For only music is able to speak to the inner spirit in its own language, whose words are expressions, and whose arguments are feelings. Only on the wings of music can we best make the flight to unseen space; and music is the only medium through which our astral body goes out from its clay prison and walks among the Celestials, in the realm of the ethereal universe. Music is the language spoken by angels. Such a religion was given to the ancient Hebrews by Moses. They had not an Aristotle to utilize the universe of philosophy, but they had

Heman and Asaph, the great composers of the Psalms, who have brought us in touch with that hidden force of life, to feel in our nerves the divine current. They had no Alexander, to weep at having no more worlds to conquer, but they had King David, who wept at seeing his own nothingness, when his spirit was carried away on the wings of music, to see the grandeur of nature and the greatness of the Ruling Power. Those nations whose cradles were rocked to the soft sounds of music, as the Hebrews and the Greeks, were higher in civilization than the mighty Romans and Persians. Music was the Mosaic religion; hence there is, in the Pentateuch, no law regarding prayer, nor any hint about the nether-world or life hereafter. Those mysteries are revealed to us by the inspiration of music — our spiritual elevator. Music is indeed an elevator — whence its Hebrew term, *Shir*, meaning *song*, *wall*, and *elevation*. The poets and singers were called *Meshorer*, as they were the elevators of the people. It is curious to note that most of the Hebrew leaders, even including women, were poets or singers — as Deborah, Miriam, and others. In order to establish a place where music could be cultivated, Moses ordered the building of the Temple, which was not, indeed, a place of worship, but merely a national college of music. And for that reason he prohibited the building of places of worship in any city, town, or village. (The building of synagogues and temples in modern Judaism is against the law of Moses). The charge of the college was given to the priests and Levites. But as the Hebrew music was in its infancy, and only three kinds of instruments were known at that time, (viz., the *shofar* or ram's horn, the *taf* or clapper, and the *chazozro* or flute), the Levites had not much to do, and to keep them from being idle, Moses made of them simple laborers, as Temple porters and carriers. As musical notes were unknown at that time, the instrumental playing uncultivated, we may regard the Mosaic music as the primitive evolution of the famous Hebrew national music.

The Father of Hebrew Music

King David, to whom is ascribed the authorship of the Psalms, was more than a poet, singer, or artist, and deserves the title of "father of Hebrew music." Himself a gifted poet and composer, he was also a good organizer — a talent so seldom found in an idealistic nature. David was the first to uplift music as an art. He ordered that the Levites should no longer be porters and carriers, but only singers, and players of instruments. Four thousand singers were by him selected from the tribe of Levi to be devoted to music, and placed under the three famous drill-masters, Asaph, Heman, and Jeduten, who were the chief composers of the music of the Psalms. The elevation to that dignity was an immense step in the development of the divine art. Musical notes, and the invention of a variety of instruments, were the outcome of that elevation. (The orthodox Jew will never listen to the strains of the organ, on the legendary ground that the organ was one of the numberless instruments of the Temple, which the Gentiles took wherewith to praise another god). But no matter how we must admire King David as a reformer and an organizer, we cannot forget him for excluding, from the art which ennobles the heart and widens the feelings, the women who, before this era, had shown a talent for it. The Rabbis have excluded the daughters of Abraham from the study of the law, designing their position at the loom, with the result that Jewish women are very ignorant in matters of their own history and religion. The excluding of women from the Musical College bore the same results. Jewish women have been tolerable pianists, but very poor composers, and their hearts are void of any of that idealistic touch so marked in their Gentile sisters.

Well-organized, and equipped with various instruments, the choir of the Levites became a highly respected body, and the Temple became the hope of the nation, whither came the people for shelter or refuge, seeking consolation not from an oracle teller, but rather from the songs that flowed sweetly from the lips of Zion's singers. In the *Hebrew Standard*, of New York, last year (under the title "Centuries Gone By") the writer gave a brief outline of the service order of the priests in the Temple. To the readers of *Music* he presents a sketch of the devotees of the music, the Levites. When organizing that body, King David regulated and clearly defined their mission — that they should every morning thank and praise the Lord with songs and instruments. As the body had a membership of more than twenty-four thousand, they were divided into sections of two thousand each, each section to serve a month in the Temple. These sections were again divided into companies of five-hundred each, one of which served each week. The company for the week was called *Mishmor*, meaning *watch*, as the members of the company were compelled to watch at their posts, and to sleep in the basements of the Temple. The discipline was a rigid one. If the lord of the mansion (the title of the Temple director) found, on his rounds, a Levite in a position not in harmony with the Temple regulations, he burned his clothes and beat his backbone with his club. Throughout Jerusalem when the people heard a cry in the night, coming from the Temple, they shook their heads in a pitying way, and said, Oh it is the cry of a poor son of Levi, who is now clubbed for not keeping the regulations. At sunrise, while the priests were preparing the morning sacrifice, arrayed in linen, the five hundred of the company, stood each at his *Dushan*, or *stand*, upon which lay the text with musical notes. The space allotted to the orchestra was in balconies, one over another like our galleries, in the shape of the half moon, so that the drillmaster might face them all alike. The companies were divided into small parties, of singers, cymbal players, etc. When the signal was given, the drillmaster waved his little flag, and the music began to sound. The same was repeated at the Evening Offering.

Every day had its selection from the Psalms, and the Talmud records that on the day of the destruction of the First Temple, which was on the ninth of the month of Av (our August), when the Chaldeans entered the Temple, the Levites sang the last verse of the ninety-fourth Psalm: "And he shall turn over them their sins, and in their wickedness he shall destroy, destroy them, God our Lord." "Curious," remarks the Talmud, "that on the same day of the same month the Second Temple was destroyed; and when the Romans entered, the Zion singers were repeating the same verse of the same chapter." From that record we learn that each day had its chapter from the Psalms, so, as the Psalms served the nation for a calendar, we are not surprised to hear of the same chapter on the same day of the month, four centuries later. From the same record our modern concert singers might take a lesson—not to be disturbed by any noise. Think of the Levites singing at their posts while the Temple was in flames! Such an orchestra must have been a sublime amusement, as everything aided to stir up the audience into an awe of joy. Even the structure of the Temple, with its splendid acoustic properties, helped to magnify that orchestral splendor. Voices were cultivated to high degree. There was in the Temple, so says the Talmud, a man, by name Gebuni Ben Cherus, whose duty it was to call every morning: "Rise, ye priests, to your work, and ye Levites to your songs." Agrippa, that Jewish king who was by blood an Edomite, by heart a Roman, by external appearances a Jew, and in character an all round hypocrite, was once in Jericho, a distance of three miles (not English) when, hearing the crier's voice at this distance, he rewarded him! Another anecdote told of Hugras Ben Levi, the master of voice culture, is that when he began to sing the priests tumbled backward, from the powerful current of his voice! On festivals, such as Purim, Pentecost, and the Tent-feast, the Hallelujahs (as Psalms 114–119 inclusive) were on the program for the day. Those Psalms were very ancient, written and composed by unknown authors, and from their jovial, musical tenor can be taken as songs of national victory. How the College of

Music affected the nation can be judged by the sentiments of the Talmud, which says that song is a labor which requires labor, and again, in a gnomic stanza;

> "When heard in music's sound
> All dance around,
> The matron with gray hair
> As the girl of seven fair."

King David will always live in the memory as the father of Hebrew song. Should all else fall into oblivion, his immortal song will still resound through the realms of space.

The Psalms

Homer and the Homeric heroes, are sleeping the long sleep and are seldom disturbed save by some old schoolmaster. Virgil is making much dust in the museums somewhere, in a forgotten corner known only to the librarian. Even the genius of Shakespeare appears mainly on the stage, and were it not for the aid that mimicry gives him, the living would hardly care for the great immortal. But King David lives, and will live until the last man shall break down by the calamity of our perishable mortality. His Psalms are sung by our sweet little ones in the Sunday schools, as well as by the pigtailed pagans in the far empire of China. No matter what creeds a religion decrees, the Psalms are counted among them. No matter what God or how many — if one or three — you worship, you can hardly approach Him, or them, without a salutation from the Psalms. Because the Psalms voice as no other literature does the spirit of worship, their melodic tongue is the language by which the individual spirit can most easily communicate with the Universal its inexpressible desires and wishes, a language understood by angels and seraphim — the sacred language of music. Such a music is the music of the Psalms, and what a variety! In them one finds the deep heartbreaking tones of a Beethoven, as well as the smooth, light, laughing, comic song of an Offenbach; the silent, sweet whisper of love's longing, as well as the wild galloping Hallelujahs suggestive of Wagner's *Walküre*. In the Psalms is contained the music of the past, present and the future. What wonder, then, that their publisher and editor, King David, lives, and will live, in the grateful memories of the lovers of the best music!

Authors and Composers

According to legend, the authors of the Psalms are Adam, Melchisedech, Moses, David, Asaph, Heman, Ethan, Jedutan, Abraham, and the sons of Korach. The historic authors and composers, besides the unknown writers, are six — David, Heman, Ethan, Asaph, Jedutan, Moses, and the sons of Korach. The chief writer seems to have been David. The oldest songs were the Hallelujahs (Psalms 140–150 inclusive), and the latest additions, "On the Rivers of Babylon."

The Instruments

The instruments were as follows: (1) *Shofar*, or ram's horn; (2) *Nehel*, or organ; (3) *Ngoh*, or love's harp, a harp similar to our banjo; (4) *Taf*, or clapper; (5) *Kinor*, a harp or psalter; (6) *Chalil*, or flute; (7) *Minim*, or cymbal; (8) *Zilzal*, a half drum, bordered with brass clappers; (9) *Shiminith*, an eight-stringed violin; (10) *Gittith*, a harp of Gath. Besides these national instruments we find in the Psalms others whose names indicated a paganistic origin — as *Al Tashcath* (mentioned four times, Ps. 57; 58; 59; and 75), an instrument used by the Arabs; *Ajeleth Hashachar* (Ps. 22) the morning star; *Gazelle*, an instrument probably used by the Greeks; *Shushan Eduth* (Ps. 60) "evidence of Shushan," a Persian instrument named out of respect for the Persians, as Shushan was the name of the Persian capitol; *Shoshanim* ("lilies") an instrument made in the shape of lilies.

Peculiarities

With the exception of those chapters whose writers and composers are unknown, the first verse of every chapter contains instruction to the drillmaster as to what instrument to employ, as well as the name of the author of the text and of the music. The drillmaster is called *Lamnazeiah*, and that word is in most chapters the first in the first verse. The word *Shir* at the beginning of a chapter, told the drillmaster that the chapter was to be sung without instrumental accompaniment. Such chapters are brief, as Ps. 70, with short sentences. Prominent among them are the fifteen Songs of Degrees, which were sung by the Levites going up the fifteen degrees (or stairs) to their stands, a song to each degree. These songs are distinguished by their brevity, and are without instruction to the drillmaster, owing to their well-known popular national air. If the word *mismor* occurs at the beginning of a chapter, the chapter is for both voice and instruments. The word *maschil* (mentioned ten times, Ps. 32; 42; 52; 53; 54; 55; 64; 78; 88; 89) means meditation — as about the historic events of the nation at large, or about man's own individual nothingness. In the former theme the song assumes more of a musical recitative, as in Psalm eighty-nine. Hence its first verse is simply marked, "*Maschil Iton Esrachi*." Among the simple recitatives we may place Psalm one hundred and nineteen, famous for its alphabetical meter. The individual meditations are composed corresponding to their texts. Sometimes the first verse of the chapter contains detailed instruction, as in Psalm eighty-eight, which reads as follows: "*Shir mismor l'b'nai Korach, Lamnazeiah al mahaloth leanoth maschil l'Heman Esrachi*." Rendered into English it reads: Song for voice and instruments, to the sons of Korach (as composers) to the drillmaster, the flute, low tones, to Heman the Ezrahite (text writer). The word *Lehaskir*, "to remember," told the drillmaster to repeat the refrain (mentioned in Ps. 38 and 70). As a rule all the Hallelujahs, most of the Meditations, some which are ascribed to David, and those under the heading *Tiphila*, "prayer," are without the prefaced first verse denoting text, theme, character, and method of handling. As they were very popular they needed no introduction. A peculiar character is the word *Selah*. Some think it is from the root *Sal*, meaning to uplift; but to my mind it is an instruction to the drillmaster to pause by that verse. *Selah*, S L H as written in the Hebrew, is the initial of *Simon* (signal) *Lamnazeiah* (to the drillmaster), and *Has* (to pause). *Selah* is often found in the Proverbs as well as in Job, whose musical notes are the same as those of the Psalms.

Music of the Psalms

The music of the Psalms, with the exception of the Hallelujahs, Prayers, and some of the Meditations, is in character minor and diffused in a variety of tones, from the silent worshiper of love to the high vibration of lamentation. The music of the Hallelujahs, on the contrary, is in a minor key, rising gradually from a joyful cry of victory, to the most jovial shout of a Bacchanalian. Owing to the suffering of the exiles after the destruction of the Temple, Hebrew music has suffered too, by losing something of its originality, through the strange influence of surroundings. The people, being always on the move to escape persecution, forgot the meaning of the ancient musical notes; and the music, passing as tradition from father to son, became erratic, and underwent many alterations. This can best be explained by a brief sketch of the state of the Hebrew nation.

The Hebrew nation as it now exists can be divided into three classes, differing in types and qualities: the Polish Jews, the Sephardic Jews, and the Jews from Yemen. The Polish Jews, after the destruction of the Temple, made their way to Russia and Poland, through Persia, and with slight changes have maintained throughout the centuries their Semitic, Hebraic, national character. Vigorous, industrious, speculative, they manifest a stubborn religious inclination to ultra-Orthodoxy, but without superstition. They are for the most part good Hebrew scholars, and music lovers; hence the ancient Temple music has been handed down with slight changes. Especially has the music of the Psalms been kept in such veneration that as if by the phonograph of time there are still reproduced the melodies sung by the Zion-singers, two thousand years ago. In Russia, and in Galicia, where orthodox Judaism reigns, societies known as *Chevrei Tehilim* (Psalm societies), the records of whose existence is as long as the years of the exile, are to be found in every village, town, and city. The purpose of those societies is to gather in the Synagogue every Sabbath afternoon and chant the songs of David to their old melodies, from the first to the last of the one hundred and fifty. In the writers boyhood it was a source of inspiring delight to him to hear those ancient songs sounding across twenty centuries. Some of those societies will rise after midnight on cold winter nights, and gather in the Synagogue to sing Psalms, electrifying the soul to vibrate higher impulses until it is touched by the divine current of joy. If a man is given up by the doctors, the Polish Hebrews seek the balm of Gilead in the Psalms. They gather, ten or more together in the Synagogue, and sing selected chapters of the Psalms, the initials of which correspond to the initials of the person on whose behalf they appeal to God. It is owing to those societies, and to religious veneration, that the music of the Psalms is not a thing of the past. The music of the Psalms has shown a marvelous power in creating the music of the synagogue, and those secular national airs so peculiar to that people. Of all the Jewish race, the Polish Jews are the greatest lovers of music, and the most gifted musicians, as certified by the works of Meyerbeer, Mendelssohn and Rubinstein.

The second class of Jews in the Hebrew race is the Sephardim, or *Spaniolen*, as they are called by their Polish brethren. The Sephardim are the descendants of those Jews who lived among the enlightened Moors, when the crescent moon shone over the Alhambra, and who were driven out by the Spaniards. After the expulsion, these Jews sought refuge in Turkey and

Asia Minor, and in Tunis, Algiers, and Morocco. They differ from the Polish Jews in every aspect of life, and even in the pronunciation of the sacred Hebrew language. It seems that the Sephardim have inherited the bad qualities of the two nations, among whom they lived. They are as lazy as the Moors, and as proud as the Spanish Hidalgos. Void of ambition, which marks the life of the Polish Jew, lacking in religious speculation — the manifestation of brain motion — the Spaniole wastes away his time in the gloomy cosmic outlook described and outlined by superstition. Monotonous as in his life, so is his music — monotonous, deplorable lamentation — and one can hardly distinguish between a funeral march and the movement with which the bride is escorted to the home of her new master. Life had no effect upon them, and in spite of the existence of the Psalms societies, as in Russia and in Poland, they have been unable to reproduce the sacred songs.

The third class of the Hebrew race consists of the Jews of Yemen, in Arabia. There is a peculiar legend among them (also mentioned in our written folklore) which suggests an explanation of their typical character and their fondness for music. The legend declares that when Zion's singers at the Rivers of Babylon with their harps hanging on the bulrushes, and bemoaning their national fall, the proud captors in a hilarious mood demanded, "Sing us an air from Zion's sweet melodies!" The Levites in despair, with a patriotic inspiration, severed their fingers from their hands with their teeth, and while the blood was gushing forth, replied, "How can we sing?" With this in mind we can understand the famous reply in the Lamenting Psalm, "By the Rivers of Babylon we sat down and wept." The legend further states that as a reward of their patriotic deed the Almighty sent a cloud to carry them into a far-off land, even to happy Arabia, where they still live in the folklore as the Children of Moses, or the red Jews (Moses was a Levite). It is perhaps more likely that the victorious, enlightened Chaldeans were so deeply impressed by the heroic deed of the Levites, that they rewarded them with liberty, whereupon they migrated to Yemen. The red color of their hair, the peculiarity of their type, and their fondness for music, may explain this legend.

In type these resemble neither the Jews of Poland, nor the *Spaniolen*, and are the most peculiar people of the race. With the patience of Job they have borne their long centuries of persecution without losing a bit of their originality. They claim to have migrated from Jerusalem long before the destruction of the Temple, and certainly present the real Hebrew Semitic type with a slight Chaldean cast. They are not naturally so erratic as the Polish Jews, nor so lazy as the *Spaniolen*. Since the settlement of Yemen they have never dared look elsewhere for another dwelling place, until within the last decade, when they have begun to flock to Jerusalem in expectation of the coming of the Messiah. It was in Jerusalem that the writer first came into contact with this peculiar people. In pronunciation of the Hebrew tongue they agree with their Polish Hebrew brethren. Pure as they are, uninfluenced by their surroundings, they have in that purity preserved the music of the Psalms in a better condition than have the Jews of Poland. When the writer first heard them sing the Psalms, he was transported by a magic spell, and seemed to be in the midst of the living men who sang these sacred melodies to the great Jehovah two thousand years ago. The Jews of Yemen are not only good Hebrew scholars, but they are also well versed in the ancient Chaldean tongue and literature. They have also preserved the ancient Chaldean melodies, which partake neither of the monotonous Arabic touch, nor the soft Hebraic tenor, and which are yet of an undeniably Semitic origin. Those strange melodies are a link between Asiatic and European music, and in their strains "God save the Queen" might have been sung when Semiramis, that ambitious queen, ruled the waves of the Euphrates, long before there was a king in Judea.

Sacred Synagogue Melodies, and Profane Melodies

A hundred years before Christ, the struggle between Pharisees and Sadducees assumed an ugly attitude, and resulted in a separation. In the *Hebrew Standard* (in 1893 in an article entitled "In Centuries Gone By"), the writer described at length that unfortunate struggle. In this paper he will confine himself to that important outcome of the struggle, not mentioned in the *Standard*, the birth of the Synagogue music. The Pharisees believed, like Christ, in the spirit of the Scriptures; hence they did not consider the Temple as the only fit place in which to worship Jehovah. The Sadducees, on the other hand, stuck to the letter, that there should be only one Temple to the one God. The former thought sacrifice a bygone custom, and no longer in harmony with the advanced thought of the time. They said that "no altar upon which animals' blood is shed, is the table of the Lord, but the table of man, where benediction is said, is the altar of the Lord." But the Sadducees thought otherwise, and the dispute resulted in the building of synagogues, with plain musical and prayer services without the ceremony of sacrifice. The best known synagogue was the Temple at Alexandria, built on the model of the Temple at Jerusalem, but with Hellenic taste in architecture and ornament. That Temple was so beautiful that the Talmud says, "He who has not seen that Temple has never seen what beauty is." The first priest who conducted the service was the famous Chonow, a genuine priest, clad in the robes of Aaron. After having served in the capacity of high priest, he was driven from his position through the intrigues of his brother, and fled from the Temple of Jerusalem. In Alexandria, that city wherein Aristotle's philosophy was the commentary to the Bible, it was, of course, impossible to have a service with animal sacrifice; so the service contained songs and prayer — songs of Psalms with Zionistic composition, but breathing an Hellenistic air. Soon after, many other synagogues were built on the same plan, even in Jerusalem, and the Talmud tells us that at the time of the destruction of the city there were four hundred such worship places in the City of the Lord. As instrumental playing was not allowed on the Sabbath outside of the Temple, the synagogues adopted "vocal orchestras," and voice culture began to be studied scientifically. The music of the Synagogue, and of the early Christians, who were still considered Jews, was that of the Psalms with slight variations from that of the Temple, due to country and surroundings. When in the course of time, Christianity evolved into a separate religion, with new doctrines and dogmas strange to Judaism, the music of the Psalms, too, was undergoing evolution, hand-in-hand with the church of Christ, and the Psalms were sung to Ghetic, Roman and Greek airs, but not to the old Zion melodies. The synagogues, less subject to outside influence, kept the strains of Zion's music longer. When many centuries of persecution had followed the Destruction, and a great desire for restoration began to manifest itself among the Hebrews, influences and views unknown among the ancients created a new literature, and the new poetry that always is at the head of a new literature. As from the natural position of the nation there was no disposition to listen to the language of the flowers, to the whispers of love, or to the words of gaiety, its poets turned to God and the circumstances of their people for subjects for their poems. The first of these poets was Rabbi Lazar Ha Kalir, a Palestinian Jew, whose birthplace and time are unknown, as are those of most of the poets. His poems found their way to those Jews who marched on the dark road of exile, from Palestine through Persia into Russia. There they soon found composers to set them to music, about half of which was taken from the Psalms, the other half being their own work, owing to a new meter and style. After Kalir other poets arose, each finding his own composer, and in that way was formed the great Jewish prayer book, the compositions in which are known as the "Music of the Synagogue." But no matter in what way the music of the Synagogue was brought into existence, we shall always recognize it as due to the music of the Psalms, and especially is this recognition easy in the so-called Sinaitic songs (sacred as if given from Sinai) — music applied to certain prayers or meditation on the Atonement, New Year's day, and certain festivals. When, a century ago, Bonaparte began to bear the torch of civilization to the far, uncultured North, and the Jewish race began to see a ray of hope shine through the clouds of its life, it was the Synagogue music which began first to show a revival, and a return to the ancient music of the Psalms. The Russian and Polish Jew is a great lover of music. He can be without a Rabbi, but he cannot worship his God without a composer, a *hazzan*. One can find poor orthodox communicates without a rabbi, but they always have a *hazzan* with a princely salary. The writer once asked an orthodox Jew why, when the reformed Jews paid their rabbis such salaries, the orthodox Jews paid it to their drillmaster and let the rabbi starve. The Jew replied, "We know the Bible as well as the rabbi, but we want to learn something that we do not know, and that we get from the *hazzan*, and we hear the voice of God calling us through the music." When a good *hazzan* is present in an orthodox city, it is no uncommon thing for the people to remain in the Synagogue the whole day, under the spell of the music. The slightest shadow upon the character of a rabbi will cost him his position, but the *hazzan* may, like "Bob Ingersoll," have his own way in religion, and it will not cost him his music stand — no matter what hypocrisy he exhibits at the sacred shrine, singing Psalms to Jehovah, to whom his heart is not devoted. That fact speaks enough for the great love of music manifested by the Polish Jew. The *hazzan*, as a rule, is assisted in the service by a regular male choir, females not being allowed to sing in the Synagogue by orthodox Jews. The choir varies in numbers according to the size of the community, sometimes numbering twenty, and including all the vocal parts, from soprano to bass. The favorite composition of the orthodox Jews is the "Thought" — a composition peculiar to these people, and in character, as its name denotes, a fantasy. The *hazzan*, before beginning a favorite piece, prefaces it with an array of thoughts, losing himself in a chaotic delirium of tones, which correspond to the piece which the harmony (the choir) is going to sing. These composers have done a great deal to receive the Jewish national music, especially that of the Psalms. Their compositions are called Jüdish (Jewish), to distinguish them from the compositions of the Reformed Jews, which are merely imitations of church music, and not Jewish. Such composers as Pasternak, Jeruchom, Hakatan, and the famous Balbesil from Wilne are worthy of niches in the temple of fame, along with Mozart, Beethoven and Wagner.

The influence of the music of the Psalms can be traced in another direction — in the folksongs, or so-called "profane" melodies. Of course the Psalms have not had as great an influence upon them as upon the music of the synagogue, and yet the primary atom in their evolution was the music of the Psalms. Composers of that sort of music show their genius in nationalization. They take a Meyerbeer, an Offenbach, and nationalize him in such a way that one can hardly recognize the origin. Famous among composers of this class are Beril the Blind, the poet Wolf Ehrenkranz, and the modern Abraham Goldfaden, the father of the modern Jewish stage.

To the Lovers of Music

Often when listening to sacred music, or church songs of the Psalms, I have been astonished to find my ear deaf to these sweet, melodious sounds. They are strange sounds, not the sounds of the Psalms. Hence I never was affected. My proposition is to form a society of musical scholars with prominent orthodox *hazzanim* to convert Milton's translations of the Psalms, as they are nearer the Hebrew meter, into the ancient music of the Psalms, comparing the ancient notes with the modern. I also might take into account the pure ancient melodies of the Jews of Yemen. Should my proposition go into effect through my present article, I would feel greatly rewarded for my hard labor.

8. The Music of the Ghetto (1898)
NAPHTALI HERZ IMBER

Melodies of the Mystics, or "Chasidim"

IN RUSSIA AND GALICIA, the bulk of the Jews belong to the well-known sect of "Chasidim" (pious ones), whom I styled in the *Jewish Exponent* the "Jewish Salvation Army."

In regard to their outside method of worship they deserve that title, but concerning the ethics of their cult they might be called "Jewish Theosophists." The sect has been known since a century ago under the name of "The Chasidim," as founded by the wonder rabbi, the Jewish Mahatma, Israel Baal Shem Tov (man of a good name). They believed in the reincarnation ere a Madam Blavatsky taught it to the Gentiles, and the secret astral body revealed a hundred years ago by the great Mahatma, while he used to smoke his pipe, ere a Blavatsky told it to her inner circle when smoking cigarettes. (As Madam Blavatsky was a native of Russia, she got the theosophy copied from the Chasidim there, giving it out to the ignorant Gentiles as new revelation). That particular sect is only a transfiguration of the ancient Jewish sect, the Essenes, transformed in other respects according to the circumstances and ages, which are constantly working upon every organic or inorganic system of this life. Their chief belief besides the Jewish religion is the Cabala, or mystic teaching which I traced back to its greatest exponent, Jesus the son of Sirach Hanosri (the sawman or the carpenter), who lived two hundred and fifty years before the Christian era. In the middle ages that teaching was known only to a few worthies until it began to illuminate the darkest half of Asia with the luster of a great optimistic ray from Israel Baal Shem Tov a century ago. He said that the only thing which uplifts the mortal to the sphere of the immortals is joy, and he claimed that the Almighty was more pleased when he (Israel Baal Shem Tov) smoked a pipe, than by the long prayers of the rabbis.

In the midst of our alarming and charming life of the nineteenth century of culture and civilization, the Chasidim live a life like those in the hermit kingdom of Korea. Their connection with their Talmudical brethren and with the natives is more mechanical than a real one — the Chasidim live in their own spiritual world, that unseen universe, of which neither Kepler nor Herschel had any idea. They are real "Children of the Ghetto," whom culture has not yet touched with its noisy vibration.

If you come into a city town in half Asia, in Russia and in Poland, you will find three classes of Hebrews, corresponding to their three kinds of worship houses. The one is the Synagogue, built in the Gothic style, a place kept very sacred, and it is only opened at the hours of prayer. The worshipers there as a rule belong to that class who are religious without knowing why. They are recruited from the all day life Jews.

The second worship house is called "The Beth Hammedrash" (house of research); it is built in the style of a village mosque in the Orient. The house is devoted to worshipers as well as to students. The worshipers there are the conservatives with strong Talmudical belief to the letter. In both of those worship places a hired *hazzan* (melody maker) is appointed with the spirit of the Hebrew melodies. As a rule the *hazzan*, who is hired by the city, prays always in the synagogue.

The third worship place is the "Klaus" (an old German term for monastery). The Klaus has the appearance of one of the storehouses which adorn the Ghetto, and no one would ever dream that this is a place for worshiping God, and if it had not inside the sacred shrine with the sacred screen, we would take it either for a free reading room or for a club house for gossips. This place is commonly called by the Jews "The Chasidim Stibel" (the little house of the Chasidim). As a rule each Ghetto has many Klauses as each bears the name of the Rabbi or Mahatma in whom the said congregation believes. The Klaus has no *hazzan* nor choir, for every one is a born singer, and, in time of prayer, the visitor will think that he is in Bayreuth hearing the hundred various voices of Wagner's music in Brunhilde. Indeed those sacred Ghetto melodies and the mode of their execution suggests to one the question if Wagner has not worked after the model of Ghetto music.

The Mahatma

The wonder rabbi, or the Mahatma, is, as a rule, the descendant of the first prominent disciples of Israel Baal Shem Tov. Each Mahatma has people in every town, who form a congregation; and the Klaus is called by the surname of the Mahatma, and so are called his followers, as the "Belzer Chasidim" or "Alska Chasidim," meaning Chasidim who believe in the wonder Rabbi of Belz or those who believe in the Mahatma of Alesk. The descendants of Baal Shem Tov are held in the highest esteem and sacredness, and each of them is known by the pet name "The Grand Child."

The wonder rabbi is worshiped like the idols of the ancient pagans, and his word is law. He is the living oracle, to whom thousands from all corners of the land come with applications in one hand, and with the Shekel in the other, to beg the Rabbi to alter the rolling wheels of fate. Not only Jews, but Gentiles of higher order are to be found among the peculiar crowd of the Ghetto who come impulsed by the same human desire — to have a niche in the future. Thousands are the daily visitors; some come with their imbecile children and others come to apply to the rabbi to keep away the grim messenger from the deathbed of their nearest and dearest.

His followers, the Chasidim, no matter whether rich or poor, make a pilgrimage twice or three times in a year, specially before the New Year and Atonement Day, when there may be more than ten thousand followers from all corners of the land to pray with the Mahatma. They believe, as even the Talmudical Jews believe, that on the New Year's day the heavenly court is at the celestial bench to decree the fates of man. Satan (or Uncle Sam, as he is called by those mystics) plays the part of prosecuting attorney, while the good angels are pleading on behalf of suffering humanity. The Mahatma, when he gets his "Aliath Neshama" (soul accession to heaven or going out by his astral), wrestles with Satan, and of course Satan gets the worst of it, and so the decrees are made favorable to the Children of the Ghetto through the powerful influence of the wonder rabbi; hence they are eager to be present at that day in his Klaus, as he carries their prayers right to the throne of the Most High. Often the Mahatma takes a trip round the land, and on such occasions the Klaus of the city becomes a most interesting sight, worthy of seeing and hearing those mystical melodies, which probably were sung by the Essenes two thousand years ago in the wilderness of Judea.

The Klaus
(The Worshiping Place of the Chasidim)

The Klaus, as I said before, has not the outside appearance of a worshiping place, neither does its inner appearance denote it as such. You can find in the morning, while the reader says the prayer before the sacred shrine, and some or many are clothed in their white prayer mantles — you will find many of them sitting around drinking their white coffee, or liquor, or gossiping about the newest miracle of the Mahatma. The Chasidim like liquor very much, as they regard it as a medium of inspiration; yet in spite of their fondness for it, you never can find a drunken Chasid, and it seems that even when the devil is used for a good purpose he turns out an angel.

The gloom which is cast in most of the worshiping houses is partly due to the strictness of the prayer drill and partly to the gloomy sermons of the rabbis. That cast is missing in the Klaus, for the Chasidim are not bound by a prayer discipline and worship regulations, and "worship as you please" is the motto of the Klaus, for when they get into the inspiration of prayer they seem not to conceive where they are and their spirits move upon the surface of celestial nothingness. Not only is the Chasid gesticulating, he shows a restlessness as the tiger in the cage. You will find him pacing up and down while praying, lifting up his hands in a motion resembling our baseball players, as if he intended to catch some flying demon. Often he will make a jump, as if he is trying to fly direct to heaven. While praying it will appear to the stranger that the whole house is a musical training school and the people practicing voice culture. Here, by a certain sentence, he will give a roar like a lion reaching the highest pitch of the organic D, while a moment later he will let out a trill in the soprano, so that you will think that some canary bird is nestling in his throat. He will while praying perform all the evolutions, gymnastical vibrations, from the soft motion of a stage actor, to the whirling dance of a ballet girl. In his melodies, he tries to outdo the Seraphic Celestial choir, who spend their whole existence in singing.

The optimistic view of life manifests itself in every movement of this earth. A Chasid never grieves; no matter how time and circumstances may press him hard, he cheerfully will accept them, and in order to escape temptations he will leave his wife and children to the care of the Almighty, while he will trust in his wonder rabbi, the Mahatma. He will go there often on foot to sit in his Klaus, eating from the free lunch given daily by the wonder rabbi. (The Klaus of the wonder rabbi maintains a free lunch on the expenses of the wonder rabbi, for which he has a special fund, and hundreds of Batlonim, "Idlers," as they are surnamed, are fed daily).

There the "Idler" sits until the rabbi finds an opportunity to work on his behalf good will in heaven. (The idea of "good will," or, in plain English, if the heavenly court is in good humor, is an established fact amongst the mystics of all nations, as they try to make a God more humane and man more than divine.) In every city, village or town in Russia and in Poland where there exist Chasidim, there you can find their Klauses open day and night full of people, some reading the books of the Zohar (the light), that Bible of the mystics (although they cannot translate to you a line of it), while others are sitting along the benches in such an attitude as those idle onlookers in America's hotels.

They sit and gossip about everything on earth from the concert of the European powers and the wars to come till the expected coming of the Messiah and the horrors which will herald its coming. Of course the recent wonders wrought by their Mahatma are interwoven in the long thread of the gossip. The wonderful tales of their Mahatma's power inspires them often to ask the sexton for a drink of liquor. The sexton of the Chasidim has many duties to perform; not as those of the Synagogues and other worship houses, whose business is to attend to the dead, and keep clean the worship place, the sexton of the Chasidim has the duty of attending to the living, to provide them with the nectar as a medium of inspiration that they may be able to visit the unseen by his own unseen astral.

Below the sacred shrine there he has a box, which represents his little saloon, containing a bottle of white whisky and a few eggs and some cakes. He sells to the Chasidim per glass, and the charges are as in other saloons. Another of his duties is to illuminate the windows of the Klaus on the death day of Rabbi Simon Bar Jochai, the author of the *Zohar*, and to provide a good provision of the nectar. I asked a Chasid once: "Why do you need such a common medium as liquor for an inspiration to spirituality?" He answered: "In order to get the highest we must get the push from below, as the balloon can not go high until it gets a push from below."

The Chasidim are the most good-hearted fellows I have ever come across on God's green earth, for in everything they see only joy and the gloomy side of things they never look on. In the night their Klaus is converted into a free hotel, and you can find the weary wanderers, or tramps, stretched along the benches snoring while the Chasidim are gossiping. Music is their religion, and here lies the secret of their happy temper. The Sabbath day, especially at the third meal (the orthodox Jew eats three meals on the Sabbath), which takes place a half hour before sunset, is the most interesting celebration among the Chasidim. On Sabbath they believe that each man has another soul in addition to his own on the eve of the Sabbath, and it departs from him on the outgoing of the Sabbath. Many Cabbalistic songs in the Chaldean language were written by famous Cabbalists in honor of the great soul and the Sabbath queen. The immortal poet Heine has immortalized that celebration only in the way orthodox Jews celebrate, but he did not know the ways of the Chasidim and how they celebrate it. While the Jews of other denominations are spending their time in hearing the sermons of wandering rabbis or studying Talmudical lore, the Chasidim in their Klaus spend the day as others, with the exception that neither cigarette nor pipe smoke fills the Elysium of the mystics.

A half an hour before sunset, while the Jews go home for their third meal, the Chasidim prepare the tables of the Klaus for a social entertainment. The one table is reserved for the Haute Valeue of the sect, the others have no tablecloths, as every Chasid brings his own meal to the religious picnic. At the dressed table their local leader occupies the seat of honor and some wealthy man among them sends fishes, while others donate the loaves. It begins now to be dark, and the Jews of other denominations are by this time at home doing and pursuing their daily work in their designed stations of life; but the Chasidim are still celebrating the Sabbath, and the Klaus is under cover of darkness, as their mystic life is. The leader drinks the first cup of wine and breaks the loaves, distributing them among the people; the same he does with the fishes. Such a ceremony reminds one of the last communion of Christ. Those who cannot reach the table have in their pockets their picnic loaves and fishes. After the leader says some mystical lores in the name of the Mahatma, they begin to sing the well-known Chasidic mystic song for the occasion, known as the "Benei Heichala" (children of the palace). Their Chaldaic songs can hardly be translated, for in another language they turn to be vulgar love poems, yet in the esoteric meaning they cover the deepest thoughts ever conceived by a philosopher. They sing — and the song is a song no mortal can play, for it is the most stirring and touching ever vocal music is able to produce; during the song every one present joins in the singing and it is marvelous that such a multitude without any director executes the pieces very satisfactorily, and you will never hear a false turn from one of them. The closing is the singing of Psalm 144 sung in a popular Jewish traditional air.

The evening prayer is said, the candles lit, and a new proceeding of a particular celebration comes, which is known as "Melave Malka" (accompanying the Queen Sabbath by her departure). The meal, or, better, the menu, consists of "Borsht" (soup made of beet sugar), a few eggs and loaves of bread and a bottle or two of brandy. When the banquet in honor of the queen is finished, which is often at ten o'clock in the night, then again music of a mystical tenor is heard, and it reaches the highest pitch of inspiration when they, as by an impulse, form their mystical dance.

The music is accompanied by tambourine, which is to be found in every Klaus; the tambourine is a half drum in the shape of a circle and little bells are distributed round its wooden borders. Music and dance were the first used by primitive man in paying attributes of admiration to the higher powers. Drum and bell were the first primitive play instruments, through which the primitive divine music was executed.

The most primitive religion was the Phallic cult, a religion well represented by the primitive play instrument of the bell and the drum. Their clappers and drums symbolized the organic instruments by which the Phallic cult was worshiped. The deep mysticism of these mystics has a philosophical leaning to the Phallic cult, hence its corresponding play instrument, the tambourine, is sacred to them. Their dance is as peculiar as their music. They dance by forming a large circle, one's hand on the shoulders of the others, and while they are whirling around to the strains of the mystical tambourine so that they cut Madona faces, they kick with their legs outside the circle as if to drive away somebody. The kicking means to kick away Satan and his host, the "Klipos" (underdeveloped evil spirits, the word denotes shells, they can be styled to their meaning spiritual bacteria). I have seen pleasures enough for my short life, I have sat at banquets where royal nectar (champagne) flowed in streams, and each cup was presented by a beauty worthy to be enlisted as a houri in Mohammed's Paradise; yet I confess that I never had such elevating pleasure as when I sat at the parting banquet to Queen Sabbath, and that unspeakable mystic power of mystical melodies carried me off from the earth to enjoy sights unseen and feel that elevating pleasure, for which we all now linger.

The Mahatma's Melody (Dem Rebins Nigin) or The Throwing out of the Astral

When the Mahatma once a year makes his tour through the land the Klaus always serves as a reception room as well as a banquet hall. The banquet is given by his faithful on the Sabbath days, and among the wonderful treasures which my memory has collected it has also preserved the "Melody of the Mahatma." The Mahatma, who is now mummified in the coffin of my recollection, or whom I have now in my mind, was of medium height, with a face shaped like a full moon, and carried a belly as big as the big drum of the Salvation Army. It was Friday evening he entered the Klaus, which was packed to suffocation. He went, escorted by the noblest of the sect, to the prayer stand before the sacred shrine. Donned in his silk Kaftan, he covered it with the white prayer mantle and began to lead folks to welcome Queen Sabbath. It was not a prayer meeting, as it resembled more a musical concert with a variety program. The first word of the prayer he uttered sounded as the harsh commanding word of a general ordering the soldiers to break up camp and to march. Then he began to pray in such a powerful and tremendous voice, which made the very roof shake and the people tremble; then following the roar of his war cry followed a song in a minor key resembling the cry of a babe intermingled with thrills and shrills in rapid succession, all in the strain of the mystical melodies, the real "music of the Ghetto." The jumps, the dance, the springs, made manifest the highest pitch of his inspiration and it seemed to speak, with the Psalms, that all his bones praised the Almighty. The uncountable multitude joined in, and there was a real Wagner concert, for every tune, from the roar of the ocean to the silent whisper of the rose, was represented. The singing, praying and jumping lasted from six o'clock in the evening till eleven o'clock in the night, five hours without pause or rest, and yet neither was the throat of the Mahatma nor of the multitude sore nor did they show symptoms of being tired. When the prayers were at an end, then the ceremony of handshake begins, and every one, young and old, comes to shake hands with the wonder rabbi, and say good Sabbath. Then the table is prepared for the banquet. The one I witnessed there were two tables arranged in a delta shape. The Mahatma occupies the head seat, and each member is placed in accordance with his rank in the sect and the station he occupies in life. The multitude is satisfied to fill out the vacuum and causing a helter skelter by each attempt to move on. The menu consists of fish, meat and puddings. First he sanctifies the wine, and taking a sip from the cup he presents it to the most prominent member near, who presents it to the other, and by such means the cup makes the round trip, and any one thinks himself in grace if he can only smell from it, not to speak of drinking. The plate of soup is now before the wonder rabbi. He takes two spoonfuls from it, then the multitude begins to battle for the drops of soup, as if it was the "elixir of life." When the first dish is finished, the signal is given, and the multitude begins to sing the Cabbalistic poem written in the Chaldean tongue to the strain of the rabbi's "Nigun" (melody). Every Mahatma has a different strain from those who believe in another wonder rabbi. When the last sound of his favorite song echoes away into the vacuum of an unseen space, the Mahatma gets his full divine inspiration. He turns his weary head aside, closes his eyes, and a death silence reigns as if the multitude were a petrified solid mass, for the rabbi throws now his own astral, goes to heaven to get new revelations in mystic lore. The Prophet Elijah went to heaven in a chariot of fire and by horses of the same element. The Mahatma of the Theosophists cannot throw out his astral until he falls into a cataleptic fit (indeed, every one who is afflicted with that terrible affliction says he goes into a trance to shield his trouble). But the Jewish Mahatma cannot go to heaven through his astral until preceded by the sweet strains of music. How sublime — how grand — to be carried on the wings of the muse to the celestial realm of happiness, beyond mortal's grasp! The trip to heaven there and back does not last long, a half an hour or more, then the rabbi awakens and tells them the new revelations he got there above, and after those mystical hints the multitude breaks out into joyous music again until late at night. The same is repeated in the morning and in the evening, when the tambourine calls them out to the mystic dance.

The Character of Mystic Melodies

That real music of the Ghetto, those deep, mystical melodies, are distinguished from the present and ancient "Hebrew Melodies" known under the name of "Golus Lieder" (songs of the exile), or the Synagogue melodies known as the "Sinaitic Tunes." The two latter are on the minor key, Oriental through and through, while in the mystic melodies, in spite they are on the deepest minor key, there is the manifestation of a strange, unknown touch, which gives them that joyous sound, that cheerfulness which is missed in the "Hebrew Melodies" as well as in the "Sinaitic Tunes." They are more of the character of victorious musical marches, and I do not know any nationality to which I shall claim the inclination of those deep mystic melodies. While in the Hebrew melodies or in the Sinaitic songs, no matter how cheerful the text may be, the melody will always betray its nativity, the exile, and the ear will understand the groan of the suffering Zion singer. Again those mystic melodies, even a funeral march of them will sound out that cheerful sound of hope, that joyous elevation, which will make us to forget the mournful text. It is a mystery in musical psychology. It seems that music has no nationality, it is only the product of the temper of the composer or producer, the optimistic view and cheerful life of the Chasidim, so their music is only a manifestation of themselves. If it is not so, then what is it? Both are Jews, both drink from the bitter cup of the exile, and both are lamenting the fall of Jerusalem, and both hope for the restoration and a Messiah, yet how different is the expression of their music. Another peculiarity of those mystical melodies is that they are adaptable to any text, and you can apply a funeral march to the text of a nuptial march and it will sound as cheerful as the occasion requires. The music of the Ghetto is deep, a music whose singers fight by its powers the forces of Satan and his demons, a music which lifts up the mortal to the loftiest spot of eternity, a music by which we can throw out our better self, the astral, and being conscious of what we hear and see, is more powerful than the hypnotic musical power of a common Svengali. Wonderful is that music, its singers and composers! Without the study of general "bass," without being able to write or read the notes, they compose, they sing, and as soon as a favorite song is composed it is in a short time traveling the whole land from the Volga to the blue Danube. I have observed that those who are trained to play or to sing from the notes are unable to take the sense of hearing into activity. The musicians of half Asia play all the arias you want by the aid to the sense of the ear. Many have tried to sketch the lives of the Ghetto, but he who lives in a city of culture can never comprehend them, as you cannot comprehend their music. He who wants to understand the children of the Ghetto must be a child of it. It is a pity that such a most interesting music has not reached the drumskin of modern musicians. We have wine music, church music, Jewish music, Gentile music, Oriental music and Occidental music, but we have not yet mystical music, which is more of musical need, for music alone is a mystical power, and he who is not of a mystical temper can never comprehend its powerful touch. The Jewish theaters in New York City may be given the credit of having imported into America some of those mystical melodies. I say some, for it needs a good deal to hear them play in preservation in notes for the benefit of those who are always lovers of divine science. Should my present sketch call the attention of music lovers to that mysterious music of the Ghetto and to their mystical melodies, I will feel greatly rewarded.

9. Jewish Singers (1910)
Mendel Silber

IT WOULD INDEED APPEAR STRANGE, were we not to find excellent singers among the people that had already in earliest times cultivated the art to a degree that made it possible for four thousand singers to be employed in the Temple service. The song, in fact, was very much used by the Jews in ancient times, as may be seen from the numerous songs in the Bible as well as from the account of the festivals and celebrations which were always accompanied by singing. And though after the destruction of the Temple and throughout the diaspora the Jew was naturally more given to "saying *selichot*" (solemn memorial prayers) than to "singing the song of the supreme on a strange soil," yet, in modern times, as soon as he was allowed to breath a purer air and to see a brighter light, the harmonious sounds of Jewish song again ascended heavenward. It is from the nineteenth century on, therefore, that we have renowned representatives among the Jews of both sacred and secular songs.

Thus, while Solomon Sulzer, the Vienna cantor, Louis Lewandowski, in Berlin, and S. Naumbourg, cantor in Paris, were engaged in attuning traditional songs of the synagogue service to the music of modern masters, Giuditta Grisi, Clara Heinefetter, and Guilia Grisi were at the same time, in the same cities, winning laurels in the opera. And as the years rolled on Jewish song in the synagogue as well as on the stage rose to a higher degree of perfection and prominence. This can be seen from the fact that while H. Goldberg's name was spreading as a great cantor, his son, Albert Goldberg, was a recognized master of the opera, and Leonard Landau achieved fame in both, first as a celebrated cantor and then as an unexcelled opera singer.

If we leave the comparison between the sacred and secular fields, the singers of the synagogue and the stage, which comparison might be sustained by innumerable examples, we shall learn that this particular art "knows no sex" and finds its favorites in every country and clime. The sisters Grisi, to whom reference has already been made, are, together with Giuditta Pasta, prominent prima-donnas among the Italian Jewesses. In Germany we have five sisters, Clara, Eva, Fatime, Kathinka, and Sabine Heinefetter, all of whom were towards the middle of the last century celebrated singers. In the same country are also distinguished Pauline Lucca, Jettka Finkelstein, Sophie Koenig, and Jenny Meyer. Poland has produced the remarkable singer Lola Beth, Denmark, Henrietta Nissen, Hungary, Therese Rothauser, France, Colestine Nathan, England, Rosa Olitzka, and in this country two Jewesses are making a fine record on the stage of the Metropolitan Opera House of New York.

That the number of Jews who have gained a national and even an international reputation as great singers, must by far exceed that of Jewesses can be readily understood. The well-known modesty of the Jewish woman and the extraordinarily deep affection and attachment of Jewish parents to their children have kept many a daughter of Israel off the stage. The man, on the other hand, among the Jews as among others, "must wager and venture and hunt down his fortune," so that he knows no barrier, save that placed in his path by nature or providence. Only a few, therefore, can receive mention here and, by following the method adopted to ascertain the most representative artists in the various countries the following names at one glance class themselves: Leopold Demuth, of Austria; David Ney, in Hungary; Nicholaus Rothmuehl, of Russo-Poland; Ferdinand Gumbert, Paul Kalisch, Ludwig Strakosch, and George Henschel (who gained his world-wide reputation after he had immigrated to England) are celebrated German artists, while in France there are few better known names than that of Jean Lasalle and England cherishes the memory of John Braham.

To these illustrious names must be added that of Heinrich Sontheim, who was not only one of the most famous singers of the last century, but who retained his voice longer than any singer on the operatic stage. As octogenarian he was still able to call forth a storm of applause, and on one occasion caused one critic to write: "He made an impression as though he was his own grandson."

Still more interesting is the career of Adolf Muehlmann, the famous baritone singer of the New York Metropolitan opera. A native of Russia (Kishineff), he attended the "Cheder" (Hebrew school) and the "Yeshibah" (Talmud school) where, for the amusement of his schoolmates he would often sing some Hebrew melody. This was not held to be in good taste for a candidate of the rabbinate (he was intended for that position) and so particular care had to be taken that no stranger was ever listening to his singing. But carelessness has always been a trait of the young, and Adolf was no exception in this regard. He was once reckless enough to sing in the presence of the town cantor, and the latter, charmed by the young man's voice, offered to teach him music. Muehlmann was delighted with the unexpected opportunity, but there were objections on all sides, as it was deemed a great wrong in the "bochur" (Talmud student), who must delve deeply into the sacred literature before he can become a rabbi, to engage in any secular occupation. However, the cantor agreed to keep the matter of instruction a secret, and after three years it became evident both to teacher and pupil that singing and not preaching was Muehlmann's rightful pursuit. He then rallied for one year in Odessa, still undecided whether or not to take the daring step, and went to Vienna, where without means and after a long and hard struggle, bordering on actual starvation, his attainments were of a nature to bring him admiration in royal courts and widespread and well-earned fame, both here and abroad.

In concluding this survey, I feel constrained to say that though, as has been noticed, the Jew has often distinguished himself as a singer, yet the traces of his abnormal life, in a field where so much depends on the physical organism, are not yet wholly obliterated. It makes one sad to think what his achievement in vocal music might have been had he not so long been imprisoned in the narrow confines of the stifling ghetto, had he, like other human beings, not been deprived of light and sunshine, of the free and fair exercise of lung and limb.

10. Composers and Players (1910)

Mendel Silber

WITH A THOROUGH KNOWLEDGE of the racial and traditional history and development of our people, strengthened and supported by a fine and fair grasp of its character, George Eliot has hinted at the exceptional musical ability of the Jew, by representing two scions of the race, Klesmer and Mirah in "Daniel Deronda" as exquisite musicians. For, if in other fields of art, his achievements are only of a recent date, in this "universal language of the heart and soul" the Jew is to be classed among both the earliest and greatest of the world. The cultivation of it, which a hostile world could not prevent and his own laws did not prohibit, nor his checkered career preclude, has been carried on by him uninterruptedly from the Davidic dynasty, through the Prophetic periods of the Temple times, in the Synagogue service and family feast, to our own age when we find him among the foremost composers and performers.

    The material in this field is, in fact, so rich that an exhaustive study of the subject would fill a volume and the mere list of names would far transcend the scope of one article. Even to give the most prominent and modern masters would necessitate much omission and compel curtness. There is literally speaking not a country that has not produced such nor an instrument that has not found the highest and most excellent expression through Jewish masters. Mendelssohn and Meyerbeer, Halevy and Hiller, Benedict and Bizet, Bruch and Bruell, Kahn, Cowen, Moscheles and Moszkowski, Offenbach and Ochs, Jadassohn, Lassen, Goldmark, and Schulhoff, are today household words with every student of famous composers and fine compositions, to the same degree of intimacy as the great Rubinstein, whose face and feature at once give evidence of genius and strength.

Nor are the Jewish performers less numerous or less notorious than the composers. Hardly has the violin ever evinced a more perfect willingness to be wielded by a human hand than under the magic mastery of Joseph Joachim. That Henri Weiniawski, whose technique has long been acknowledged to have excelled that of all other violin artists of the nineteenth century, must be placed beside the great Joachim everybody knows. It may not be so generally known, however, that Weiniawski's end was a tragic one, he being obliged to breath his last, destitute and neglected, in a Moscow hospital, but six years after, in the company of Rubinstein, his playing stirred this country to the highest pitch of enthusiastic admiration.

To realize what fine seconds these two masters have found among their own people we need but mention the galaxy of glorious names by which each of these is surrounded in his country. Countrymen of Joachim, as Leopold Auer, Jacob Gruen, Mishka Hauser, as well as Hubay, Remenyi, Nachez, and Singer have contributed not a little to make Hungary the land of wine also the home of song and music. Adolph Brodsky, on the other hand, Isidor Lotto, Charles Gregorowitsch, Sergei Rachmaninoff, Mischa Ellman, and a number of others, too many to name, are the honored friends and countrymen of the Russo-Polish Jewish genius.

In other countries we find among the most eminent violin virtuosos Heinrich Wilhelm Ernst, "the German Paganini," who on one occasion canceled a very flattering and profitable engagement at the court of the Czar because on his way there he was, at Warsaw, charged a "Jew tax." Gustav Hollaender is another very prominent name among the German masters of the violin, while in Bohemia we have Ferdinand Laub, in Austria Edward Rappolli and the famous musical prodigy, Bronislaw Hubermann, and in Romania, Arnold Rose.

Performers who have achieved greatness on other instruments are no less numerous, the piano, of course, counting the largest number of leaders. Yet the violin-cello, too, has won triumphs for many a Jewish artist. Thus we find Carl Davidow, Heinrich Gruenfeld, David Popper, Philip Roth, Joseph Sulzer (son of the great Vienna cantor), and Louis Blumenberg among the very first performers on the instrument, while Bachrich has won many a laurel on his viola, as did the Lewry brothers on the cornet, Parish-Alvers on the harp and Michael Joseph Gusikow on his own invented wood and straw violin from which he extracted his own, untutored, compositions in a manner that brought him the homage of the noblemen and notables of all Europe.

As stated before, the piano has found representation in any number of Jewish geniuses. Joseph Rubinstein (the younger brother of the famous composer), Moritz Rosenthal, George Liebling, Joseph Hoffman (whose Jewish descent is very probable, though not fully ascertained), Karl Tausig, Joseph Vieniawski, Arthur Friedheim, Anton Door, Fischof, Herz, and Gruenfeld, not to speak of Mme. Bloomfield-Zeissler, Osip Gabrilowitsch (son-in-law of the humorist, Mark Twain), Lewin and the Damrosches (Leopold and Walter), whom most or many of us have had an opportunity of hearing and judging for ourselves, are but the towering trees in the immense forest of lower but equally imposing plants.

From this brief and, of necessity, not wholly adequate review of the Jew's achievement in the field of music, his place of importance in the branch of art becomes at once clear. And we need not be surprised to find him a born leader in music. When we realize how closely allied music is to religion, both sending their roots deep down into the opaque structure of subconscious intelligence, making of the two natural associates, if not (as archaeologists claim) religion must be looked upon as the parent of music, we should really expect to find the Jew playing a most pre-eminent part in the one as in the other.

11. The Russian Jewish Folk-Song (1917)

Kurt Schindler

AS A MUSICIAN AND SCHOLAR who has earnestly and for many years occupied himself with the folk-music of many nations, the writer has been overjoyed and profoundly stirred to find that his own race possesses musical treasures of the highest value, unknown to many and unknown until a few years ago to himself.

As I am not of Russian parentage and have no other local knowledge of Russian-Jewish folk-songs than a short six weeks' trip through Russia permitted me to acquire, my information on this subject is confined to what I have been able to learn from Russian Jews in New York and from the all too scarce literature of books and music available on the subject. What little I know, however, has so thoroughly convinced me of the priceless worth of these possessions of the Jewish race, of the opportunity, yea the duty of Jewish musicians to devote their time and thought to the preservation and propagation of this racial bequest, that I hope I shall be able to impart some of my enthusiasm to others.

The Human Appeal of the Jewish Folk-Song

Like so many non–Russian Jews, I was long unaware of the very fact that a Jewish folk-song existed in Russia. My eyes were first opened when I came to know the Jewish melodies contained in the work of the great Russian composer Moussorgsky. This great innovator and seeker for the truth in music, who like none other knew how to render and perpetuate the Russian peasant song in his work, proceeded with the same meticulous — I might say ethnographical — correctness when he noted down the melodies of the Russian Jew. In his country place near Pskoff, where he spent many summers, he came often in contact with the Jews, and owing to his acquaintance with them the world is richer by two of the most superb Jewish melodies: his "Song of Solomon" and the "Plaint of the Women of Amorea" in the Cantata "Joshua" (which, I am proud to think, was the first work I ever performed before the New York public).

Moussorgsky is not the only Russian composer who wrote songs in the Jewish style. The works of Rimsky-Korsakoff and of Balakireff abound in songs under the name of "Hebrew Songs," and despite the sufferings the old Russian Government inflicted upon the Jewish race, the Russian non–Jewish composer has always understood and appreciated the Jew. In fact, thanks to the Jewish pupils of Rimsky-Korsakoff, there exists today in Petrograd a "Society for Jewish Folk-Music," which has in the last few years placed upon the market a large number of exceedingly good settings of Jewish folk-songs. The best among this set of young Jewish composers of Russia is undoubtedly Julius Engel, the widely known musical critic of Moscow; but most interesting contributions have come from men like Shallit, Shklyar, Shitomirsky and Milner. These ought to be widely known here, and if the war did not interfere to such a degree with importations from Europe, there ought to be a persistent effort made to interest the Jewish public here in them.

As matters are, we are indebted to such propagandists as Mr. Medvedyev, Miss Elizabeth Gutmann, Mr. Gideon and Mr. Pinchos Jassinowsky, for introducing them to the American public; not only Jew but Gentile, have taken lately with great interest to the Jewish folk-song.

The tremendous enthusiasm which greets Alma Gluck every time she sings that typical little Jewish song, "Meierke, Mein Sun, un weisst du vor wemen du steihst" (written down by the eminent French composer Ravel), or the applause that greets Zimbalist when he plays his "Danse Juive" (to an original Jewish tune), the extraordinary interest which my own Schola Cantorum, a chorus of 175 singers, mostly Gentiles, took in learning such Jewish songs as "Eili, Eili" and "Avrahm," as well as the outspoken praise of musicians and press for these two melodies especially — all these are signs of the times, signs that Jewish folk-melodies will mean much in the future, to us as well as to Gentile audiences. I wish every one could have seen the real emotion shown by a friend of mine, an Episcopalian priest, when I played and explained to him a little Cheder-song, which depicts so graphically and touchingly the first lesson that the tiny little Jewish boy receives from the venerable Rebbe. What I mean to convey is that the Jewish folk-song, when given in its real, unspoiled form, and arranged by thoughtful musicians with loving care, has a wonderful appeal to a public of all confessions; that its spreading will mean a better understanding of the Jew, because it speaks right to the heart in its direct human appeal.

Songs That Mirror the Pathos of a Race

The Russian Jewish folk-song has grown and was reared under the greatest oppression, the grimmest tyranny that a race ever went through. By this very oppression it has become tense, quivering, abounding with emotion; in its melodies the Jewish heart is laid open, and it speaks in a language understandable to all. Songs like "Eili, Eili" and "Avrahm," which, I confess, are at this moment the nearest and dearest to me, have such an elemental appeal that they almost take one's breath away; their musical structure is so gigantic that no one man could have invented them — they represent the collective outcry of a suffering, unbendable race. To hear them, to understand them for the first time, is like standing face to face with a prophet!

A very large number of the folk-songs of the Russian Jews are sad and serious, thus mirroring the conditions of their wretched life. Such, for example, is the song of the dying mother to her child, "Nito kein Mame," a most touching melody of deep pathos. Two other mother-songs are especially worthy of mention: the well-known cradle-song, "Unter Soreles Wiergele steht a weisse Ziegele, die Ziegele is gefohren handlen, Rosinkes mit Mandlen," with its typically Jewish intervals; and the tender song of mother-love:

> *"As ich wollt grehat dem Kaiser's M'liche,*
> *Wollt das gor nit sain bei mir asei greiss Niche,*
> *Wi dub binst mir Niche, mein Licht, mein Schein!*
> *As ich derseh dich, mein ich, die ganze Welt is mein!*
> *Schlof, mein kind, sollst mir ruhen un sein gesind!"*

> "If I had the Emperor's kingdom,
> It would not give me so much pleasure
> As you give me, my light, my beauty!
> When I see you, I think the world is mine!
> Sleep, my child, in peace and health."

One of the most widely known songs, that deal with the life of Jewish children, is "Oif'n Pripetshok" (On the Little Stove). Like the Cheder-song of which I spoke above, it describes the first lessons in religion which the little children take from the Rebbe:

> *"Oif'n Pripetshok brent a feirele,*
> *un in Stub is heiss,*
> *Un der Rebbe lernt kleine kinderlach*
> *Dem Alef Beis..."*

> "On the little stove burns a light,
> And the room is hot,
> And the Rebbe teaches the little children
> The alphabet..."

Its melody is somewhat in the style of a Polish Mazurka, but it has a little endearing turn all its own.

Lyrics of Love and Tender Partings

Another group of Jewish songs comprises love-songs and farewell-songs of the bride to her parents. Among the love-songs the prettiest that I know is to the words:

> *"Sag mir du sheins Meidele, hör nor, due scheins Meidele,*
> *Wos west du tun in aso waiten Weg?*
> *Ich wel gehn in alle Gassen un wel schreien Wesch zu waschen*
> *Abi mit dir zusammen sein."*

> "Tell me, pretty maiden, just listen, pretty maiden,
> What will you do when so far away?
> I will go throughout the town and will ask for clothes to wash,
> Just to be with you."

The farewells of the bride are invariably sad — on the eve of her marriage she thinks of nothing but all the kindness she received from her parents, and she views the future with uncertainty:

> *"Sait gesunterheit, maine liebe Eltern!*
> *Ich fohr aweck in a waiten Weg,*
> *Wu kein Wind weiht nit, un wu kein Viegele fliht nit*

Un wo kein Hohn kreiht nit...
Gott soll geben Gesund un Leben
Un mir a glickliche Weg!"

"Farewell, my dear parents!
I am going far away,
Where no wind blows and no bird flies,
And no cock crows.
God give you health and life,
And me a happy journey."

Another of these bridal songs is most interesting, because it shows the influence of the Russian peasant folk-song on its structure and make-up: I mean "Di Gilderne Pave."

"Es kumt gefloigen di gilderne Pave
Fun ein Fremden Land,
Hot sie ferloren dem gildernen Feder
Mite in graissen Schand.
Es is nit asei der gilderne Feder
Wi di Pave alein,
Es is nit asei der Eidam
Wi di Tochter alein.
Wi is es bitter, mein liebe Mutter,
A Feigele of dem Yam
Asei is bitter, mein liebe Mutter
Bei ein schlechten Mann."

"The golden peacock comes a-flying
From a distant land.
There she lost a golden feather,
Greatly to her shame.
Not so much the golden feather,
As a peacock itself,
Not so much the son-in-law,
As the daughter herself.
How bitter is it, mother dear,
For a bird lost on the sea?
So bitter is it, mother dear,
To live with a bad husband."

Exuberant Dance and Wedding Songs

In great contrast to these sad lyric songs, there is another equally large group of exceedingly gay, boisterous dance-songs, often in polka-rhythms, not always very refined, but of a forceful vital exuberance that gives them a distant note among other folk-dances.

The most characteristic, the most entrancing in its humor, is, of course, "Di Mesinke" (the wedding of the youngest daughter):

> "*Hecher, besser! di Rod, di Rod macht gresser!*
> *Gross hat mich Gott gemacht,*
> *Glick hat er mir gebracht,*
> *Hulet kinder a gantze Nacht!*
> *Di Mesinke oisgegeben!*"

> "Louder! better! the ring make larger.
> God has made me great,
> He has brought me joy;
> Dance, children, throughout the night,
> The Mesinka's married off."

Even more exuberant is a Rumanian Jewish wedding song with the refrain:

> "*Tanz wie a Chasson mit der Kalle,*
> *Pleesket, pleesket alle!*
> *Ich lach mich gut fon meine Sonnim ois*
> *En geh mir gur a Freilechs.*"

> "Dance, like a groom with his bride,
> Applaud, let's applaud, all of us!
> I laugh in scorn at all my foes,
> And have a joyous time."

A great number of these gay and jolly Jewish dance-songs can be classified as "Simchas Torah" songs — melodies that were and are sung especially upon the festival of rejoicing.

The figure of the "Chossidl," that lively, hilarious lay-teacher of religion so familiar in Russia and Poland, is the subject of a great number of Jewish humorous songs. One of these very amusingly contrasts the singing of the Chossidl with the wild strains of the Tzigane and the boisterous, gleeful shouts of the Russian peasant Ivanjke.

A Genre Group — Quaintly Humorous and Ironical

There remains a last group of Jewish folk-songs of which I have not yet spoken; little genre songs, full of quaint humor, descriptive, tinged with a subtle irony, a cheerful resignation. Thus the highly amusing:

> "*Gut Morgen Moischele dir!*"
> "*Gut morgen Yankele dir!*"
> "*Was hert sich epes, Moische, bei dir?*"
> "*Ai was sol sich heren bei mir?*
> *Das Leben is zuckersiss,*
> *Ich wer verschwartzt fin dem Kopf bis in die Fiss,*
> *Das Leben beigt, das Leben brecht,*
> *Ich wähn ich bin efscher gerecht.*"

> "Good morning to you, Moischele!"
> "Good morning to you, Yankele!"
> "What's new with you today?"
> "Ai! what news can there be?
> Life is so sugar-sweet,
> But I have the worst of luck,
> Life bends us, life breaks us,
> Yet, I trust, I am all right."

A little song of charades — known under the title "Ein Retenis" (A Riddle) is musically of a high order. It is sung as a duet, with questions and answers:

> "*Du Meidele, du feuins, du Meidele, du sheins,*
> *Ich will dir eppes, fragen, a Retenis a feins.*
> *Was is hecher far a Hois?*
> *Un was is flinker far a Mois?*"

> "Pretty maiden, Pretty maiden,
> Let me ask you a fine riddle:
> What is higher than a house,
> What is quicker than a mouse?"

To which the girl replies:

> "*Du narrischer Bocher, du narrischer Tropp,*
> *Du hast nit kein Seichel in dein Kopp.*

Der Räuch is hecher fas a Hois,
A Katz is flinker far a Mois."

"You foolish boy, you foolish simpleton,
You have no brains in your head.
Smoke is higher than a house,
A cat is quicker than a mouse."

After many verses come the last questions:

"Was is tiefer far a Quell?
Un was is bittrer far a Gall?"

"What is deeper than a well?
What is more bitter than gall?"

And the answer is:

"Di Toire is tiefer far a Quell,
Der Toid is bittrer far a Gall!"

"The Torah is deeper than a well,
And Death more bitter than gall."

I cannot finish this very brief review without mentioning what is perhaps the most characteristic of all Yiddish songs: "Si alte Kashe." This is a song of a few words, but with much subtle irony between the lines and in the ever-recurring, much modulated syllables, "Ai, ai, tradiridirom" and "trala traidim."

"Fregt di welt an alte Kashe: trala tradiridirom?
Entfert man: tradiridireinom, Ai, ai tradiridirom!
Un as men will, ken man doch sagen: traidim?
Bleibt doch weiter die alter Kashe: trala tradiridirom?"

"If the world should ask that time-worn question: trala tradiridirom?
One should answer: tradiridireinom, Ai, ai tradiridirom!
And if one wants, one may ask: traidim?
Still there is the time-worn question: trala tradiridirom?"

The resignation born of the century-long suffering of a race, a smile under tears, speaks from the strangely touching melody of this song, with its sad intervals and its gay rhythm.

The Local Influence Reflected in Jewish Music

Recently the question has been put several times before me: Is there a Jewish folk-music entirely distinctive from the music of other nations? This is not quite easy to answer. There are Jewish melodies of the Portuguese-Sephardic Jews, there are melodies of Palestine, others typical of the Caucasian Jewish races, and, finally, the songs of the great Russian-Polish pale of settlement. There is in all of these a similarity in melodic treatment, in the singular Oriental scale upon which they are founded, which corresponds to synagogue traditions. But in rhythmical structure they are widely different. To explain what I mean: the Jews of Poland sing songs in the rhythm of a Mazurka; the Jews of Lithuania have sentimental ballads rhythmically similar to the folk-songs of Northern Russia; the Jews of Middle-or-White-Russia have long drawn-out lyric melodies like the songs of the peasants there; and the Jews of Ukraine have polka-rhythms like the favorite dances of the Little Russians.

This phenomenon of rhythmical influence upon their melodies, according to the soil where Jews live, is an obvious and easily understandable one.

The Jews have a special genius for assimilation and amalgamation. This they have shown and convincingly demonstrated by the manner in which they have been embodied in all the national units among which destiny placed them. They are one with the countries in which they reside: only some part of the life of their soul, their very inner self has remained a separate entity, and it is through this bond of the Jewish soul that Jews of all countries can understand and speak to each other. Just so with their music, the rhythms vary, but the melody—the soul of the music—remains the same; and this is true not only of folk-song but of synagogue music. The melodies of the temples of France have received their share of the influence of the great period of operatic French music in the early nineteenth century, the style of Halevy; the synagogue music of Germany bears the traces of the influence of the classical masters; the Jewish music of Russia shows the vitalizing effect upon the race of living among the most thoroughly and intrinsically musical people of the world. If the Russians themselves are a musical nation, all the more have the Jews of Russia become imbued with the spirit of music. So much so that, as Rachmaninoff, director of all the conservatories of Russia, told me, the best talent in Russian music schools invariably comes from the Jews, and many Jews rank today among the most prominent composers and musical leaders of Russia.

And among them a new spirit has arisen, a spirit of frankly cultivating what is racial and typically Jewish in their musical make-up, a frank movement for Jewish folk-music, such as Rubinstein only half-heartedly, timidly dared to write it, and to which the real way was shown, as I said at the beginning, by some of Russia's greatest masters in music, Moussorgsky and Rimsky-Korsakoff.

There are hopeful signs that this movement will be transplanted to America, where it will find the happiest conditions to foster it, and I wish to say for myself that I shall endeavor to put forth my best efforts to help further this movement.

12. Hazzanim and Hazzanut (1920)

Pinchos Jassinowsky

THE ART OF *HAZZANUT*, the chants of the *hazzanim*, is a unique manifestation among our people. It began its development shortly after the destruction of the First Temple. The Jews carried to Babylon by Nebuchadnezzar formed themselves into communities and instituted *yeshivot* of learning and houses of prayer. The many Levites among the exiles, remembering the chants they had employed in the Temple service, applied the same music to the prayers offered in the alien land.

Scores of synagogues arose in Babylonia. In these precincts the exiles poured out their hearts, and offered up hopeful prayers for return to their Holy land. The saddened orisons for the devastated land and Temple brought relief to their hearts, and provided both solace and trust in a better future. When, seventy years after the beginning of the exilic period, they returned to Palestine, they brought back with them the entire repertory of liturgical music developed during their sojourn in Babylonia.

A similar process accompanied the era of the second destruction. The descendants of the early exiles, now exiled in Rome, carried with them the Temple singers and the Temple songs temporarily silenced by all-conquering Titus. It must be said that these melodies exercised a profound influence not alone upon the Jewish population, but also upon the pagan people of ancient Rome, who learned much from the Hebrew forms of worship.

The chants thus remembered and practiced by Israel were known as community prayers. However, the Jewish liturgy long antedated the exilic hymns. In the olden days, when Abraham, the first Hebrew, on God's behest crossed the Euphrates to spread the divine word among the inhabitants of the land, there were individual prayers rising from the inner needs and cravings of the individual. The first Patriarch had dispatched Eliezer, his steward, to find a bride for his son, Isaac. With gifts of great worth he traversed the lands on his quest, ultimately reaching Aram-Naharaim to bestow his master's possessions upon Abraham's distant relatives.

The shades of night were spreading over the land as Eliezer came near the city of Near. He brought his camels to rest at the well, and prepared to utter prayer to his God. "O Lord, the God of my master Abraham ... show kindness unto my master.... Behold, I stand by the foundations of water; and the daughters of the men of the city come out to draw water. So let it come to pass, that the damsel to whom I shall say: Drink, and I shall give thy camels drink also; let the same be she that Thou hast appointed for Isaac; and thereby shall I know that Thou hast shown kindness unto my master."

Had Eliezer not seen and heard the conduct of prayer in the tents of his master, he would never have thought to offer his own supplication. It is evident from Scripture that Abraham was a most worshipful man. It was he who prayed to the Creator of the universe to show mercy toward Sodom: "Wilt Thou indeed sweep away the righteous with the wicked? ... That be far from Thee; shall not the Judge of all the earth do justly?" It was he who prayed for the health and security of Abimelech. It was through his supplications for the just and the righteous that Abraham attained the admiration and devotion of all God-fearing men.

The first communal prayer of Israel was heard in Egypt, when the people as a whole, in their deep trial and bondage, pleaded for surcease of their cruel enslavement. "And the children of Israel sighed by reason of their bondage, and they cried, and their cry came up to God." From these and other incidents we first learned that, just as prayer can well up from the heart of an individual in distress, it can also rise simultaneously from the hearts of a multitude.

Jewish prayer is not solely the product of the Men of the Great Assembly, who formulated and coordinated the modes of public worship. The aim was not merely to replace the Temple service with words spoken by the lips. According to Maimonides, prayer is a positive commandment direct form the Torah, which declares in the *Shema*, "And thou shalt love the Lord thy God with all thy heart, and with all thy soul, and with all thy might," and in the ensuing paragraph, employing the plural form, "I command you this day, to love the Lord your God, and to serve Him with all your heart and with all your soul." By 'serve' is meant pray, says Maimonides, service of the heart. From the days of Moses to those of Ezra the Scribe, it was the duty of every Israelite to offer up daily prayers to the Lord.

But exposition of biblical verses is not the task of this essay. Its aim is to demonstrate the gradual development of Israel's liturgy, and attainment of the present high literary and religious level. One of our most prized creations as a people is the musically elevated recitative that marks modern *hazzanut*. Both through its content and form it has thrilled not alone the regular attendant at synagogue services, whose spirit is already permeated with longing and prayerful remembrance of olden glories, but it has given the highest aesthetic pleasure to everyone with an appreciation of emotion in music. It may well be said that the majestic chants of the synagogue service have been of more powerful effect upon the souls of the listeners than the prayers themselves. For when Israel was in exile, prayer chanted was the deepest expression of folk emotion, awakening the spirit of the people, and mitigating the sorrowful experiences engendered by a hapless life in an alien environment. The prayers that are sung are part of the cantorial art of earlier days, and now our regular liturgical expression.

The full humanity of any person never so surely reflects the image of God as when he is engaged in prayer. No great art, no skilled artist, can so affect the heart of man as does a simple silent prayer wafting from a heart fully attuned to the divinity in every human soul. There is no fire to melt steel so powerful as the warm-hearted prayer that bends the iron will of man and brings him closer to those writers which heaven would instill within him.

The first exponents of prayer, the *hazzanim* (*shelichei-tzibbur*), popular representatives — came from the people. The precentor was the man considered outstanding in the community. He was expected to possess the virtues of good appearance, character, learning, and an acceptable voice. To hold this place among the people was a matter of honor, for which many householders strove. So great was the desire to attain that post, that often prominent men were given bribes to further the candidacy of various aspirants. In ancient days men actually sought to buy their way into the honorific high priesthood; against such ambitious men did the prophets and later leaders powerfully fulminate. It was a Jewish precept, in fact, that any prayer representative who ascended the platform against the actual will of the congregation was not entitled to hear the *Amen* after the conclusion of blessings recited to him. As time went on, the art of synagogue singing developed; a skilled professional class of cantors arose; and the right to recite the prayers aloft was taken from communal wrangling; and assigned to designated and able chanters of the Hebrew melodies. First called *baalei tefillah* — masters of prayers — they were later designated *hazzanim*, and then, in modern times, cantors.

The earliest *hazzanim* were not singers alone, but also poets, liturgists, who composed new hymns and prayers. Eliezer Kalir, who in the tenth century served as cantor of a small Italian town, was the writer of many liturgical forms — laments, *selichot, yotzerot* — in acrostic form. A later cantor and poet of note was Meir of Worms, who authored the famed *Akdamut*, sung on *Shavuot*. The great commentator Rashi, his contemporary, wrote of Meir as "my colleague, my master, and prayerful representative of the people, faithful and venerable." To this day that unique festival prayer is sung according to a special and impressive chant, out of which many additional hymns have been derived.

In various parts of Europe were to be found similarly gifted cantors and poets. There were R. Joseph Alkalay, cantor of Sicily; the composer and writer, Isaac Sahud, who flourished in Spain; R. Moses the Elder of London — none of whom was possessed of great technical musical knowledge, since the music of that day was still in developmental form. But they were highly talented and pious men, marked by that religious fire and fervor which impelled them, while singing, to pour their very hearts out to the Lord. Their chants were actually improvised from the emotions that welled from their souls in prayer; their musical expression was dictated by inner feeling. This tendency toward improvisation in conduct of religious service is not to be found in the history of any other religious group. For this reason our melodies have to this day remained thoroughly flexible, attuned to the emotions of those chanting them before a congregation of worshipers. These were never mere hymns or prayer songs; they have always been actual expressions of the spirit of the singer in his moment of devotional ecstasy.

However, *hazzanut* itself, in its history, has been marked by many alterations and developments, both toward betterment and toward decline. These changes can be traced to the actual vicissitudes of Jewish exilic life, with its long story of persecution and martyrdom. Not always have Jewish leaders looked with approval upon the current progress of the cantorial art. Often the learned men, cold reasoners and researchers in the law, did not hold sway over the minds of the people. They stood above the run of Jewry and looked down upon them. But the masses were interested in the teaching and convoluted philosophic reasoning of the more enlightened savants; instead of the problems of Jewish law, they sought spiritual nourishment for their starved souls. Far from the *pilpul* and involved thinking of the learned classes, they sought only serenity and forgetfulness in their religious ardor. Rather than be instructed concerning the nature and fearsomeness of God, they preferred to yield their soul to their Maker with the trust and faith of innocent children. Life was so difficult that they were perpetually seeking some haven or refuge; let the intellectuals feed their minds — they wanted only to soothe their innermost emotions. The common man was not concerned over the arduous theological and scientific searchings of the learned; to sing the wonders and gifts of the Lord was all they required. Love, reverence, wonderment, and thankfulness were their métiers.

In the song of the *hazzan* the people found what they had so long been seeking. New congregations in far-flung communities were built about the art of the cantor. And as that art developed, however, spiritual leaders began to look askance at the cantor; on many occasions had spiritual leaders in Israel found fault with similar expressions of Jewish spirituality through the instrumentality of the human voice. This attitude was existent even in the days of the First Temple, when the priests developed a feeling of jealousy toward the great popular chants of the Levites. It was quite natural, therefore, that in the exile a like attitude should repeat itself. It was much aggravated when cantors began to strike out for themselves musically and employ new hymns and musical forms, different from traditional modes. The cantors must not be blamed for creating such differences; it was a truth even in the days of Moses that, while the folk were seeking interest in alien cultures, their representatives in song tended to adopt musical and devotional forms taken from their environment. The new songs were strange to the ears of the masses, who showed their displeasure. Two opposing streams in Jewish life — the centripetal and centrifugal — are evidenced in the whole story of the development of synagogue song.

The quarrel did not long endure, however. In ensuing years there arose numbers of religious *hazzanim* or high musical talent, who were completely devoted to employing their capacities in the interest of their people. The voices of some of these later cantors were of the highest caliber; the power of their prayers was aptly named *shaagat ha-ari* — "the roar of the lion." The people were overwhelmed by the strength and melodic beauty of their singing. Yet there were also *hazzanim* who had no voices at all, but were thoroughly capable of the art of liturgical music. Unable to express themselves with their own vocal chords, they turned to choir singing and emotional vocal expression to attract the *mitpallelim* of the congregation. Chief representative of this class of wailers and weepers was Nissi Belzer.

The synagogues in which these men served were as a rule without large means, unable to maintain both cantor and singers. For this reason the cantors would regularly appear in adjacent communities on Sabbaths, so that the fees thus amassed might cover the deficits created in their own communities. As a result the wandering singers were able to spread knowledge of Jewish liturgical music in towns that would otherwise never have learned to understand and appreciate it. The success of these tours was out of the ordinary; the worshipers listened enthralled to the prayerful song. The cantors were pursued by the populace everywhere, and often they were carried aloft on the hands of their admirers.

The tremendous influence of the wandering cantor on the people can be indicated from a single example. Once Nissi Belzer and his choir conducted a Sabbath service in a small town, with vast success. The company was scheduled to depart for another town, but the inhabitants pleaded that they remain with them for another Sabbath service. This was obviously impossible. The people, seeing that neither pleas nor offers of more money were of any avail, stationed themselves on the outskirts of the city, and when the coaches bearing the singers approached they demolished the wheels and compelled them to stay over. This shows the power of Blezer's art; though he lacked a musical voice, his form of prayer was sufficient to bring more than ordinary satisfaction to the ear of the ordinary listener. All were fascinated by his melodies and his artistry. His excellent large choir aided in creating this impression among the worshipers. The choir singers, many of them, also became distinguished cantors under his tutelage. It was a mark of high distinction to say that any *hazzan* had once sung for the famed Nissi Belzer. His pious and heartfelt synagogue songs became musical canon, and may later composers built their music upon his foundation.

In later days both rabbis and householders opposed the extension of the new synagogue music, because of the added time required to present it. This, along with the too lengthy discourses of rabbis and itinerant preachers, created many difficulties in the service of the synagogue. As the difficulties multiplied, many a thoughtful congregant began to contemplate the emergence of a more controlled form of cantorial artistry. There was also an effort to reduce the rambling discourses of the chance preacher to the limited confines of the modern sermon.

In East Europe, in Russia and adjacent lands, there arose the modern type of synagogue, great edifices boasting trained cantors and choirs. In the West came the temples of the *Kultus-Gemeinde*; and in America the Reform temples, centers, and other contemporary developments of the synagogue. The spirit of emancipation wafting through all progressive countries was largely responsible for the new movement. As the ghetto walls fell, and revolutionary movements gained power in European lands, all this was reflected in the life of the synagogue. *Hazzanut* derived from the traditional European forms was developed under such auspices.

Solomon Sulzer pioneered the new movement. His work, *Schir Zion*, became the basis for synagogue and choir singing throughout the world. In the ordered chanting developed by Sulzer and other moderns, worshipers found both joy and spiritual comfort. Always despairing over their condition, suppressed by their enemies, oppressed by blood accusations and other false charges, they achieved a measure of solace and serenity in the elevating tones of synagogue melody. If men wonder how Jewry was enabled to live through hardship and persecution, let them comprehend the extraordinary power of our many minor sanctuaries in providing new strength and substance for the Jewish soul. Our sacred song also raised our repute among our neighbors. Men who came to harm us were softened by the strains that swept from our places of worship into the heart of the world. Frequently representatives of the government attended the synagogue, eager to hear the chants that brought delight to them as well as to the regular worshipers. They marveled that, after they had written off the existence of Israel, that people was still in position to erect such splendid synagogues and indulge in such magnificent songs and prayer. Thereafter it was easier for our professional intercessors to obtain remission of harsh decrees and to gain the good will of the rulers.

The song of the synagogue raised worshipers to the highest human realms. They felt again that their strivings were not directed to mere personal or selfish aims, but toward preservation of people, of faith, of love of God, and all things worthwhile in the existence of humankind. It was brought home to them that above the material efforts of life, their true duty was to provide for family and community in such a manner that children and all others might grow to honor the Lord and His highest ethical teachings. And as God spoke to Israel through the Torah, they in turn spoke to the Master of the universe in their formal supplications. The cardinal attributes of Jewish striving have been Repentance, Prayer, and Charity. All that Israel does must be carried on in the name of God. The Jewish concept of God's unity was spread among the nations, among the Christian churches and Mohammedan mosques, adding their own substance to the prayer of our ideals.

Tremendous are the emotions engendered by the voice of the cantor. It carries the episodes of Israel's long sad history back into the recollection of every worshiper. From generation to generation our song has accompanied us; it has lightened every burden. It has given us the perennial hope that our redemption is still to come, and that life will yet be beautiful. Raptly do we plead, as we stand in prayer, "Grant peace, welfare, blessing, grace, loving-kindness, and mercy unto us and unto Israel Thy people." In the days when brigands were granted carte blanche to rob and oppress and murder the citizenry, the Jews in their ghettos chanted this prayer: "Open my heart to Thy law, and let my soul pursue Thy commandments.... If any design evil against me, speedily make their council no effect. Do it for the sake of Thy name." Jubilantly do we ply the people with peace. In such words and chants is concealed our racial strength; these are our armies, our government, our power. One can sense the true might of Israel in the exclamation. "And the Lord shall be King over all the earth: in that day shall the Lord be one, and His name one!"

Part III
Reviving Jewish Music

Introduction

MARTIN BUBER (1878–1965), the renowned German-Jewish social and religious philosopher, was among the first to advocate a "Jewish renaissance." Calling for the "resurrection of the Jewish people from the partial life to full life,"[1] Buber demanded that Jewish scholars expand their field of study beyond Judaic literature, and devote attention to all aspects of the Jewish experience. He was particularly critical of nineteenth-century *Wissenschaft des Judentums* (Science of Judaism), which, in his view, lacked an appreciation of Judaism as a living cultural reality. Scholars of the *Wissenschaft* dedicated their efforts almost exclusively to the historical study of Jewish texts, but, as Buber lamented, were largely unconcerned with the preservation of Jewish identity. With this criticism, Buber foreshadowed a position that would come to dominate Jewish studies in the twentieth century, when scholars — dissatisfied with years of assimilationalist tendencies — expressed renewed interest in cultural distinctiveness.

Idelsohn, for instance, spent most of his career championing music's role in this cultural renaissance. He wrote passionately that "The day on which every Jew will come to realize that there cannot be a Jewish renascence without a revival of Jewish music — for just as it is impossible for a man to live without a heart, so it is impossible for a people to live without its folk music — on that day will the renascence become a reality."[2] And, arguing for the active creation of nationalistic Jewish music, Idelsohn declared, "That great song, born of the Jews, preserved by them, and in the course of centuries developed by them, can continue to grow through musicians, born Jews, reared in a Jewish environment, steeped in Jewish folklore and folk-song, vibrant with Jewish sorrows, joys, hopes, and convictions — faithful sons of Israel."[3]

As this statement suggests, the revival of Jewish music was in large part an effort to restore Jewish folk melodies, both sacred and secular. The earliest pioneer in this regard was Salomon Sulzer (1804–1890), an Austrian cantor-composer and influential reformer of Jewish liturgical music. The first half of the nineteenth century witnessed the emergence of Reform Judaism in Germany and Central Europe, which brought modern European aesthetics into the synagogue service. Following Protestant practice, the Bible and liturgy were read, not chanted, an organ was introduced, and Jewish hymns were sung to the music of Christian composers. Sulzer, who advocated a more moderate reform, was troubled by this abandonment of traditional Jewish music, and sought to "renovate" traditional synagogue music by taking into consideration Western musical norms. In the preface to his collection of synagogue music, *Schir Zion* (1840), Sulzer described his mission: "I see it as my duty ... to consider first the traditional tunes bequeathed to us, to cleanse their ancient and decorous character from the later accretions or tasteless embellishments, to restore their original purity, and to reconstruct them in accordance with the text and the rules of harmony."[4]

This section begins with two biographical sketches chronicling Sulzer's personal and professional life. Benjamin Franklin Peixotto's (1834–1890) essay opens with his visit to the World's Exposition at Vienna in 1873, where he saw Sulzer perform, and continues with an overview of Sulzer's life both inside and outside of the synagogue. Interestingly, Peixotto, who was an American lawyer, diplomat, and communal leader, published this article in 1890, the same year both he and Sulzer passed away.

Adolph Guttman (1854–1927), a rabbi who served in Syracuse, New York, offers a more intimate portrait of Sulzer's life and legacy. Guttman pays special attention to Sulzer's personality, describing his kindness and generosity in family and social life, and the pleasant and jovial character for which he was well known. Of particular note, Guttman describes Sulzer as a "prince of well-doers," citing his work with various charitable organizations, and the free instruction he gave to fellow cantors and singers.

In 1895, Gustav Karpeles (1848–1909), an accomplished literary historian, delivered a speech in honor of Louis Lewandowski's fiftieth anniversary as music director. After Sulzer, Lewandowski (1821–1894) was the most prominent and influential synagogue composer. He was the first Jew admitted to the Berlin Academy of Fine Arts, and after 1840 served as choirmaster for the Berlin Jewish community. In this capacity, he reproduced traditional melodies in his cantorial recitatives, though he favored a "church-like" approach to four-part choral writing, following the style of Mendelssohn's choruses and oratorios. Karpeles praises Lewandowski's contributions to Jewish music, saying, "You have remodeled the divine service of the Jewish synagogue.... Under your touch old lays have clothed themselves with a modern garb — a new rhythm vibrates through our historic melodies, keener strength in the familiar words, heightened dignity in the cherished songs."

Next are two essays by Joseph Reider (1886–1960), who was professor of biblical philology and librarian at Dropsie College in Philadelphia. Reider was primarily an expert in Hebrew and ancient Near Eastern languages, and taught a variety of related courses at Dropsie College, including Hebrew Grammar, the Book of Job, and the Aramaic Papyri of Assuan and Elephantine. In addition to his extensive textual studies, Reider also published several papers on Jewish music, many of which offer informed critiques of the state of synagogue music in his day. With these writings, Reider displayed his mastery of Jewish musical history and technique, and argued well his call for the purification of American synagogue music. This is the theme of his essay, "Secular Currents in Synagogal Chant in America," which describes numerous historical examples of foreign melodies — both secular and sacred — that have entered the synagogue, and commends efforts to "purge our liturgy of foreign excrescences and preserve the primitive Jewish tunes in a more or less integral state."

Following this, Reider addresses more generally the need for a Jewish music revival. Most significantly, Reider contends that folksongs should be the basis of Jewish musical creativity, writing that, "while listening to the strongly racial creations of Liszt, Dvořák, and Tschaikowsky, I have yearned for a great Jewish composer who could lay hold upon the many genuine tunes current in the dusky ghettos, and yield them into a mighty symphony expressing Jewish fears and hopes, Jewish passions and emotions, throughout the ages."

Jerome H. Bayer's essay, "The Future of Jewish Music," determines that "only that music is Jewish which reflects the Jewish spirit." According to biographical information published with this study, which originally appeared in *The Menorah Journal* (1919), Bayer "devoted himself for many years to musical study, and has been a pioneer in awakening interest in Jewish music among various circles in California ... and has composed several pieces of music which profess Jewish motifs or inspiration." It is this adherence to traditional synagogue modes and melodies that Bayer finds most crucial for the vibrant future of Jewish music.

Lastly is a selection by Louis Grossman (1863–1926), an Austrian-born rabbi who succeeded Isaac Mayer Wise (1819–1900) as rabbi of Congregation B'nai Yeshurun in Cincinnati. Grossman also taught ethics, pedagogy and theology at Hebrew Union College, and took special interest in religious school education. In this essay, "Music in the Religious School," originally published in his handbook *The Aims of Teaching in Jewish Schools* (1919), Grossman stresses the role of the educator in facilitating a Jewish music revival. Among other things, Grossman argues that synagogue music should be a subject taught in all religious schools, not only because of its intrinsic educational value, but because it stimulates a deeper involvement in religious life. Grossman recommends that teachers expunge "alien hymns" from the curriculum, noting the common practice at the time of singing texts from Christian hymnals, and suggests that schools provide sheet music for home use in the "hope that we may touch the hidden springs of the sentimental kinship in our families by the magic of song."

Notes

1. Martin Buber, "Jüdische Wissenschaft," *Die Welt* (1901); reprinted in Paul Mendes-Flohr and Jehuda Reinharz, eds., *The Jew in the Modern World: A Documentary History* (New York: Oxford University Press, 1980), p. 212.

2. Abraham Z. Idelsohn, "The Value of Jewish Music in the Present Day Jewish Renascence," in *Avukah Annual*, ed. Leo W. Schwartz (New York: American Student Zionist Federation, 1930), p. 83.

3. Abraham Z. Idelsohn, *Jewish Music in Its Historical Development* (New York: Schocken, 1929), p. 29.

4. Salomon Sulzer, preface to *Schir Zion*, ed. Eric Werner (New York: Bloch, 1954).

13. Solomon Sulzer: Reminiscences of Vienna (1890)

BENJAMIN FRANKLIN PEIXOTTO

IT WAS, I THINK, during the World's Exposition at Vienna, in 1873, that I first heard the celebrated *hazzan*, Solomon Sulzer*, who recently, after a life approaching the nineties, passed away.

It was not to hear him, that, with two eminent friends, Prof. Dr. Lazarus and Berthold Auerbach, of Berlin, who were also on a visit to the Kaiserstadt, that we went to the Temple. Our desire was to listen to our eloquent friend, Adolph Jellinek, the justly renowned rabbi, whose discourses and writings had exercised so mighty and powerful an influence not only upon Austrian but Continental Judaism.

Dr. Jellinek's sermon was a masterpiece and fully sustained his reputation as one of the most enlightened and progressive of modern thinkers, and we enjoyed it beyond measure. But there was one thing in the Temple service which to me, at least (for my friends had often heard him before), was as unexpected as it was hallowing, and this was the singing of the great Cantor, Solomon Sulzer. And when I was told that this was only the remnant, so to speak, of a voice that had enchanted all Europe, I marveled what such a voice must have been in its prime. The life of this celebrated cantor and composer, happily prolonged to his eighty-sixth year, is full of romantic interest and deserves a place in the pages of this publication, the *Menorah*.

Solomon Sulzer came of a family originally named Levi, who, in the days of direst persecution, had been driven forth, with twenty other families in

---

**Salomon Sulzer is often referred to as "Solomon" in English-language publications.*

the little congregation, from Sulz in the Voralberg. Settling in Hohenems, they preserved the memory of their loved home in their surname.

Sulzer's parents were persons of means and influence. Joseph Sulzer, the father, owned factories and houses in Hohenems, and possessed accomplishments then rarely found among Jews. The mother, Fanny Sulzer, was also a woman of high culture, and of strong character besides. They delighted, too, in music, since we read of the many occasions on which Frau Sulzer persuaded her husband to take her to hear the opera at Munich or at Innspruck. What that meant at the beginning of this century may be imagined when even now the Jew of a Polish city, who claims to be orthodox, would visit the theater in trepidation and by stealth.

Solomon was a bright and merry child and full of mischief, thereby constantly exposing himself to danger. Once he ventured into a mountain torrent, and immediately swept away, was with difficulty rescued by an intrepid peasant. It is illustrative of Sulzer to learn that after years he settled a liberal pension upon this man. The escapade decided his future career. His romantic mother clad the boy in white garments, and dedicated her child to the service of his Maker. They sent him to a Talmud school at Endingen in Switzerland, and afterwards to Carlsruhe to study music. Developing an exquisite voice and great musical talent, young Sulzer thought to become cantor in his native town. But the good folk of Hohenems like those of other lands did not believe in the genius of their townsman and it was only the due and formal appointment of the Emperor which procured him the position at a salary of $50 per year, while he was himself giving his bass chorister $100 — with board and lodging in his father's house.

Anecdotes are told of Sulzer at this time which picture him as a combination of physical vivacity and serious piety. He was passionately fond of riding, and would often be met galloping madly into town to be in time for afternoon prayer. He is said once to have plunged wildly down a precipitous mountain side in order to reach the synagogue in time. He organized a choir in his synagogue and wrote the music for it. He even introduced a string orchestra to weddings, for the Kaiser's birthday. Soon his ability became widely known, and young as he was, he was called to the cantorship of the Viennese Temple, when the famous Mannheimer was invited from Copenhagen to fill the post as preacher. The Vienna Congregation, proud alike of their eloquent minister and their sweet voiced *hazzan*, showed appreciation of the latter's unique talent by bearing the cost of his studies under the most eminent musicians of that musical city. In time, Sulzer himself became professor at the Conservatoire, and director of the famous Vienna Men's Choir.

The greatest musicians of the day flocked to the Temple to hear the artist-*hazzan*, and he was held in deepest respect in Gentile musical circles long before his co-religionists began to pride themselves upon his merits. He numbered many eminent men his intimate friends, and traces of their work may be found in his great compilations. Thus, the 92nd Psalm, in his *Shir Zion I*, is from the pen of Schubert. Liszt was also a warm admirer of Sulzer, Meyerbeer was delighted with him; the British Attaché, Lord Westmorland, was often to be met at Sulzer's. The *hazzan* was invited to sing at the Court, and was requested by the Arch-Duchess Sophia to become her "Hofkapellensänger." This Sulzer declined, but he accepted with much pleasure the formal title "Obercantor."

Prince Metternich often invited the athletic *hazzan* to join him in his sporting expeditions. This came to the ears of his wardens, and drew forth their reproaches. On the next occasion his Highness had to go without Sulzer, who had replied, "My Wardens forbid it." The Prince-Chancellor accordingly addressed his invitation regularly to the wardens, who had the good sense to put a pleasant face on the matter. Hearing that he was entirely in his true element in the synagogue, he attended at the Temple one Friday evening, and stayed greatly edified until the close of the service. Naturally, all the Jews of Austria felt themselves highly complimented. On another occasion, Sulzer was walking in the park, when a music-loving aide-de-camp of Kaiser Ferdinand accosted him and invited him to the Palace to look over a newly arrived collection of rare musical manuscript. The *hazzan*'s excuse that he was not dressed for the Palace was laughingly put aside. After the manuscripts had been examined he was begged just to sing one of Schubert's songs. Sitting down to the pianoforte he sang as exquisitely as ever the door meanwhile opening and disclosing the two Arch Dukes, one of them the present Emperor Franz Josef, who is said to have planned the affair. Sulzer went home with their warm praises ringing in his ears.

Happily Sulzer's genius was fully acknowledged outside as well as within the circle of his own coreligionists. He was an honorary freeman of the city of Vienna, a Knight of the Franz Josef Order, holder of the "Imperial Royal Gold Medal for Art and Science" of Austria and of the "Imperial Russian Gold Medal for Art and Science," an officer of the Turkish "Medjidieh," and honorary member of many societies and corporations. The *hazzanim* of America sent him a large gold medal, and various congregations presented him with as many as thirty *kiddush* cups. Sulzer had sixteen children, ten of them daughters all happily married. The family was artistic and musical, and the father's gifts have been handed on to the third generation.

14. The Life of Salomon Sulzer (1903)

Adolph Guttman

IF EVER A MAN IN PUBLIC LIFE has received befitting recognition from his contemporaries and won for himself a place of honor in the hearts of posterity, it is that master of the art of music, the regenerator of the synagogue service, the preserver of the old traditional melodies, the sweetest in Israel, Salomon Sulzer. Of him it may be truly said: "He is like a tree planted by the streams of water, that bringeth forth its fruit in its season, whose leaf does not wither, and whatsoever he doeth prospereth."

Early Life

At the foot of the old castle of Ems, where Count Rudolf wrote his "Barlaam and Josaphat" and within whose walls the treasure of the "Nibelungen Lied" was found and lifted, there lies the beautiful little town of Hohenems, whose Jewish community forms to this day one of the most progressive and intelligent congregations in Austria. Here, in the "Judengasse," stands the neat little house in which on the thirtieth of March, 1804, one Sulzer first saw the light of the world. "My earthly life," he says, "I owe to two of the noblest beings that have ever walked the earth. All I am and all I have, I owe to my good parents in whom deep spirituality, genuine goodness and strong common sense were happily blended. They were my joy and my delight during their lifetime, and I remember them with love and reverence after their death." His ancestors belonged to one of the best and oldest Jewish families, which in consequence of the expulsion of the Jews of Sulz, Vorarlberg, in 1744, moved to the neighboring little town of Hohenems, where they were permitted to live in peace and tranquility under the benign protection of the Count of Hohenems. In 1809, when the Austrian Jews had to assume surnames, they changed their name from "Loewy" to "Sulzer," in memory of the place of their former residence. Sulzer's father, Joseph, was an honest, useful, generous man, successful in business and respected by all. When in 1816, a dire famine caused much distress and suffering among the poorer classes, he erected a weaving mill, in order to give employment to a large number of men that were without work. Sulzer's mother was a woman of a wonderful depth of affection, and with a profound religious nature. From her he received his love for the beauties of nature, his artistic temperament, and his deep faith in God.

"Who taught me to sing? Was it in the first place my earliest teacher, the esteemed Mr. S. Eichberg, and then the sun and the moon, the mountains and the valleys of my dear native land, more sublime and lovely than anywhere else in the world! Then the roar of thunder, and the stars shining bright in the nightly heavens, citadels and castles, the weather-beaten relics of conquered barbarism, the neighborly Switzerland, 'frisch, frei and fromm,' and the deep grief at the sad condition of my coreligionists, which early filled my heart, and last but not least, my serene, inspired mother, all of these were my teachers and made me what I am, a singer of Jehovah!"

At a very early age Sulzer gave evidence of extraordinary talent and aptitude for song. He received a thorough instruction in Hebrew, in music as in all other branches of secular education. In his ninth year a marvelous saving of his life from the swollen creak of his native town served to produce upon the young mind a profound religious impression, and encouraged by his mother, who had already consecrated him to the service of the Lord, he decided a few years later to become a *hazzan*.

At the age of thirteen, on his *bar-mitzvah*, he led the entire Sabbath service in the synagogue of Hohenems. His rich, magnificent soprano voice, his fine execution, and his perfect rendering of the Hebrew text, excited the admiration of old and young. He was abundantly gifted to fill the position of Cantor, his extreme youth alone stood in the way. By the intervention of the authorities a leave of absence for three years was granted him, in which he might mature and perfect himself in all things necessary for the office to which he had been elected.

Wanderjahre and Return

"So ergriff ich dann den Wanderstab," he writes, "and went to Switzerland where I studied diligently under cantor Lippman and prepared myself for my future calling. Our journeys through Elsace and Lorraine, which reminds me of the old man and the youth in Uhland's ballad, were attended with great triumphs and gave me a deeper insight into the needs of the synagogue worship. At the close of two years, after a brief visit to Hohenems, I started for Carlsruhe, where I spent one year studying music and composition. I returned in 1821, a youth of seventeen, to my native town, to lay my first fruits upon the altar of the Lord. My heart was filled above all with the thought of putting an end to the neglect into which public worship had fallen."

The youthful cantor brought zeal and enthusiasm into the performance of his duties, thus dissipating whatever misgivings still lingered in the hearts of some of his congregation. The various wholesome improvements which he introduced in the synagogue, as well as the enchanting power of his song lifted the service to a high plane, increased the devotion of the worshipers, established order and decorum, and won him the hearts of all. The fame of this young master-singer had spread abroad in the land and upon the recommendation of Dr. Mannheimer and several influential merchants who had heard him in his home-synagogue the Viennese Jewish Congregation extended an invitation to him to officiate on a Sabbath in their newly erected temple. He came, sang and conquered, and was duly elected cantor, which position he for 56 years filled to the glory of God and to the honor and blessing of Judaism.

Activity in Vienna

With a heart full of tender feelings he departed from his home congregation and entered a field whose limits of influence were to be bounded only by the limits of the civilized globe. We give the story of this period in his own words, as he described it many years later: "I need scarcely mention that here, too, I found everything in a state of chaos. I saw immediately that the development of the song service of the synagogue could only be a restoration based upon historical foundations. The old traditions were not to be abolished, their forms alone were to be modified and harmonized with the laws of modern art. The old were to find again what had become dear and familiar through long associations, and the young to be made susceptible of it. The heart of the fathers had to be reconciled to that of the children, and the aspiring youth to be filled with reverence for the feelings of old. Arduous labors were in store for me, and I entered upon them with all my soul. First of all the pronunciation of the Hebrew had to be improved, the old melodies, that had become national, sought out and arranged in an artistic form. New musical creations were also needed, and in this I was generously assisted by such masters as Seyfried, Schubert, Fischoff and others. In the midst of my own congregation, my efforts to bring about a reconciliation between the past and the future and to pave the way for progress and betterment, met with the fullest appreciation, and I count as one of the happiest recollections of my life the moment when truth gained the victory in the great and noble soul of the sainted preacher of Mannheimer, who had long cherished the thought of radical reform, such as had been planned in the 'Berliner Culturverein,' and on his own accord admitted that the course which I had taken was the only correct one, the one that alone would lead to the desired goal. The Lord's blessing was visibly on the side of our undertaking. It found favor with the most intelligent congregations. The Viennese Ritual rose to be the pattern and the regulator, and the melodies of our temple met with a hearty reception in the widest circles, even beyond the sea."

It was, indeed, an educational mission which Sulzer performed. The political emancipation of the Jews and their entrance into the larger life of the world had to be preceded by the modification of their distinctive traits acquired through centuries of oppression and persecution. This regeneration could proceed only from the synagogue which was the center of the Ghetto life. To reform the service and the liturgy of the synagogue was to reform the Jew himself. Who will dispute Sulzer's claim to the credit of having accomplished this great work and worthily filled the place providentially assigned to him by the side of the famous preacher Mannheimer? Like the latter, Sulzer, too, was saturated with the fiery zeal which he needed in the battle against the opposition in his own camp and against the police domination of his time. He collected the scattered pearls of the old songs, arranged them artistically for choral uses, and in two volumes of *Schir Zion* he gave his coreligionists a work which has become the common possession of the Jews in both hemispheres. "As there were old schools of the prophets," says Dr. August Frankl, "So Sulzer, by his *Schir Zion* has founded schools for the sacred song, whose temple is the world." Doubtless others have contributed to the reform of the Jewish liturgy, and thereby brought order and devotion into the synagogue service, yet the greatest credit is due to Salomon Sulzer who in justice must be called the regenerator of the Jewish public worship, the creator of a soul-inspiring musical liturgy.

Sulzer As Cantor

But great and far-reaching as were the work and influence of Sulzer as the regenerator of the synagogue music, his greatest influence, above all, he wielded as cantor in the House of the Lord. Here he was unsurpassed. The temple was his home, the altar before the ark his throne. No one who saw and heard him in the Seitenstettengasse-temple doubted that God had put him into that office.

He was a prophet whose lips the flaming seraph had touched and cleansed, and prepared for the delivery of his message to his coreligionists. I must leave comment on his style to others who are judges of tone and form and method, but this I know that his style was his own. It was as natural to him as is its own song to the nightingale. No wonder, then, that men as they entered the temple could not resist the voice of song which fell on their ear; and no wonder that, once having entered, they should be fascinated by the scene which met their eye, and touched, thrilled and refreshed should leave saying: "Surely God is in this place; this is, indeed, the house of God, and this is none other than the gate of heaven." So from Sabbath to Sabbath his temple was crowded to its utmost capacity. People of all classes came to hear and worship and none could ever forget the fascinating mixture of tenderness, earnestness and pathos which he breathed into the services. We cannot forego to give here a few graphic descriptions of the impressions he made upon and the delight he gave to those who ever heard him.

Franz Liszt writes: "In order to hear Sulzer sing, we went to the synagogue where he was musical director and cantor. Seldom have we experienced such an overpowering effect upon the chords of divine adoration and human sympathy, as that evening when we listened to his outpouring of praises to the God of the ancient covenant."

Professor Hanslick, in 1866, writes in the *Neue Freie Presse*: "Old Sulzer is one of the most popular persons in Vienna. Who does not know him with his remarkable characteristic head, his curly grey locks, his round, fiery eyes and the energetic, large mouth? The man, who half a century ago, a youth then barely seventeen, led the congregation of his native town in prayer, and then for upwards of forty years charmed the musical Vienna with the splendor of his voice and the pathos of his expression is still active and in unbroken vigor, having lost neither his voice nor the ardor of youth. Today, as 30 or 40 years ago, scarcely a visiting musical artist leaves Vienna without having once heard the famous cantor." On the occasion of his retirement from active service in 1881, Dr. Ludwig Frankl, the oldest officer of the congregation, addressed him as follows: "As at the entrance of the temple at Jerusalem there towered two pillars ingeniously wrought in stone, so did you stand in our sanctuary associated with a man who already rests in peace. He glorified God in words, you in song. When you sang we heard now the shout of joy from Mount Zion, and then again it was like the sad notes of the harp by the rivers of Babylon. Our hearts beat in rapturous joy when you greeted the Sabbath bride, and strength and comfort filled our souls when, like the trumpet of the resurrection, you raised your lamentations at the open graves."

And Dr. Adolph Jellinek, Sulzer's co-worker for many years, said of him: "That voice, who can describe it? Its strengths and its softness, its richness and its tenderness, its fervor and its pathos. That voice charmed, overpowered and inspired, opened the gates of heaven and penetrated the depths of the soul. That was the expression of an honest, tender heart. For he was, in the fullest sense of the word, a 'messenger of the congregation.'"

Sulzer As Singer — His Popularity

Sulzer shone not only as the great temple-singer, but also as the best Schubert-singer. True art does not confine itself to just one sphere, its boundaries reach far and wide, and thus Sulzer went outside his temple to contend for the palm, which Liszt, Schubert, Schuman, Seyfried and others ungrudgingly awarded him. Archbishop Pyrker, who heard him sing Schubert's 'Allmacht' at a court-concert, was so moved that he walked up to him with outstretched arms, intending to bless him with the sign of the cross, but remembering that he was a Jew, fell on his neck and wept tears of joy.

Great marks of honor are flowered upon him from all sides. He was the possessor of the Franz Joseph and Medjidje Order, also of the Great Gold Medal of Austria and Russia for Art and Science. He was the recipient of diamond rings from Emperor Ferdinand, Emperor Franz Joseph and the Great Duke of Baden; of a gold medal from the Duke Maximilian of Bavaria, as well as a gold medal from America struck especially for him. The municipality of Vienna honored him with the freedom of the city, and the Sacred College of Rome made him an honorary member.

Gold and silver wreaths were presented to him, also addresses and diplomas from musical societies, as well as from Jewish congregations in all parts of the world. His own congregation lost no opportunity to do him honor and to show him their appreciation of his work. This was the case in 1856, when he had been their cantor 30 years. Then in 1866, when he celebrated his 40th anniversary; again in 1874, on the occasion of the anniversary of his 70th birthday; again in 1876 in celebration of his golden jubilee, and when in April 2nd, 1881, he resigned his position, after an active service of 56 years, he received an ovation from the men and women of his own congregation and from the people of Vienna in general, such as seldom falls to the lot of mortals. All joined in the song of gratitude for the celestial delight which his song had given them.

Sulzer's Social and Family Life

Sulzer was one of the most popular persons in Vienna. Jews and non-Jews esteemed and revered the man who, though a great artist, did not forget that he was a man, and who at times was ready with help and advice for all, irrespective of creed or class. Sulzer and benevolence are synonymous. It is not easy to exaggerate when speaking of his generosity. He was never too tired to say the cheering word, nor too busy to do the kindly deed. He had a great, loving heart. Once he did a man a great favor and the man, grasping his hand, said, "I hope soon to have an opportunity to return your favor." "Don't wait for me," he replied, "return the favor to the first man that asks for it." Everything about him was colossal, his figure, voice, brain and heart. In him "mercy and love met together, righteousness and peace kissed each other."

His whole life was a song, a song as sweet and beautiful as that which he sang. His generous nature manifested itself in many ways. In order to awaken and foster the germ of true art in others, he unselfishly gave free instruction to a large number of pupils who by their achievements at home and abroad have shed luster upon the name of their master. For several years he served as professor at the Conservatory of Music in Vienna without accepting any compensation. He was one of the founders of the "Soup and Tea Institute," also of the "Institute for the Blind" of Vienna; president of the "Children's Savings and Aid Society," vice-president of the "Aid Society of Tyrol and Vorarlberg," in which capacity especially he proved himself a prince of well-doers. One must not have lived close to him to form a correct estimate of the good he has wrought and the noble acts he performed, and which alone explains his popularity with his contemporaries.

But it was in the home-life where the tender, sweet sides of his nature were fully revealed. For his family he had the deepest affection. To his children he was the companion, the partner in every joy, the comforter in every sorrow. In 1827, he married Franziska Hirschfeld, who belonged to one of the best families of Hohenems. It was a marriage of hand and heart. This union was blessed with fourteen children, some of whom have fallen heir to their father's musical talent. The oldest son was conductor of the Court Orchestra and the youngest a solo cellist at the Opera House in Vienna. Two of his daughters have won fame as singers and musicians in Austria, France, Spain and Italy. "I have," he writes, "made every effort conceivable to give each one of our fourteen children a good education, so as to fit them for life's duties and enable them to fill a worthy place in society. With God's help we have borne the frequent recurring separations, which were severe trials to us, and today after so many years, we can look back upon them with great self-satisfaction."

Sulzer's Humor

Sulzer was a perfect child of nature, frank, jovial, entertaining and bubbling ever with wit and humor. He was an excellent mimic and his stories would set the gravest in a roar. We reproduce a few amusing incidents as he described them. "A Jewish lieutenant in the Austrian army once sought the hand of my daughter. He had *one* star on his coat collar, but hoped soon to be made captain, and then to be wearer of three stars. 'Very well,' I said, 'let us wait, for you know, Es wird nicht angebissen, bis *drei* Sterne sichtber sind.'"

"Mr. Sonnenthal, the famous actor at the Court Theatre of Vienna, while spending a few days at Geneva, Switzerland, was attracted by a beautiful churchlike structure standing upon a hill. He ascended and presently found himself in front of the Jewish temple. Being led inside by the sexton he noticed a large book upon the desk bearing the inscription: *Schir Zion* by Sulzer. When Mr. Sonnenthal exclaimed, 'Unser Sulzer!' then slipped from the lips of the sexton the remark, 'Ah so!'"

The End

After a brief illness Sulzer passed away January 17, 1890, at the age of 86. His funeral, a most imposing one, was attended by representatives of every class and creed, Jews and non-Jews, every denomination vying with each other in paying tributes of respect to their common brother. Drs. Jellinek and Güdeman delivered eulogistic addresses, and many cantors, from Austria and Germany participated in the funeral services. The Jewish community of Vienna erected a magnificent monument upon his grave; yet his most enduring monument is the great service he rendered to the sacred cause of synagogue worship. Sulzer is dead, but his work lives on. A noble, useful life is never lost; the memory of the righteous is a continuous blessing. They scatter with generous hand the precious seeds, and posterity reaps the golden grain. Let us thank God for the useful, blessed life of Salomon Sulzer, who for more than 60 years has given his strength and genius, and has labored incessantly and with sincerity of motive for the glory of his God and for the honor of his people.

Such is the record of Salomon Sulzer. It is the record of a man who was loyal to duty and truth, loyal to God, himself and his fellowmen. He has left us a priceless heritage and it is ours to develop and to perpetuate it.

> Press on! Press on! Do not fear,
> From age to age his voice shall cheer!
> What'er may die and be forgot,
> Work done for God, it dieth not.

15. Music of the Synagogue (1895)

Gustav Karpeles

Ladies and Gentlemen: Let the emotions aroused by the notes of the great masters, now dying away upon the air, continue to reverberate in your souls. More forcibly and more eloquently than my weak words, they express the thoughts and the feelings appropriate to this solemn occasion.

A festival like ours has rarely been celebrated in Israel. For nearly two thousand years the muse of Jewish melody was silent; during the whole of that period, a new chord was but seldom won from the unused lyre. The Talmud (Yoma, 38a) has a quaint tale on the subject: Higros the Levite living at the time of the decadence of Israel's nationality, was the last skilled musician, and he refused to teach his art. When he sang his exquisite melodies, touching his mouth with his thumb, and striking the strings with his fingers, it is said that his priestly mates, transported by the magic power of his art, fell prostrate, and wept. Under the Oriental trappings of this tale is concealed regretful anguish over the decay of old Hebrew song. The altar at Jerusalem was demolished, and the songs of Zion, erst sung by the Levitical choirs under the leadership of the Korachides, were heard no longer. The silence was unbroken, until, in our day, a band of gifted men disengaged the old harps from the willows, and once more lured the ancient melodies from their quivering strings.

Towering head and shoulders above most of the group of restorers is he in whose honor we are assembled, to whom we bring greeting and congratulation. To you, Herr Lewandowski, I address myself to offer you the deep-felt gratitude and the cordial wishes of your friends, of the Berlin community, and, I may add, of the whole of Israel. You were appointed for large tasks — larger tasks have you successfully performed. At a time when Judaism was at a low ebb, only scarcely discernible indications promising a brighter future, Providence sent you to occupy a guide's position in the most important, the largest, and the most intelligent Jewish community of Germany. For fifty years your zeal, your diligence, your faithfulness, your devotion, your affectionate reverence for our past, and your exalted gifts, have graced the office. Were testimony unto your gifts and character needed, it would be given by this day's celebration, proving, as it does, that your brethren have understood the underlying thought of your activities, have grasped their bearing upon Jewish development, and have appreciated their influence.

You have remodeled the divine service of the Jewish synagogue, superceding elements of devotion and sacredness. Under your touch old lays have clothed themselves with a modern garb — a new garb vibrates through our historic melodies, keener strength in the familiar words, heightened dignity in the cherished songs. Two generations and all parts of the world have hearkened to your harmonies, responding to them with tears of joy or sorrow, with feelings stirred from the recesses of the heart. To your music have listened entranced the boy and girl on the day of declaring their allegiance to the covenant of their fathers; the youth and the maiden in life's most solemn hour; men and women in all the sacred moments of the year, on the days of mourning and of festivity.

A quarter of a century ago, when you celebrated the end of twenty-five years of useful work, a better man stood, and spoke to you. Leopold Zunz on that occasion said to you: "Old thoughts have been transformed by you into modern emotions, and long stored words seasoned with your melodies have made delicious food."

This is your share in the revival of Jewish poesy, and what you have resuscitated, and remodeled, and re-created, will endure, echoing and re-echoing through all the lands. In you Higros the Levite has been restored to us. But your melodies will never sink into oblivious silence. They have been carried by an honorable body of disciples to distant lands, beyond the ocean, to communities in the remote countries of civilization. Thus they have become the perpetual inheritance of the congregation of Jacob, the people that has ever loved and wooed music, only direst distress succeeding in flinging the pall of silence over song and melody.

Holy Writ places the origin of music in the primitive days of man, tersely pointing out, at the same time, music's conciliatory charms: it is the descendant of Cain, the fratricide, a son of Lemech, the slayer of a man to his own wounding, who is said to be the "father of all such as play the harp and guitar" (*Kinnor* and *Ugab*). Another of Lemechh's sons was the first artificer in every article of copper and iron, the inventor of weapons of war, as the former was the inventor of stringed instruments. Both used brass, the one to sing, the other to fight. So music sprang from sorrow and combat. Song and roundelay, timbrels and harp, accompanied our forefathers on their wanderings, and preceded the armed men into battle. So, too, the returning victor was greeted, and in the Temple on Moriah's crest, joyful songs of gratitude extolled the grace of the Lord. From the harp issued the psalm dedicated to the glory of God — love of art gave rise to the psalter, a songbook for the nations, and its author David may be called the founder of the national and Temple music of the ancient Hebrews. With his song, he banished the evil spirit from Saul's soul; with his skill on the psaltery, he defeated his enemies, and he led the jubilant chorus in the Holy City singing to the honor and glory of the Most High.

Compare the Hebrew and the Hellenic music of ancient times: Orpheus with his music charms wild beasts; David's subdues demons. By means of Amphion's lyre, living walls raise themselves; Israel's cornets make level the ramparts of Jericho. Arion's melodies lure dolphins from the sea; Hebrew music infuses into the prophet's disciples the spirit of the Lord. These are the wondrous effects of music in Israel and in Hellas, the foremost representatives of ancient civilization. Had the one united with the other, what celestial harmonies might have resulted! But later, in the time of Macedonian imperialism, when Alexandria and Jerusalem met, the one stood for enervated paganism, the other for a Judaism of compromise, and a union of such tones produces no harmonious chords.

But little is known of the ancient Hebrew music of the Temple, of the singers, the songs, the melodies, and the instruments. The Hebrews had songs and instrumental music on all festive, solemn occasions, particularly during the divine service. At their national celebrations, in their homes, at their diversions, even on their journeys and their pilgrimages to the sanctuary, their hymns were at once religious, patriotic, and social. They had the viol and the cithara, flutes, cymbals, and castanets, and, if our authorities interpret correctly, an organ (*magrepha*) whose volume of sound surpassed description. When, on the Day of Atonement, its strains pealed through the chambers of the Temple they were heard in the whole of Jerusalem, and all the people bowed in humble adoration before the Lord of hosts. The old music ceased with the overthrow of the Jewish state. The Levites hung their harps on the willows of Babylon's streams, and every entreaty for the "words of song" was met by the reproachful inquiry: "How should we sing the song of the Lord on the soil of the stranger?" Higros the Levite was the last of the Israelite tone-artists.

Israel set out on his fateful wanderings, his unparalleled pilgrimage, through the lands and the centuries, along an endless, thorny path, drenched with blood, watered with tears, across nations and thrones, lonely, terrible, sublime with the stern sublimity of tragic scenes. They are not the sights and experiences to inspire joyous songs — melody is muffled by terror. Only lamentation finds voice, an endless, oppressive, anxious wail, sounding adown, through two thousand years, like a long-drawn sigh, reverberating in far-reaching echoes: "How long, O Lord, how long!" and "When shall a redeemer arise for this people?" These elegiac refrains Israel never wearies of repeating on all his journeyings. Occasionally a fitful gleam of sunlight glides into the crowded Jewish quarters, and at once a more joyous note is heard, rising triumphant above the doleful plaint, a note which asserts itself exultingly on the celebration in memory of the Maccabean heroes, on the days of *Purim*, at wedding banquets, at the love-feasts of the pious brotherhood. This fusion of melancholy and of rejoicing is the keynote of medieval Jewish music growing out of the grotesque contrasts of Jewish history. Yet, despite its romantic woe, it is informed with the spirit of a remote past, making it the legitimate offspring of ancient Hebrew music, whose characteristics, to be sure, we arrive at only by guesswork. Of that medieval music of ours, the poet's words are true: "It rejoices so pathetically, it laments so joyfully."

Whoever has heard, will never forget Israel's melodies, breaking forth into rejoicing, then cast down with sadness: bringing out their notes to the skies, then sinking into the abyss of grief; now elated, now oppressed; now holding out hope, now moaning forth sorrow and pain. They convey the whole of Judah's history — his glorious past, his mournful present, his exalted future promised by God. As their tones flood our soul, a succession of visions passes before our mental view: the Temple in all its unexampled splendor, the exultant chorus of Levites, the priests discharging their holy office, the venerable forms of the patriarchs, the law-giver guide of the people, prophets with uplifted finger of warning, worthy rabbis, pale-faced martyrs of the middle ages; but the melodies conjuring before our minds all these shadowy figures have but one burden: "How should we sing the song of the Lord on the soil of the stranger?"

That is the ever-occurring *motif* of the Jewish music of the middle ages. But the blending of widely different emotions is not favorable to the creation of melody. Secular occurrences set their seal upon religious music, of which some have so high a concentration as to call it one of the seven liberal arts, or even to extol it beyond poetry. Jacob Levi of Mayence (Maharil), living at the beginning of the fifteenth century, is considered the founder of German synagogue music, but his productions remained barren of poetic and devotional results. He drew his best subjects from alien sources. At the time of the Italian Renaissance, music had so firmly established itself in the appreciation of the people that a preacher, Judah Muscato, devoted the first of his celebrated sermons to music, assigning to it a high mission among the arts. He interpreted the legend of David's Aeolian harp as a beautiful allegory. Basing his explanation on a verse in the Psalms, he showed that it symbolizes a spiritual experience of the royal bard. Another writer, Abraham ben David Portaleone, found the times still riper; he could venture to write a theory of music, as taught him by his teachers, Samuel Arkevolti and Menahem Lonsano, both of whom had strongly opposed the use of certain secular melodies then current in Italy, Germany, France, and Turkey for religious songs. Among Jewish musicians in the later centuries of the middle ages, the most prominent was Solomon Rossi. He, too, failed to exercise influence in the shaping of Jewish music, which more and more delighted in grotesqueness and aberrations from good taste. The origin of synagogue melodies was attributed to remoter and remoter periods; the most soulful hymns were adapted to frivolous airs. Later still, at a time when German music had risen to its zenith, when Bach, Handel, Haydn, Mozart, and Beethoven flourished, the Jewish strolling musician *klezmer*, a mendicant in the world of song as in the world of finance, was wandering through the provinces with his two mates.

Suddenly a new era dawned for Israel, too. The sun of humanity sent a few of its rays into the squalid Ghetto. Its walls fell before the trumpet blast of humanity. On all sides sounded the cry for liberty. The brotherhood of man, embracing all, did not exclude storm-baptized Israel. The old synagogue had to keep pace with modern demands, and was arrayed in a new garb. Among those who designed and fashioned the new garment, he is prominent in whose honor we have met today.

From our short journey through the centuries of music, we have returned to him who has succeeded in the great work of restoring to its honorable place the music of the synagogue, sorely missed, ardently longed for, and bringing back to us old songs in a new guise. An old song and a new melody! The old song of abiding love, loyalty, and resignation to the will of God! His motto was the beautiful verse: "My strength and my song is the Lord"; and his unchanging refrain, the jubilant exclamation: "Blessed be thou, fair Musica!" A wise man once said: "Hold in high honor of Lady of Music!"

The wise man was Martin Luther — another instance this of the conciliatory power of music, standing high above the barriers raised by religious indifference. It is worthy of mention, on this occasion, that at the four hundredth anniversary celebration in honor of Martin Luther, in the Sebaldus church at Nuremberg, the most Protestant of the cities of Germany, called by Luther himself, "the eye of God," a psalm of David was sung to music composed by our guest of the day.

"Hold in high honor our Lady of Music!" We will be admonished by the behest, and give honor to the artist by whose fostering care the music of the synagogue enjoys a new lease of life; who, with pious zeal, has collected our dear old melodies, and has sung them to us all the ardor and power with which God in His kindness endowed him. "The sculptor must simulate life, of the poet I demand intelligence; The soul can be expressed only by Polyhymnia!"

An orphan, song wandered hither and thither through the world, met, after many days, by the musician, who compassionately adopted it, and clothed it with his melodies. On the pinions of music, it now soars withersoever it listeth, bringing joy and blessing wherever it alights. "The old song, the new melody." Hark! through the silence of the night in this solemn moment, one of those old songs, clad by our maestro in a new melody, falls upon our ears: "I remember unto thee the kindness of thy youth, the love of thy espousals, thy going after me in the wilderness, through a land that is not shown!"

Hearken! Can we not distinguish in its roots, as they fill our ears, the passage of a music of the future, of love and goodwill? We seem to hear the rustle of the young leaves of a new spring, the resurrection foretold thousands of years agone by our poets and prophets. We see slowly dawning that great day on which mankind, awakened from the fitful sleep of error and delusion, will unite in the profession of the creed of brotherly love, and Israel's song will be mankind's song, myriads of voices in unison sending aloft to the skies the psalm of praise: Hallelujah, Hallelujah!

16. Secular Currents in the Synagogal Chant in America (1918)

Joseph Reider

THE DISTINCTION BETWEEN religious and secular music is not readily admitted. There is a considerable group of people, some of them very learned in the art and science of sound, who claim that music *per se* is one and indivisible, either good or bad, grammatically correct or wrong, and that the colored moods or feelings we experience at a recital are simply due to association of ideas. Thus a chant or anthem becomes to us a sacred composition because we hear them in a cathedral or synagogue instead of a music hall or theater. The world-renowned *Miserere* given in the Sistine Chapel at Rome during the holy week is used as an illustration. This famous performance, over which tourists enthuse and rave *ad extremun*, when noted down and analyzed outside the cathedral atmosphere, as was done surreptitiously by Mozart, proves to be prosaic and simple to the marked degree. They also cite instances of sacred oratorios, like Handel's *Esther* and Mendelssohn's *Elijah*, being offered on the operatic stage and evoking feelings quite contrary to those evoked within the cold Gothic walls of the oratory. That there is a modicum of truth in this assertion is evident with anyone conversant with the influence of the environment on such a sentient being as man. Indeed, even apart from this, it must be admitted that what we generally characterize as holy and secular melodies are not as far apart as we are prone to think. They often merge together so that we are not able to distinguish their line of demarcation. Nevertheless, the division of music into religious and secular is legitimate, and is justified not alone by time-honored usage but also by essentially differing characteristics which serve as criteria for determination of the artistic status of a certain melody.

To begin with, all true religious tunes have a certain breadth, strength, dignity, and simplicity, which are rarely met with in secular songs. These stern qualities are obtained in various ways, such as the use of slow movement, the employment of only one note or syllable, the use of common time, major or augmented intervals, and, last but not least, an upward diatonic progression. The opposite is true of secular tunes, which are generally florid and melismatic, fugal and mellifluous, having slurs and appoggiaturas, with the result that two or more notes are given in one syllable, employing mostly triple time, minor or diminished intervals, and chromatic progression. The one represents innate reverence, the other innate flippancy. To make their relation still clearer by a simile, sacred stands to secular music as Gothic architecture stands to the building style of the Renaissance: it is pointedness versus rotundity, masculinity against femininity, ruggedness instead of suppleness. The same relation obtains in painting between the early Church style as exemplified in Fra Angelico on the one hand and the Renaissance style of Raphael, Michael Angelo and Rubens on the other; in the former we find perpendicularity and a suggestion of infinity, in the latter roundness and perfection and nothing left to the soaring imagination.

The nearest approach to religious song is the Gregorian chant of the Catholic Church which admittedly goes back to Temple music at least as far as content is concerned. This chant has various ramifications, but all of them portray a self-surrendering faith, the humility and abnegation of a pietistic soul, subjective resignation and extinction of egotism. The most typical representative is the famous *Cantus Pere Grinus*, which Jesus of Nazareth is supposed to have intoned to the *Hallel* on the Feast of Passover (comp. Mark 14, 26). It is a primitive and elementary tune, consisting of two short phrases, one ascending and the other descending, terminating in the minor *la*, so characteristic of the Orient; nevertheless it is full of strength, dignity, and beauty. Its antiquity may be vouchsafed, even aside from the well-authenticated tradition by dint of what of we know of the origin of human speech and song. It has been determined beyond any doubt that originally all music was religious and consisted in intensive speech-song, a kind of dramatic recitation, with as much rigidity and as little floridity as possible. The speech was dominant, the song subservient, and this is exactly what we find in these rugged tunes, as anyone may convince himself by hearing the *Sanctus* and the *Gloria* of the Eucharistic service. Another example of general and antique religious song, more familiar to us Jews, is the well-known tune *Leoni*, which is sung at some congregations to *Yigdal* on Sabbath eve. It is so pathetic and reverent, self-denying and God-exalting, that it is hard to find its equal in the whole Jewish liturgy. Its ancient Jewish origin is attested to not merely by the characteristic minor key, but also by the almost monotonous simplicity represented by the constantly reoccurring phrase of upward progression. I might also mention the world-renowned tune for *Kol Nidre*, which in its basic outline barring the abbellimenti and fioriruri of ambitious composers, is deeply religious and soul stirring. Or I might refer to that powerful and all-engulfing hymn of the Sephardim at the close of the Day of Atonement, *Eil Nora Alila*, which in my mind is always associated with Luther's *Eine feste Burg*, both being ascendant and aggressive in the highest degree.

But all these genuine tunes are rare exceptions in our liturgy. For the most part our ancient hymns have undergone a radical metamorphosis, due to various internal and external factors, but chiefly to the strange environments to which the Jews found themselves at the entrance of the Diaspora. Under the conditions of flux and re-flux, of continuous immigration and emigration, in which the Jews henceforth found themselves, it was inevitable that even their closely guarded and strictly observed chant should be affected by current popular melodies. As a matter of fact, it can be maintained with a considerable degree of certainty that the synagogal chant was never absolutely pure and uncontaminated, that there was always some leaven of folk-song mixed with the pabulum of the hymn. But with the supremacy of ecclesiastical over secular music until the end of the Middle Ages this admixture was not noticeable, being of a negligible quality and therefore enjoying the connivance of the clergy. It was only during the Renaissance, when popular got the ascendancy over ecclesiastical music, that the contamination of the chant began to grow apace. It was the natural result of the process of secularization, which was supreme and dominant in the Christian Church of those days and culminated later on in the excrescence of the Muggletonians in England and the Salvation Army brotherhood in America, in the revival methods of the Protestant John Wesley, who borrowed some of the Devil's best tunes in order that all of them might not be thrown away upon an unworthy service. The Jews, without even a hierarchy to restrain them, proved excellent imitators in this attractive and seducing practice. As an authority on the subject, Francis L. Cohen, expresses it very succinctly:

> Beginning with the sixteenth century it became a frequent practice among Ashkenazim as well as Sephardim, to adopt melodies foreign to the synagogue, and to liberally reproduce there the folksongs of the country. Many *hazzanim* would

themselves compose melodies for the service, but these would be influenced rather by the popular music of the day than by the Jewish spirit of the older tunes. The larger number of the tunes henceforward introduced bear plain token of their outside origin, to which indeed many of them are clearly traceable. Such are the liturgical hymns for Sabbath, and for Hanukah, and other similar occasions, the larger portion of the melodies which characterize the three festivals, together with nearly all, if not quite all, of the hymns for singing in the home circle, according to the good old Jewish custom. Much of this adopted music is of a jingling prettiness; some little of it, however, well worth preservation.

The subject of secularization is highly interesting and fascinating not only from the religious but also from the musical standpoint, and I intend to deal with it at some length on another occasion. Here I want to touch upon it only insofar as it affects the various practices in our American synagogues and temples. Corresponding to the three great classes of the Jewish population in America, viz. the Spanish, the German and the Russian-Polish Jews, we can diagnose three distinct tendencies in the treatment of synagogue music: the Sephardim retain their love for Moorish and generally Oriental folk tunes, the Ashkenazim indulge in operatic airs and oratorio themes, while the Russian-Polish Jews, in addition to their love for Slav and generally eastern European melodies, imitate everything melodious in the musical register. Some of these tendencies manifested themselves already in the Middle Ages, but they became accentuated with the advance of time and the consequent evolution of new musical forms. With the immigration of the Jews to the new continent these practices were transplanted here and continued their undisturbed development.

With reference to the Spanish and Portuguese the dictum of Carl Engel still holds true: "In the synagogal hymns of the Sephardic Jews," he says in his work *National Music*, "who were expelled from the Spanish Peninsula at the end of the fifteen century, distinct traces and characteristics of Moorish music are still preserved." These characteristics, as anyone acquainted with Arab music knows, are primarily chromatic and inharmonic scales, built up of semitones and demi-semitones, instead of whole tones and half tones as case in the diatonic mode of the Europeans. It is the nature of these chromatic intervals that they yield a certain softness and effeminacy which we style minor mode. Another feature is the nasal twang, so common in the Orient, and no doubt the result of the peculiar scale system. The impression on a cultivated ear is something doleful and lugubrious, or else of something cold, turgid and anemic. This canorous style, with some modification, of course, found its way into the Sephardic synagogue at an early date and has since become naturalized there, so much so that the claim is often heard that it represents the oldest form of synagogue music and probably goes back to the Temple service. Thus the hymn *Az Yeshir Moshe* is claimed by the Sephardim to be the oldest melody of the synagogue. Whether there is any basis for this claim, I cannot discuss now; but I want to state my doubts in the face of the newly published collection of songs of the Yemenite Jews (Idelsohn, *Gesaenge der jemischen Juden*, Leipzig 1914). The Yeminite Jews, as is well known, remained without any outside influence for nearly two thousand years; and if any Jewish chant is to claim a hoary antiquity and perchance Temple ancestry, it is certainly the Yemenite chant with its pristine simplicity and elementary structure, its small range and narrow compass, its paucity of modulation and monotony of modes, its diatonic and often pentatonic scale. The Sephardic chant, on the other hand, is quite elaborate and developed, has a variety of motives and modes, a high range of tonality, a great number of scales, a system of modulation, and last but not least, chromatic intervals. The *piyyutim* are crooned in the *Irak* (Dorian) mode, but quite frequently also in the *l'Sain* (Hyper-Dorian or A minor) and the *l'Sain-sebah* (A minor with G sharp modern harmonic minor), reminding us of the romantic folksongs of the Iberian Peninsula and the cooing ditties of medieval Provence. In this connection it is interesting to quote the Rev. D. J. Sola, from his book *Ancient Melodies of the Liturgy of the Spanish and Portuguese Jews* (1857):

> When the Sephardic ritual became fixed and generally established in Spain, and was enriched by the solemn hymns of Gabirol, Judah ha-Levi, and other celebrated Hebrew poets, chants or melodies were composed or adapted to them, and were soon generally adopted. It would, indeed, have been most desirable that the sublime ways of our pious poets should have ever been found combined with equally sublime and sweet strains by devotionally inspired musical composers of our own nation. But this was not always practicable; and at a very early period it became necessary to sing these hymns to the popular melodies of the day; and in most collections we find directions prefixed to hymns replete with piety and devotion, that are to be sung to the tune of *Permetid, bella Amaryllis, Tres colors in una, Temprano naces, Almendro*, and similar ancient Spanish or Moorish songs — a practice no doubt very objectionable, for obvious reasons, and from which the better taste of the present age would shrink.

The profanation became so universal that hardly a congregation escaped it. Its traces may be pursued in the *mahzorim* coming from the Orient, a great majority of which bear superscriptions on the head of each *piyyut* indicating by first line the popular melodies to which the *piyyutim* were to be sung. From the standpoint of musical history this material is quite important.

It is also interesting to note that the Reverend Leeser states on one occasion that the hymn *Ki Eshmera Shabbat* was publicly caroled forth by an adventurous songster in a most respectable congregation to the popular love tune of "Meet Me by the Moonlight Alone," and by another, to well-known song *Partant pour la Syrie*— a practice which he condemns in strong terms.

The Sephardim, in their process of secularization, never went beyond the folksong. There is only one instance of an attempt to introduce operatic airs in their service, probably in imitation of the flourishing German temples. In Leeser's *Occident* of Dec. 1, 1859, a correspondent from New York states that "for some time past there appeared in the Jewish papers an advertisement for singers 'a la opera,' for the Portuguese Synagogue of this city; the thing went so far that an advertisement even appeared in a London periodical — but the electors at a recent meeting, with scarcely a dissenting vote, refused to permit any such folly to be introduced in place of good old fashioned orthodox worship."

The Ashkenazim have likewise been good adepts in this art of secularization. They were particularly subject to such influences, living as they did in the heart of musical fermentation, in a land where new forms were cropping up overnight and where harmony was marching in the cloud-capped eminencies of triumph and glory. The folksong with its charming simplicity and melodic sweetness naturally exerted great influence, as may still be seen in a minute examination of the hymns. To point out every such instance in the Ashkenazic hymnal would lead us too far astray. A few instances will suffice for the present. Thus the grave and pathetic hymn *Ledavid baruch* is sung at the close of the Sabbath to a jolly dance tune, notwithstanding the fact that it contains such weighty words as "Man is like to vanity, his days are but a shadow that passeth away." Similarly the hymn *Hodu l'adonai* for the first days of Passover bears the earmarks of a dance melody, though in its present form it is already attuned to a more serious purpose. Notwithstanding the subject of the prayer requires a lively tune, we expect something more refined and dignified, something broader and weightier, *maestoso* instead of *allegro*. Again, the song *Echad mi yodea* for Passover night is in imitation of a Catholic vesper which was current in Germany during the fifteenth century and was itself patterned after a monkish drink song. Though in the minor key, it has that droning and doleful quality, that flattened intonation, which somehow we associate with the moldering monks in a gloomy convent. Another Passover tune, the famous *Had Gadya*, is of foreign origin and of a secular nature. Gay and lively, of terpsichoreal measure and rhythm, it is a typical Provencal folksong of the type that was current during the latter part of the Middle Ages. It is known to have been incorporated in the Ashkenazi ritual during the sixteenth century. The very popular and sweetly hymn *Moaz zur yeshuati* sung on Hanukah is dressed in the melody of a Lutheran chorale, entitled *Nun frent euch, ihr lieben Christen* ("Now rejoice, ye dear Christians") or *So weiss ich eins, das mich erfreut* ("So one thing I know that gladdens me"). Incidentally it might be remarked that in some places of Eastern Europe this hymn bears the melody of a medieval folksong entitled *Die Frau zu Weissenburg*.

But more potent than the folksong was the influence of the larger and more artistic works such as chorales, oratorios, and operas, which, by dint of their novelty and dramatic dimensions, appealed very strongly to a people steeped in misery. The introduction of operatic airs in the German synagogue had been a notorious practice during the first flush of the Reformation, and this practice persisted throughout the ages until late in the nineteenth century, when, owing to the beneficent activity of men like Sulzer and Lewandowski, the evil was partly stamped out. The process of introducing these airs was slow. As Francis L. Cohen puts it: "It need not be imagined that these foreign airs were at once admitted into the synagogue. They would have been freely used with hymn songs sung in the home circle, as seems later on to have been the usual practice of the German Jews. Then, when their secular origin was forgotten, the melodies would finally have found a place in the synagogal hymnody, and would be jealously treasured as the more purely Jewish music." In this way, the synagogue service was overburdened with ariosos and cavatinas, traces of which can still be found in the Ashkenazic liturgy. This zeal for imitation was intensified with the entrance of Reform, whose main purpose was to beautify the service through the introduction of good music, both vocal and instrumental. The traditional chant was discarded as too primitive and un-harmonic, not suited to the powerful resources of the organ, and in its stead were introduced opera arias from various composers. In this unnatural adaptation the only extenuating circumstance is the fact that they chose their secular airs from the best composers in the field, among them Hayden, Bach, Handel, Beethoven, Mozart, Rossini and Mendelssohn. A particular favorite was Meyerbeer, who, because of his Jewish provenance and faith, was drawn upon very extensively, despite the fact that he was never capable of writing religious music and that of all the operatic composers in those days he was one of the lightest and thinnest. The airs from his *Africaine*, *Huguenots*, *Prophete*, and *Robert le Diable*, filled the Reformed temples for more than a generation, and some of them may still be detected there. There are also instances of borrowing of Lutheran chorales which, in their turn, have been derived from popular songs. All these things have been transplanted to America, where, as might have been expected, they were considerably augmented by Anglican anthems and Methodist revival songs. Even Moody-Sankey revival tunes and Salvation Army ditties found their way into some German temples. The result was a Christian-like service of an inferior kind, with a concert-hall flavor in it. It is such performances that a writer in the *American Hebrew* of June 10, 1887 has in mind when he complains of the fact that the choirs in most of the temples sing the most outrageously inappropriate melodies. Says the writer:

> It is sometimes absolutely grotesque to hear the tunes associated with amorous or dramatic passages in operas, sung to words of religious import. The most ridiculous lack of aesthetic taste is displayed. Seldom is there any true solemnity or other natural emotional force expressed by these choirs. Nothing but declamatory phrasing and sensational yelling and screeching utterly at variance with the character of the service. The whole thing is disgusting to the true artistic temperament, which realizes that melody should be wedded to verse and that the tune itself should be of such a nature that even without the words the hearer should be able to judge of its character. This was possible with the ancient *En Kelohenus*, *Yigdals*, *Adon Olams* and other characteristic Hebrew melodies, but it is utterly impossible with the present hotch-potch concert in the temple.

The Sunday morning service in particular served for a display of virtuosity. At that time the choir, made up largely of non–Jews, would intone "O du mein holder Abendstern" from Wagner's *Tannhauser* or, "I dreamt I dwelt in Marble Halls" from Balfe's *Bohemian Girl*. Then would follow Christian hymns and anthems such as the *Old Hundred* and the *Doxology*. As evidence may be cited the fact that in 1887 Dr. Gustav Gottheil of Temple Emanuel, New York, issued a volume entitled *Hymns and Anthems Adapted for Jewish Worship*, in which under five headings (Worship, God, Man, Israel, Four Various Occasions), he offers a collection of hymns, mostly by Christian writers. He draws upon Tate and Brady, Watts, Wesley, Doddridge, Bowring, and Montgomery, as well as upon Whittier, Emerson, Hosmer, and Chadwick, and several native sources. That conditions are the same in our present-day temples may be seen from an examination of the latest *Union Hymnal* published in 1914. This contains more foreign than traditional Jewish material, and although the foreign material is of the highest character and by some of the world's greatest composers, nevertheless the greatest part of it, from its association with the concert room, remains secular and irrelevant to divine worship.

Another practice of the Reform Synagogues should be mentioned here. It has become a custom with some of them to give Handel's *Judas Maccabeus* on Hanukkah, for no other reason but that the subject of the words is biblical. However, the music is anything but sacred, its floral style reminiscent of the bravura school of Italian opera. In fact, Handel is known as one of the most unchurchly of choral composers, in complete contrast to his contemporary Bach, whose compositions are ponderous and pregnant with religious fervor. Also Mendelssohn's *Elijah* is sometimes given there, notwithstanding the fact that, unlike his *St. Paul*, this is an opera as well as an oratorio, having been presented a number of times on the theatrical stage.

The Russian-Polish Jews adopted primarily Slav melodies in their ritual. The Hassidim of Poland and Russia in particular were wont to appropriate folksongs of their Slavonic neighbors for their liturgical hymns. Hence the peculiar characteristics of their chant, which is built on the harmonic minor and has great rhythmic freedom. An outgrowth of this is the unduly florid and excessively embroidered style of the so-called "Polish *Hazzanuth*," which has its counterpart in the Greek Church and is a natural concomitant of every purely melodic style of music. These *fiorituri* and *contrappunti alla mente* take the place of harmony. Trills, shakes, quavers, and passages, serve as a tonic to the moroseness of a monotonous recitative.

In America the Russian-Polish Jews have gone further than that, having appropriated also popular songs and operatic airs from the theatrical stage. Everything depends on the fancy of the *hazzan*, who in many cases is ignorant of the very rudiments of music and imposes on the synagogue what he pleases. In an Ohio town, on a Friday eve, I was surprised some years ago to hear a Hungarian cantor intone *Adon Olam* to Stephen C. Foster's *Old Black Joe*. I was anxious to know whether he knew the origin of the tune, and so I asked at the end of the service. But he proved to be absolutely ignorant of its origin, nor had he ever heard of the existence of that sweet bard of negro melodies. He said he picked it up on the street, and on account of its beauty and sweetness introduced it into the synagogue. I also know an old-fashioned *hazzan* on the East Side of New York who, after hearing the famous "Siciliana" of Mascagni's *Cavalleria Rusticana* and realizing its intrinsic value and exclusiveness as a devotional air, adapted it to *Adon Olam*, thus regaling his congregation with grand opera without their having the slightest notion of it. I likewise once heard a Galacian *hazzan*, on *Yom Kippur* eve, sing the fine *piyyut Yaaleh* to Liszt's second rhapsody, while a Hungarian cantor, with great pain, did it to the *Rakoczi-March*. *The Last Rose of Summer* is likewise popular in some East Side synagogues, where it is sung in violation of time and meter and with little regard of its technical suitability to the particular *piyyut*. It is enough that a melody is sweet and mellifluous, sad and lachrymose, in order to be accepted by the Polish *hazzan*, who rarely worries about its provenance.

In conclusion, it is interesting to note that also the melody of *Hatikvah*, the *cheval de bataille* of the Zionists, which of late is being used for *Shir ha-ma'alot* and other liturgical purposes, appears to be foreign and secular, as its main theme occurs in Smetana's symphonic poem entitled *On the Moldau*. I am aware of Dr. Pool's contention that this tune is rather an adaptation from the old Sephardic tune to *Hallel*. However, aside from the authentic information and certain knowledge of the fact which Dr. Pool claims to have and which I dare not impugn, the assertion is based on the similarity on the first or ascending figure or phrase in both melodies. But this is not sufficient as a criterion for authenticity, for the same inceptive figure or musical germ may be found also in other compositions of various lands and ages. In fact, the progression, *la, ti, do, re, mi*, is characteristic of the minor mode and is quite common in folksongs of all climates. I found it even in English folksongs of the Elizabethan period. One thing is certain, that Smetana did not derive his melody from the Sephardic *Hallel*. As is well known, this Bohemian composer utilized popular tunes of Bohemia as themes to his larger compositions. The most striking thing is that there is more similarity between *Hatikvah* and Smetana's melody than between the former and the Sephardic *Hallel*, especially with reference to the second or descending figure. However that may be, in its present elaborate shape it appears more like a folksong than an ecclesiastical chant, and hence is inappropriate for liturgical use.

It is just to add that efforts are being made now, here and elsewhere, to purge our liturgy of foreign excrescences and preserve the primitive Jewish tunes in a more or less integral state. The St. Cecilie movement, which aims to restore the plain chant within the Catholic Church, was no doubt instrumental in this direction. However that may be, towards the end of the nineteenth century there grew up cantors' associations in Germany and Austria whose main purpose was to purify and beautify the synagogal chant, and even propagate it among the people through periodic sacred concerts. In this country there was formed the Society of American Cantors, which was succeeded in 1908 by the Cantors Association of America. It has branches in Chicago, New York City, Philadelphia, and San Francisco. It meets annually to discuss the most important phases of synagogue music, and though so far it has not accomplished much, there is reason to believe that it holds out a good promise for the future.

17. A Revival of Jewish Music (1919)
JOSEPH REIDER

Part I

THERE ARE STILL PEOPLE who require an apology from one who presumes to speak about Jewish music. They cling to the belief that the Jews never had a music of their own, but like parasites have fed on the tonal systems of neighboring nations. This, however, is not true if by music we understand not only the modern harmonic structures but also the everlasting and eternally youthful melodic foundation.

The Bible and the Talmud contain ample records of the tonal fertility of the ancient Jews, and it is a well-known fact that many Temple melodies were transplanted into the hymnal of the primitive Christian Church. These edifying airs may still be traced in many Gregorian and Ambrosian chants which are framed either in the grave and majestic Dorian or the sad and pathetic Aeolian mode, so characteristic of the Orient. They are easily discernable in the liturgy of the Byzantine or Greek Church where the chant failed to progress as rapidly as in the Western Church, and where it still finds itself in the chrysalis stage of polyphony instead of the butterfly stage of harmony. Even a musical tyro can recognize very close kinship between the *a capella* style of the Oriental hierarchy and the *hazzanut* style of the eastern European ghettos: not only did both manage their liturgy without musical instruments of any kind, but even their scales and progressions are very often alike.

It is useless to speculate now upon what might have been the future of

Jewish music had the Jews remained in Palestine and led an untrammeled existence there. As it is, Christianity seized upon the existing material and through centuries of ceaseless shifting and combination produced that magnificent framework of modern times which is justly styled "the youngest and greatest of the Arts." The Jew, isolated as they were in the ghettos and steeped henceforth in legalistic activities and mercurial pursuits, could no longer keep pace with this great development. Nevertheless, retired like a marmot in his den, they continued to foster music in its melodic aspect, as may be seen from casual statements in medieval Rabbinic literature. Anyone who wants to convince himself that music was alive among the Jews during the Middle Ages should read the interesting chapter entitled "The Triumph of Music Over Its Opponents" in Leopold Löw's *Die Lebensalter in der jüdischen Litteratur* (p. 305 ff.). The love for music manifested itself in a number of ways. In the synagogue the *hazzan* (cantor) and his *meshorerim* (male choir) regaled the congregation with sad and pathetic airs, partly traditional and partly improvised and embellished with shakes, trills, roulades, and other fripperies of a questionable character. At home suffering and tantalized Israel, both young and old, gave vent to their grief in plaintive strains and heartrending threnodies. Moreover, instrumental music continued a chary and precarious existence through the activities of the so-called *klezmer*, a miniature orchestra playing at weddings. An imposing figure in connection with the latter was the Marshallik or Badhan, who improvised both lyrics and melodies in the spur of the moment. It is unfortunate that these melodic productions were never written down and fixed forever through notation. We might have possessed a wealth of material serving to illustrate not only the state of mind but also the aesthetic taste of our people in these trying days.

The Slow Development of Jewish Music

It is a fallacy to assume that this music, with all its poverty and one-sidedness, experienced no growth or development whatever until very recent times. Nor is it fair to refer to it as exclusively melodic or homophonic music. Like its Byzantine prototype it soon reached the stage of polyphony and initial harmony as far as these may be applied to the human voice. In the days of the Reformation choral song was the rule in western Jewish communities, and, like Hucbald, the Flemish monk, in the tenth century, Jewish precentors were evolving the *fauxbourden* or *organum*, a kind of diaphony or descant consisting in one voice singing the melody while another voice keeps up a drone on one note, or possibly alternating notes, either above or below.

At the same time in Italy, where Jews fostered music even to the extent of establishing musical clubs and societies, Solomon de Rossi, a descendant of the famous De Rossi family of which tradition says that their ancestors were brought to Rome in the time of Titus, attempted, probably for the first time in the history of the Jews, to write music for the synagogue in an up-to-date manner. His compositions, as published by Naumbourg in 1877, are for four and eight voices and are written in the elaborate polyphonic style of Palestrina. It is known that De Rossi intended a revival of Hebrew music, but he was steeped too much in the ecclesiastical modes of the Catholic Church to be able to an independent style and a genuine mode of expression. There is nothing characteristically Jewish in his thirty-three canticles and anthems, and they could as well be chanted or played in a cathedral. Likewise, there is nothing Jewish except the name in the so-called "Jewish Operas" of Antonio José da Silva, a baptized Jew from Brazil, born in 1705, who won great fame by popularizing the *Modinha* or Portuguese romance.

The real and genuine Jewish music, the spontaneous and self-evolved song, continued its oral existence until the middle of the nineteenth century, when some of the most important liturgical chants were noted down and developed by the great cantors Sulzer, Lewandowski, Naumbourg, Aguilar, and many others. The secular tunes or folksongs, however, as being ephemeral and transitory, and more or less influenced by foreign environment, were neglected for another generation. Not that they lacked treatment altogether: attempts had been made to utilize them for the Yiddish stage which came into existence in Southern Russia and Galicia during the latter half of the last century. Especially noteworthy is the effort of Abraham Goldfaden, the first great Jewish theatrical manager, who unconsciously wove many folksongs into his widely known operas *Shulamith* and *Bar Kochba*. But this treatment by men who hardly had any notion of the canons of composition and whose interest was purely commercial was far, far from satisfactory and anything but exact. The scientific construction of modern times was still wanting.

The Awaking of Interest in the Folksong

But times change. With the rise of Zionism and the regeneration of the Jews, the self-effacement of the days of emancipation gave way to a self-consciousness which strove to express itself in many ways, not the least being musical self-expression. Jewish artists and musicians, taunted and ostracized in European circles because of their physical features and racial characteristics, turned to their own people for inspiration and appreciation, and, after due study of the psychic traits and spiritual nuances of the sleepy giant, discovered that he, too, possessed ideas and ideals worth dreaming and singing about. As soon as this was realized a search was instituted here and there for an idiom appropriate enough for the expression of Young Israel's aspirations, and a desire grew up among young artists to found, in accordance with the spirit of modern times, a national school of Jewish music. The plan is still in the experimental stage, but enough has been done already to deserve our attention to its various phases and to warrant its auspicious consummation.

It is evident that no really national school of music can exist without the folksong. It is the national or popular songs that reflect the peculiar characteristics of a people, its mental state and temperament, its passions and emotions, its innate qualities and defects, its woes and weal, its dreams and ideals. This self-revelation is accomplished by various means, among them being a peculiar time and rhythm, a unique scale progression, a striking cadence, and certain other traits too complicated to enumerate here. It is due to these apparently insignificant differences that the German folksong is characterized by strong sentimentalism, the French by light cynicism, the Italian by exaggerated lyricism, the Spanish by passionate explosion, the Russian by woeful resignation, the Ukrainian by hedonism and absolute joy, the Afro-American by melancholy and nostalgia. And when a composer wants to stamp his music as national he must employ the folksong of the particular nation as a basis or theme for variations. This principle is not new. It was Father Eximeno who enumerated it in the eighteenth century in the following statement: "It is on the basis of popular national songs that every people must construct its artistic system." In fact we find Beethoven introducing Russian tunes into his Quartets dedicated to Prince Rasumowsky. Rossini does the same in his highly successful opera *Il Barbiere di Seviglia* [sic]. Gluck employs in his ballet *Don Juan* a popular and well-known Sephardic fandango, i.e., a rapid dance in triple time, which was afterwards used by Mozart at the end of the third act of his opera *Le Nozze di Figaro*. The serenade in Mozart's *Don Giovanni* is said to be an Italian popular air. Even the prolific Handel was not deterred from laying hands upon ready material when it suited his purpose, as may be seen from the fact that the theme of the sweet Pastorale in his *Messiah* was derived from the Pifferari, Italian peasants, who during Christmas sing their pastoral songs in the streets of Rome and Naples before the shrine of the Holy Virgin. Weber likewise, in the first act of his *Oberon*, introduced an Arabian melody which was brought from the East by the well-known traveler Niebuhr; and in the third act he made use of a

Turkish dance-tune which had previously been published in Laborde's *Essai sur la Musique*.

But these were only isolated cases, executed as a rule without consciousness and almost always without a definite plan or tendency. The real propaganda for the nationalization of music and consequently for the utilization of folksong in larger compositions began towards the middle of the nineteenth century, with Glinka in Russia, Moniuszko in Poland, Smetana in Bohemia, Erkel in Hungary, Grieg in Norway, and Söderland in Sweden. These men enlisted their lives for the benefit of the songs of their own peoples, thus creating national schools of music all over Eastern Europe, which still constitute a powerful stimulus towards truthful and forceful expression as opposed to the artificial vehicle of the great intellectual composers of Western Europe. This nationalistic tendency which has given us the most beautiful compositions in the world repertoire promises to be the most dominant and effective throughout the twentieth century.

The Folksong Must Be the Basis of Jewish Music

Taking all this into consideration, it becomes clear that Jewish music, to be distinctly Jewish, must be based on the Jewish folksong in its various ramifications. This folksong, neglected for two thousand years, must be resuscitated and become the cornerstone of the new edifice. And it is right here that signs of a revival have been noticeable of late years. A number of efforts have been made to gather up Jewish songs and edit them in attractive shape. The great collections by S. M. Ginzburg and P. S. Marek, entitled *Jüdische Volkslieder in Russland* and published in 1901 in St. Petersburg, contains 375 Yiddish songs picked up in the ghettos of southern Russia. Here in America Platon Brounoff has harmonized a number of Yiddish songs imported to the East Side from across the seas. Another instance is Dalman's *Jüdisch-deutsche Volkslieder aus Galizien und Russland* (Berlin 1891). However, the most remarkable collection is the great corpus of Jewish songs in the Orient now in process of publication by A. Z. Idelsohn of Palestine. Idelsohn is a graduate of the Berlin Controversy and has been teaching music in the school of the German Hülfsverein at Jerusalem for a number of years. While in Palestine he made a thorough study of the Jewish folksong, both synagogal and secular, and now, with the help of the Kaiserliche Akademie der Wissenschaft in Vienna, the Gesellschaft zur Förderung der Wissenschaft des Judenthumus in Berlin, and the Zunz-Stiftung of Berlin, he is on the way to publishing his work in six volumes. The first volume dealing with the songs of the Yemenite Jews appeared in 1914; the succeeding volumes will treat of the songs of the Persian, Babylonian, Syrian, Spanish-Portuguese, and Moroccan Jews. It is also interesting to know that Idelsohn, unlike other collections, employs strictly scientific methods, such as a phonograph apparatus with plates for melodic impressions, yielding very exact results. Besides these larger collections there are numerous instances of smaller editions of single songs or groups of songs.

In Europe, particularly in the eastern parts comprising great Jewish populations, there has been marked activity. Beginning with the twentieth century, folklore societies have been established in Germany, Russia, and Austria, for the purpose of collecting the many folksongs scattered in the fast fading ghettos and preserving them in notation for permanent use. Hundreds and thousands of historically important and aesthetically beautiful songs have thus been saved from oblivion. But for those efforts who knows whether we could now sit comfortably in a concert room and bask in the somber and melancholy strains of such songs as "Sehnsucht," "Avram, Avram," or "Otavorite vorata." Moreover, societies of musicians have been established for the harmonization and concert performance of these songs. The most noteworthy of these are the Verein zur Pflege hebräischer Musik in Berlin and the Society for Jewish Folk-Music in Petrograd. At the head of both institutions are Jewish musicians of high repute and acknowledged masters of composition, whose zeal is tireless and whose aim is to do for the Jewish song what Schubert, Schumann, and Franz have done for the German song. Outside of these organized efforts there are individual attempts to further the folksong, such, for instance, as was carried on by that unparagoned German-Jewish monthly, *Ost und West* of Berlin, during the last years of its brief existence. In its pages may be found settings of many songs by Arno Nadel and other young composers of Berlin.

The Appeal of Jewish Music to Americans

Here in America a manifold activity is being manifested in artistic circles which hitherto had kept aloof and even deprecated such efforts. It is no longer surprising, in fact it is becoming customary and even fashionable, to include a Jewish number in the program of great artists, most of whom, curiously enough, are of Jewish extraction, though generally styled Russian, Bohemian, Hungarian and American. To mention but a few: Alma Gluck has endeavored to popularize Ravel's version of that exquisite little gem *Meierke, mein Sun, un weisst du vor wemen du steihst?*, while her gifted husband, the violinist Efram Zimbalist, created a furore with his arrangement of the *Danse Juive*. The organist and composer Kurt Schindler and his Schola Cantorum, a chorus of 175 singers, mostly Gentiles, make it a point to render in public concerts such genuinely pathetic and deeply stirring songs as *Eili, Eili, lomo asavtonu?* and *Avrahm, Avrahm, Batjka nash*. Elizabeth Gutman of Baltimore carries throughout the country the message of our Chassidic songs, some of which, like *Macht der Chossidl*, have become popular even among non–Jews. Others who render substantial help in the elaboration and propagation of the Jewish folksong are J. Medvedieff, Platon Brounoff, Henry Lefkowitz, Henry Gideon, Pinchos Jassinowsky, and Morris Clarke. Our religious song is likewise fostered by special societies, such as the Cantors Association of the United States and the recently formed Zimrath Yah Society of New York, whose purpose is to give sacred concerts at stated intervals and thus popularize the synagogal melodies of great antiquity.

This itself is an unusual phenomenon. Time was when Jewish songs were looked upon as trivial and monotonous, insipid and jejune, at best as soft-livered and lackadaisical melodies of doubtful origin and eclectic ancestry. It is enough to recall the verdict of Voltaire in the sixth letter of the Dictionnaire: "Restournez en Judée le plus tot que vous pourrez ... vous y exécuteriez a plasir dans votre detestable jargon votre detestable musique" (Return to Judea as soon as you can ... and there perform at leisure your abominable music in your abominable jargon). The more recent indictment of Jewish music by Wagner is well known. Wagner contends (*Das Judenthum in der Musik*) that the tendency of music by Jewish composers like Mendelssohn and Meyerbeer is to be sweet and tinkling without depth, effeminate and enervating, horizontal rather than vertical, flat and superficial. However, even the aesthetic taste is subject to evolution and the law of mutation. As was stated above, the latter half of the nineteenth century witnessed the triumph of nationalism in music, particularly in the countries of eastern Europe, where the folksong partakes of Oriental characteristics. Side by side with this the process of importing Oriental tunes to western Europe, auspiciously begun by Felicien David, was continued by Salvador-Daniel, Saint Saëns, and others, whose fancy was struck by the peculiar scales and exotic rhythms of these songs. In this way Europe and America developed a taste for Oriental and likewise Jewish songs, which, garbed in a harmonic guise, lose much of their exoticism and bizarrerie. Besides, there is more tolerance now and a willingness on the part of one people to try to understand the musical idiom of another, and it is freely conceded now that the music of almost every nation has charms which we can appreciate if we enter into its spirit without bias or prejudice. Hence a musical program of purely Jewish compositions, lasting approximately two hours, no longer shocks a metropolitan audience as it would have done years ago.

The Folksong of the New Palestine

It is gratifying to see that the Jews do not rest merely on the laurels of the past. While this work of summarizing two thousand years of song is being carried on in the Occident, a new species of Jewish folksong is being developed in the Orient, in the cradle of the Jewish race, on the plains of Sharon and on the hills of Judea. As might have been expected, this new song of the colonists in Palestine, while retaining the form of the old songs, has an entirely different content, resounding with the gay notes of the new carefree life. It is no longer sad and gloomy, plaintive and melancholy, cooing and droning, but rather firm and manly, joyous and hopeful, brimful of verse and resilience, elasticity and sinuosity, and buoyancy and warmth. A good illustration is the harvest song known as *Po beerez* which, on account of its popularity, has been carried even to the American shores and in Zionist circles vies with the famous *Hatikva*. Though in the key of A flat minor, it is surcharged with enthusiasm and joy of life, and lacks even that note of yearning which is so evident in the melody of *Hatikva*. Other neo–Palestinian songs, as exhibited in Idelsohn's collection entitled *Shirim*, partake of the same characteristics. Their outstanding feature is a perfect melodicity found only among the Mediterranean peoples. From these harbingers of song it is easy to foresee what the future holds for us in Palestine by way of a national music.

Part II

I must revert here to the charge frequently made that the Jewish folksong, unlike the folksong of other tribes and nations, is not altogether indigenous and independent but partakes of characteristics of the songs of neighboring peoples. This charge is supported by a reference to the Moorish traits of the songs of the Spanish-Portuguese Jews or the Russian elements in the melodies of the Russian Jews. Traces of foreign origin have been found even in our much-vaunted national hymn *Hatikva*, which exhibits a striking resemblance to the main motive in Smetana's symphonic poem entitled *On the Moldau*. But it must be maintained that such points of contact do not invalidate the national character of a song. Melodies differ from verbal compositions in that they travel far and wide, penetrating even the remotest corners of the inhabited globe; but in every new locality they assume special characteristics before they become naturalized, and it is these additional nuances that stamp them as national.

An example may be adduced from Arabic music. As told in the *Kitab el-agani*, the great poetical anthology of the Arabs, Ibn Misgah of Mecca, during the reign of the Caliph Moawiya the First (A.D. 661–680), listened to the songs of certain Persian builders from Iraq, and picked up such of the tunes as pleased his fancy best, adapting them to Arabic poems. Later on he even went to Persia and Greece to study their music, but in introducing the airs of these countries into Arabia he modified them in such a way as befits the Arab ear. There are numerous instances of folksongs common to two or more nationalities. Carl Engel (*Introduction to the Study of National Music*, p. 2) refers to the well-known German "Dessauer Marsch" which, he maintains, is of Italian origin. "After Prince Leopold of Dessau had stormed Turin (in 1706), the conquered Italians met him with this march to do him homage. The taking melody pleased the German soldiers, and soon their trumpeters began to blow it upon their instruments. When it had been transmitted by them to Germany, the people soon Germanized its Italian flourishes." Engel refers also to a curious instance of transplantation in Courland. Of a number of German songs, translated into the Lettish language, and introduced into Courland by some gentlemen, a few became popular among the peasants. After some length of time these songs exhibited a remarkable change: originally in major, they were now sung partly in minor, and a rude kind of accompaniment was added. An instance familiar to everyone is the melody of "My Country" which in England is sung to "God Save the King" and in Germany to "Heil dir im Siegerkranz"; yet every one of these nations considers it their own.

And so it is true that many Jewish folksongs find their counterpart in the song collection of other peoples, which is natural under the circumstances existing between Israel and the nations for two thousand years. But when these melodies were transplanted into the Jewish fold they underwent a process of transmutation in conformity with the Jewish spirit and character. Major became minor; cadences on the tonic were changed to the mediant; the leading-tone, the most dependent tone on the diatonic scale, turned independent and often figured as a climax; the frequent progression in thirds and fifths gave place to augmented seconds and fourths. Moreover, certain melismata and roulades were added to each cadence, resulting in a gloomy and crepuscular atmosphere in keeping with the physical surroundings. The foreign tunes, in other words, were Judaized, and henceforth they became the property of the Jewish masses — folksongs in the true sense of the word.

The Inspiration for a Great Sonata or Symphony

But more important, from an artistic standpoint, than the Jewish folksong *per se* is the fact of its utilization in larger compositions, such as the sonata and symphony, without which no modern music can exist. Very often, while listening to the strongly racial creations of Liszt, Dvorák, and Tschaikowsky, I have yearned for a great Jewish composer who could lay hold upon the many genuine tunes current in the dusky ghettos and wield them into a mighty symphony expressing Jewish fears and hopes, Jewish passions and emotions, throughout the ages. Such a composition, sounding the abysmal depths of Jewish misery and the loftiest pinnacles of Jewish faith, would be greater testimonial to us than a thousand books trying to depict our situation among the nations. Yet this dream is nearing realization and the difficult task will surely be consummated in the not distant future. Already there are symptoms of individual efforts among some of our young composers, who are indefatigable in their search for an adequate form and a distinct style. I wish to call attention particularly to a group of composers in Russia, among them Engel, Schalitt, Skliar, Shitomirsky, and Milner, all pupils of the Russian master Rimsky-Korsakoff, who employ Jewish songs in their compositions for piano and orchestra and strive otherwise for a singular and original expression. In France Maurice Ravel follows the same course. Even Leo Ornstein, of New York, whose ultra-modern methods puzzle the entire musical world, makes use sometimes of Hebrew songs and chants, as may be seen from his latest sonata for cello and piano dedicated to the cellist Hans Kindler. In fact, every Jewish composer is susceptible to this modern trend which is bound to lead to the cloud-capped eminence of fame.

Rimsky-Korsakoff, who was so sensitive to the national idiom of a people, stated on more than one occasion that a time will yet come when a Jewish Glinka will be born. Today his Jewish pupils, laboring in the field of Jewish music, vie with one another for that much-coveted title. Whether or not a "Jewish Glinka" is latent in their midst it is hard to tell, but their influence is far-reaching and is exerted even on non–Jewish circles. They are responsible for some Jewish elements in the works of Rimsky-Korsakoff, Glazounoff, Krein, and others, and generally for the interest evinced by the Neo-Russian school for ghetto songs. While Jewish composers like Mendelssohn and Meyerbeer, Rubinstein and Mahler, were loath to utilize their own folksongs, a genuine Russian like Moussorgsky introduced two Jewish melodies in his cantata *Joshua*: the "Song of Solomon" and the "Plaint of the Women of Amoria." "New times, new songs." The new current of life that circulates in the reawakened body of the Jewish people is affecting even the outside world, who are dazzled at the modern phenomenon of *Jupiter redivivus*, and, with undisguised sympathy and genuine good will, endeavor to draw their inspiration from it. This explains the rumor from Catholic Rome that the poet Gabriele d'Annuzio is preparing a text for an opera dealing with the pregnant history of the Jews. The score is to contain a number of Jewish traditional melodies whose authenticity and antiquity are beyond doubt. This is only a beginning, and other works are sure to follow. But after all, this outside influence is only incidental. The real creation of Jewish music can only come through Jewish composers who have lived a Jewish life among their brethren and witnessed their weal and woe, hope and tribulation, and who, above everything else, believe in the future of our people.

The Work of a Great Jewish Composer: Ernest Bloch

Of these more and more are forcing themselves to the front, but the most notable instance is Ernest Bloch of Geneva, Switzerland, now resident in New York. For years Bloch has been struggling to find a medium of expression, a new style for his ideas about Jews and Judaism, and after many failures he succeeded in creating something novel and original which at once made him prominent and brought him to the fore as a great Jewish composer. His originality manifests itself in a number of devices employed dexterously and opportunely. Among these is the elliptic rhythm with its element of surprise and excitement, and pure minor with its vague cadences and suspended finales, Oriental chromaticism and enharmony, continuous modulation producing a spontaneous change of mood and color, and, regretful to say, some dissonance and cacophony *a la* Strauss and Schoenberg. Not less conspicuous is his handling of the orchestra: the reeds are usurped at the expense of the strings, the melody being allotted to the former; within the strings the cellos have priority over the other catgut species; the brasses and the Turkish battery are strongly emphasized, producing a rather ponderous effect.

Whether this ultra-modern system constitutes Jewish music is a question open to dispute and not to be settled with any degree of finality. After all, any standard is bound to be arbitrary, since we know so little about the nature and constitution of ancient Hebraic music. We cannot resuscitate it from Biblical records, just as we cannot reproduce Paganini's compositions even from the masterful description in Heine's *Florentiner Nächte*. But there is this to be said in favor of Bloch, that besides his strong Orientalism he seeks to imprint a Jewish stamp on his creations through the introduction not only of Jewish folksongs but also synagogal chants. This principle, as has been pointed out above, is the only true criterion for a national music, everything else being nondescript and universal. That Bloch avails himself of it may be seen from his unfinished symphony *Israel*, a work of great effect and infinite beauty, which symbolizes the spiritual significance of the Day of Atonement and winds up with a graceful and impressive chorale "Adonai Elohim." The same tendency is evident in his three Jewish poems (*Danse, Rite, Cortege Funebre*) which, according to a musical authority, "are essentially Hebraic in spirit and expression; impressive, genuinely musical, rich in color and of remarkable originality of idiom and mastery of rhythm. The *Danse* is exotic; a chromatic phantasy, now languorous, now passionate, ending with the sudden swirl of molten draperies around quickly tensed limbs. The second movement is less colorful, but more deeply emotional, suggesting the solemn observance of an ancient impressive ritual. But of the three, the final movement, *Cortege Funebre*, is most remarkable. It is the embodiment of grief, wherein Fate is inexorable. It depicts the poignancy of a great bereavement; the passionate, but impotent, lamentations of the bereaved; and finally, an abiding peace, sorrowful, yet rising above human frailties." Even more powerful are Bloch's settings of Psalm 114 (When Israel came out of Egypt) and 137 (By the waters of Babylon), the latter being intensely tragic, reaching a climax rarely if ever surpassed by any other composer.

Perhaps the most Jewish of Bloch's works is his Hebraic rhapsody *Schlomo* for violincello and full orchestra. It expresses the poignant agony and turbulent anguish of the Jewish soul in a masterly fashion. It summarizes in a few bars and measures the whole history of the Jewish Diaspora whose point of gravity lay in Prometheus-like ebullition followed by extreme enervation and periodic lethargy, a state of inertia and laissez-faire. As one of the critics characterized it: "It is a large, a poignant, an authentic expression of what is racial in the Jew. It is authentic by virtue of qualities more fundamental than the synagogal modes on which it bases itself, the Semantic pomp and color that inform it. There are moments when one hears in this music the harsh and haughty accents of the Hebrew tongue, sees the abrupt and passionate gestures of the Hebrew soul, feels the titanic burst of energy that created the race, and carried it safely across lands and times, out of the eternal Egypt, through the eternal Red Sea. It is as if an element that has remained unchanged throughout all the ages, an element that is in every Jew, an element by which every Jew must know himself and his descent, were caught up in it, and fixed there."

Jewish Music Must Remain Chiefly Melodic

Bloch is a direct product of the Jewish revival, and he endeavors to depict this revival in his music. As he emphasized it himself, the archaeological aspect of Israel does not interest him very much as musical material. His creative genius does not deal with skeletons of the past, not even with the evanescent Ghetto type, the overwrought and much abused Golus Jew. He prefers to picture the Jewish soul of the present and its hope in the future. Highly sensitive as he is, he grasps the fleeting hope and agony, joy and sorrow, of the modern Jew and idealizes them in the ethereal realm of tone. The whole psychology of present-day Israel is revealed in a series of tonal sketches and harmonic arabesques of a kaleidoscope variety, such as even a Debussy or Scriabin might envy. In this respect he resembles the ever-youthful Lilien, who, in his perfect forms and gladsome scenes of far distant and happier days, personified young Judea in its untarnished vitality.

Bloch's music, while an auspicious beginning towards a national medium of expression, is by no means the *ultima Thule* of Jewish attainment. It is felt by many that in his great zeal and search for effect he has overstepped the mark and gone beyond the boundary of *utils cum dulci*. There is certainly a suggestion of aping the cubists and futurists in the massive harmonies and crass dissonances which tend to obliterate the beautiful melodic passages. His music often suffers from over-orchestration which master musicians like Beethoven and Brahms knew so well to avoid but which is the stumbling-block of the ultra-modern school. No wonder Von Bülow, with his fine critical acumen, had to lay down his famous reminder: "In the beginning there was melody." Modern in contradistinction to ancient music is a combination of melody and harmony, but this combination must be proportionate and one of the elements should not outweigh the other. With the phenomenal development of the orchestra and consequently of polyphonic music in recent years we are apt to forget the importance and aesthetic value of the homophonic genus which served mankind for thousands of years. Victor Hugo may be right in styling harmony *la lune de l'art*, but after all it stands to melody like embroidery to cloth, and Mozart's dictum "Melody is the essence of music" still holds good. Pure harmonic music may hold sway sometime in the future, but as yet it sounds foreign to our aural nerves. Certainly in the case of Jewish music, which always was and still is largely melodic, it is hardly proper to supercede the old style with a system spung, Venus-like, fully blown and over-ripe. Even for the sake of a gradual transition a more melodic style, involving less complicated harmonies, is at once imperative. However, Bloch is only a pioneer who points out the way in a new direction and invites others to follow him. His followers may prove more successful in evolving a characteristic idiom. The field is rich, and like every new soil the more you dig it the more it yields. If only Jewish composers would turn to it and be rewarded with a rich harvest instead of playing second fiddle to European celebrities!

The Requisites of a Distinctly Jewish Music

In conclusion, it behooves us to inquire: What is to be the nature of a new Jewish music? People might differ in the details, but there are some cardinal characteristics from which it should not depart if it wants to be distinctly Jewish. In the first place it should be conceived in those oriental modes which throughout the ages have been identified as Jewish. Of these, two stand out as conspicuous: the natural minor or Aeolian mode which is common to all the peoples of the Orient and is identical with modern A minor without sharped seventh, and another mode akin to the Hungarian Gypsy scale with two augmented intervals (C, Db, E, F, G, Ab, Bb, C). The former is used mostly in religious chants, the latter is peculiar to the folksong and is more characteristically Jewish. It might be stated parenthetically that the Jews have always exhibited a peculiar susceptibility to augmented intervals, i.e., intervals of more than a whole tone, probably because such an interval is best fitted to express acute grief and poignant melancholy as found in the folksong of more than one nation. It underlies the primitive pentatonic scale, i.e., a scale of five whole tones, in which savage tribes of old and even some peoples of today express their spiritual yearning for the Elysian fields and the canopies of Nirvana. Major scales should be employed sparingly as not compatible with our manner of expression. This does not necessarily mean that our music continue to be sad and plaintive, for not always does major express joy and minor pain. The color and mood of a composition depend also on other factors besides the scale: such are the time and rhythm and kind of instruments employed. Some instruments, particularly those with valves, lend themselves to somber combinations. That a minor key may be used for a joyous mood is proved by Mozart's symphony in G minor, whose allegro spurts with laughter, whose andante is bright and serene, whose minuet is flippant, and whose finale spells the joy of life. I have already referred to the new Jewish songs in Palestine which, though written in the minor key, express unbounded hope and joy.

Moreover, it seems to me that one of the requisites is a staid and broad rhythm, except where a terpsichorean mood requires it to become more quick and abrupt. Volatility and effervescence are foreign to the nature of the Jew as a permanent state or condition. An elliptic rhythm, such as is employed by Bloch in his Jewish Poems, is certainly Oriental as far as we know the Orient today. It is the rhythm used by all great composers in writing Oriental music. But there are groups within the Orient. What Europe styles Oriental music is really Arab music as heard in the cities and villages of the North-African littoral (Morocco, Algeria, Tripoli and Egypt) and less so in the deserts of Arabia proper. The Syrians of Asia Minor, for instance, differ in their musical style from the Arabs; and so do other Semitic tribes who did not come under the direct influence of the Beduins. As to the rhythm of the ancient Hebrews, not having a living record we are left in the dark. The poetical portions of the Bible are insufficient in themselves to furnish us a clue to this labyrinth. But Eduard Sievers, one of the foremost authorities on metre in Europe today, claims to have found in the Bible a uniform and definite rhythm which may be called pseudo-anapaestic, two unaccented syllables of any quantity being followed by a long accented syllable. If this be true, my contention for a broad rhythm might claim the authority of the Bible as support.

The Wealth of Opportunities for a Jewish Composer

Another condition of the new art is an affluence of melody and dearth of harmony for harmony's sake. Jewish music, to appeal to the Jewish public, must be preponderantly melodic and euphonious instead of over-harmonic and dissonant. We cannot afford to make abortive experiments with harmonic chords and contrapuntal designs in imitation of the younger school of Occidental composers. They have Bach and Beethoven behind them, and not being able to improve upon them by way of melodicity, they are compelled to resort to a new harmonic system, if they want to create something new. With us it is different. We have a wealth of melodic material to whip into shape before we resort to mere harmonies. Let us first work up our folksongs into sonatas, symphonies, operas, and other larger forms of which we possess practically nothing. It is desirable that we develop at least one of these forms to a hitherto unattained height. It might be advisable to develop also the oratorio form. In fact, Jewish songs, being largely religious and devotional, are more appropriate for oratorio than opera. Why should not a Jewish composer seize such pathetic chants as *Leoni* and *Kol Nidre* and make them the basis for a great oratorio dealing with the fateful Diaspora? Such a work might have a great religious in addition to the aesthetic effect. At the present time our Reform congregations, in planning a sacred concert, are compelled to resort to Mendelssohn's *Elijah* or Handel's *Israel in Egypt* and *Judas Maccabaeus*, none of which are strictly religious, as may be seen from the fact that for a long time they were performed on the theatrical stage. How much more appropriate it would be if we could give sacred concerts in the synagogue with oratorios based on ancient synagogal chant.

And lastly, let me refer to a point of orchestration. The peculiar color of Jewish music might be augmented by the use of certain instruments known to be in vogue only among Jews. Of these the *shofar* or ram's horn is most prominent and of the greatest antiquity, and, having been in use in the synagogue for thousands of years, it should be employed especially in ecclesiastical compositions, such as the oratorio. It is interesting to know that Bloch employs the muffled timbre of this instrument with great effect and strong emphasis when calling attention to the Jewish ritual. Other characteristic instruments, though common to other Semitic tribes, are cymbals, lutes, and lyres, all of which have the capacity to lend a unique color to a piece of music. Our young composers will not be long in finding this out and in discovering many other mediums of forceful expression which are bound to escape the attention of a layman. The moment they do find them we shall have passed the experimental stage and entered upon the enjoyment of a growing and expanding art, and then a national Jewish music will no longer be an ideal but a reality. Let us hope that this day is not far distant.

18. The Future of Jewish Music (1919)

Jerome H. Bayer

AS A JEW, I FEEL A DEEP INTEREST in the Jewish music of tomorrow, because I believe that the future life of Israel, whether it be religious or national or both, can be profoundly influenced by music. As a musician, I feel a deep interest in the Jewish music of tomorrow, because I believe that the category of secular music will remain sadly incomplete until it contains a true expression of the spirit of Jewish idealism and romance. As a Jew, I look to Jewish music as one significant means to a worthy end; as a musician, I look to Jewish music as a great end in itself.

How can this twofold purpose be realized? My aim is to suggest an answer to this vital question. I shall treat each purpose separately, directing attention, first, to a discussion of Jewish music as a means of future development of the religious and national life of Israel.

The Peculiarities of Jewish Music

In order that we may know precisely what the Jewish music of tomorrow should be, we must know the nature and scope of the Jewish music of today. I assume that, according to a natural classification of music, only that music is Jewish which reflects the Jewish spirit, either directly or indirectly, by long association with Jewish life. With scarcely an exception, all Jewish music of the present falls into two groups — religious music and folk songs. In the first place, let us determine whether or not it contains a Jewish music-idiom, that is, a peculiarity of mode, rhythm or harmony which is characteristic only of Jewish music and which expresses the individuality of the spirit of Israel.

So far as mode and harmony are concerned there is no Jewish music-idiom. Modes used in cantillation are the same as those in the Catholic, Byzantine and Armenian churches. In the hymns and folksongs the major mode and Asbein mode of the Arabs are very largely used. Many modes are employed in Jewish music, but none is peculiarly Jewish. Nor is its harmony any more distinctive than the modes which are used.

Let us next examine the rhythm of Jewish music. The hymns and folksongs have standard types of rhythm. In the Scriptural chants, we find extreme rhythmic irregularity which depends upon the rhythm of the syllables to which the tones act as a setting, and which is employed to mark the finest shades of distinction in the sense of the text. This high degree of peculiar irregularity is, so far as I can determine, exclusively a Jewish characteristic. It has none of the naturalness of the conversational or even the declamatory recitative used in secular music, and although the Koran chants are checked rhythmically by the meaning of the text, they do not, judging from the few illustrations which I have seen, express shades of meaning as fine as those which Jewish Scriptural chants express. Nevertheless, I do not regard this extremely peculiar irregularity as the Jewish music-idiom, because I do not believe that it is expressive of the individuality of the Jewish spirit.

The True Music-Idiom

What, then, constitutes the Jewish music-idiom? It is the means of producing an effect which is found primarily in the traditional chanting of prayers and blessings, wherein the Cantor is permitted to extemporize freely, being required only to use a prescribed motive as a coda. This expression of Jewish individuality is not very definite, and without the use of notation, it can be most clearly described in terms of its effect. It awakens a unique type of emotionalism — a passionate intensity and a plaintiveness, reflecting the effect of the outer world upon the soul of the Jew, but also reflecting something far more important than that, namely, a profound religious fervor. The Hungarian Gypsy music, when saddest in the depressing measures of the mournful "lassan," never expresses more than the effect of the outer world upon the individual. These chants of Israel express that also, but they express much more than that — deep religious emotion. This effect is brought about by numerous musical devices. There is a constant change of tempo, dynamics and accent, not determined by the rhythm and meaning of the words, but revealing the emotional state of the cantor at the time when the chant is rendered. The trochaic nuance is extensively used and creates a sobbing effect which is peculiarly Jewish. The duration of the first tone of this nuance depends upon the degree of intensity which the nuance is required to express. Melisma is nearly always used in these chants, but melisma which differs from that of other types of music. It utilizes more of the scale than the Arabian "gloss"; it is seldom as wild as the flourish of the Hungarian Gypsy improvisations, and it has none of the showiness of the Italian bravura except when inferior Cantors revive the custom of a bygone period in Jewish life. At that time the synagogue was the only club of the Jew, and as a result many ludicrous novelties were introduced into the religious services to satisfy the instinct of play. These various musical devices constitute the Jewish music-idiom; they are as Jewish as the feelings of the Cantor permit them to be.

There are, however, types of Jewish music which though not containing this Jewish music-idiom, nevertheless express the individuality of the spirit of Israel, indirectly, by suggesting phases of Jewish life through their intimate connection with that life through many centuries. These types are the Scriptural chant, the traditional hymn, and the folk song.

We have thus far observed the nature and scope of present Jewish music. Let us now look to the future. Should we use this for the further development of the religious or national life of Israel? If so, how extensively should we use it and in what way?

The Musical and Spiritual Worth of the Traditional Chants

I feel confident that no type of music which could be introduced into the synagogue and the Jewish home would be capable of influencing the future development of the Jewish religious life as the traditional music can influence it. The traditional methods of Scripture reading are highly expressive and are permeated by an Oriental color; therefore they bring to the hearer, if he understands Hebrew, a true appreciation of the Scriptures and their spirit and, hence, a greater intimacy with the sources of our religious feeling. No ordinary reading of Scriptures either in Hebrew or in any other language could possibly have an equally desirable effect. If the hearer cannot understand Hebrew it is his duty to learn the language. The hymns, such as *Addir Hu*, traditional settings of *Yigdal* and *Adon Olam*, and *Ma'oz Zur*, have considerable religious value, even if they have been borrowed from the songs of other peoples; for they not only present expressions of religious sentiment in an inviting form, but they have been intimately associated with religious festivals or the Sabbath for many centuries. These hymns, if used with a sympathetic knowledge of their past, will exert an important spiritual influence. That phase of chanting which reveals the Jewish music-idiom is of paramount importance, for it is the most powerful incentive to Jewish religious development.

Even for the national development of Israel, traditional synagogue music is, I believe, equally as important as the folk song, because, whatever the place of religion will be in the Jewish nation, really to understand the spirit of Jewish nationalism one must understand the religious life which has always been closely interwoven with Jewish community life. The folksongs, as a direct expression of the community life of the Jew, are, of course, very valuable.

How extensively should this traditional music be used? Should we permit alien music to be sung and played to the Jewish liturgy? No, indeed no! How stupid it is to use music utterly lacking in expressiveness of the Jewish spirit in synagogue and in the Jewish home! But it is argued that many songs which are now regarded as Jewish have been adapted from very remote sources, for example, *Ma'oz Zur*, which was once a street song, and that through long association with Jewish life they have become Jewish; that the non-Jewish compositions which are now being used in Jewish services will also eventually become Jewish; that the contemporaneous musical fashion of the outer world has ever found its echo in synagogue music. What of it! I admit that the present music of Israel largely consists of foreign elements and I deplore that fact. Why should we drag into it more extraneous material? To substitute Christian church melodies for traditional Jewish melodies is absurd; to substitute them for those chants which contain the very essence of the Jewish spirit, is unpardonable folly. Evangelical melodies and harmonies are akin, in their similarity to the material out of which some of our hymns have been formed. But why should we substitute them for hymns which already have such rich treasures of sentiment in their measures, and which will constantly gain more significance as the years pass?

Is Jewish Music Inartistic?

The introduction into the synagogue of evangelical music is not the only innovation which has been made in modern Jewish music. We now hear

Reform congregations and even in some conservative congregations, pretentious, formal, choral music, in which choir is supreme and Cantor is forgotten, and which by its very nature is not adaptable to synagogue needs. The synagogue requires music which is natural, impulsive and flexible, through which the soul of Israel can find adequate expression. How can formal, rigid, polyphonic music, built upon classic lines and breathing the spirit of classicism, express the intense emotionalism of the Jewish soul? The fact that the oratorio *Elijah* bears a Jewish name and centers around Jewish characters, does not signify that it has any Jewishness. In a Christian church, compositions of its character are sublime; in a synagogue they are grotesque.

There are only two conceivable purposes in introducing this type of music into the synagogue — an artistic purpose and a religious purpose. Even if we were to assume that the Jewish music of today is thoroughly inartistic, as long as its use is the best means of developing the Jewish religious life through music, why should it be superceded by a type of composition which altogether more artistic cannot realize the purpose of synagogue music? But is it true that the present music of Israel is inartistic? According to the older and more classic standards wherein conventional precision is required, the chants are inartistic. According to the standards of the modern and more romantic art, which throws to the winds most of the "sacred" rules of composition, the chants and all of the traditional hymns are thoroughly artistic. What would have been regarded twenty years ago as tonal expressions of insanity are today regarded as masterly works; for music lovers believe that the most characteristic expression of an artistic idea is the most musical, regardless of the rules of the past. Each of these two sets of standards rests upon a great school of thought — the former upon classicism, the latter upon romanticism. I seek to defend neither. I only desire to suggest to the critics of present Jewish music that before they condemn it they must first understand the school of thought upon which it rests.

Let us now direct our attention to necessary changes in the rendition of Jewish music.

Suggestions for Desirable Changes

Until the synagogue choir can rival the Hungarian Gypsies in their unique talent for polyphonic improvisation, it should remain subordinate to the cantor, serving merely as his support. It is no wonder that we find the

Jewish choir of today in a loft; it is entirely too non-Jewish in its personnel and renditions to stand upon the altar of Israel.

A simple and sympathetic organ accompaniment can do no harm. Orchestras should be employed sparingly in the service, for they encourage the use of non-Jewish music.

Let us permit neither trombone nor any other modern instrument to caricature the distinctive beauty of the *shofar* tones. There is no instrument in the modern orchestra which is capable of the pastoral yet trumpet-like effect of the ancient horn of Israel. If it sounds grotesque in a modern service, the service is at fault, not the *shofar*.

Above all we need gifted and enlightened cantors; men who deeply love the romance of orthodoxy and the music that goes with it; men whose lives will develop in them the real spirit of their people; men who sing well and whose knowledge of their art is broad enough to enable them to understand the artistic worth of traditional Jewish music. Such Cantors will prove an important factor in the further development of Jewish life.

The Jewish Music That Might Be!

At present, there is really no secular Jewish music. If we would have the musical genius of the Israelite express itself in Jewish terms, we must fill him with a deep love for traditional Jewish music; we must fill his soul with the philosophic problems of the Holy Pages; we must create in him a wholehearted sympathy for the tragic life of Israel throughout the ages.

I love to dream of a mighty symphony which will express with the peculiarly Jewish religious fervor, the spirit of Israel's conception of God, man, the natural world and the human soul — four soul-stirring movements of the symphony.

I love to dream of a glorious tone-poem reflecting the spirit of the "Giving of the Law." What noble music that dramatic narrative would make — the divine inspiration of Moses, standing in solitude on a lonely mountain peak amid the raging of elements; in bold contrast, the fickleness of an ignorant people; the wrath and grief of the disappointed lawgiver; the repetition of the first episode; and lastly, the promise of loyalty to the Law which Israel has kept throughout the ages!

I love to dream of a noble music-sentence symbolizing a pastoral conception of God — a recurrence in regular rhythm of prolonged chords of desolation depicting the gloom and monotony of a vast desert whose awful silence, whose unity of color and contour suggest the eternity of God. Suddenly the sweet, mellow, plaintive tone of a far-away flute is heard, chanting a lovely pastoral melody to which the grim chords become a half-unwilling accomplishment — the shepherd of Israel unconsciously shows us God!

I love to dream of a turbulent Jewish rhapsody composed in the spirit of the chants of old and pulsating with the tragedy of Jewish life, but prophetic of future happiness!

Even the musical expression of that happiness must ever be permeated with a note of sadness, for the sadness of the Jew presents more than his reaction to an unfriendly environment; it expresses his religious fervor and must endure until the spirit of Israel fades from human life. Let us hope with full hearts that such a time may never come! Let us strive to aid the realization of our hope by encouraging a devotion to traditional Jewish music and the development of a new Jewish secular music — noble expressions of the essence of Israel's spirit in the universal language of men.

19. Music in the Religious School (1919)
Louis Grossman

Music is a means for religious influence in the Religious School or it should not be there. As a fine art it cannot be abused with impunity, not even with children. Religious music, and in our case Synagogue Music, should be a subject in the Course of Study of the Religious School, since it has an intrinsic educational value of its own. A wise teacher of music will relate it to history, to life and to character.

Children should know who wrote the music that wings Jewish devotion, they should know that Jewish songs were sung in home and community under the stress of deep piety, and they should hear the story of those who composed them. We need not be discouraged by those who say that there is no original Jewish music; it has been the vehicle of intense feeling in the Jewish home and in Jewish community, and that is sufficient. The aim of the teacher must be to restore religious music to the present-day Jewish home and to see to it that the melodies are sung as part of the pious life of the people.

Sulzer, Naumbourg, and Lewandowski should be restored to us before the droning church melodies now in vogue in our Religious School Hymnals have wrought their mischief.

That alien hymns have crept into the Jewish Religious School is due to our lack of thought on that matter, to indifference of those from whom we have a right to expect professional help, and finally to the confusion into which the subject has lapsed.

School Hymns

The hymns and responses which the children learn in the Religious School should be expressions of the religious emotion of the children while they engage in worship. They should be means for religious teaching and influence just as the other subjects of the Religious School curriculum. And in the third place, the school music should prepare for home worship and bring back into Jewish households the songs which were there in former days. No teacher has done his duty in this matter until he has assured himself that the songs he teaches in his school room have become household songs in the homes of his pupils. We must crowd out the cheap and demoralizing songs which are now current in Jewish family life. We may be able to do this by the school hymns if they are carefully chosen with reference to their fitness for the expression of genuine feeling.

The Text of the Hymns

The texts are an important feature of the hymns, and it is to be deeply regretted that so little thought has been given to their selection. For the most part texts have been taken over from Christian hymn books, on the easy assumption that they are religious. But we Jews need not borrow anywhere. We have abundant material of our own. The poems of Solomon and Gabirol and Judah Halevi are as good as, and better than those of any author of a Christian hymn book; they are, at least, more in keeping with Jewish sentiment. We can well afford to give them to our children; it is our duty, in fact, to give them to our Jewish childhood, which will quickly enough feel that they are spirit of its spirit. The text of the average School Hymnal now used in our Religious School often contradicts our teachings, and its flabby tone and stifled phraseology perplex the children and contribute much toward making Jewish child music uncongenial and repellant.

Congregational Singing

Perhaps the difficulty we experience in the introduction of adult congregational singing is to be traced to the fact that the music forced on the congregation is alien, and the hesitation of the congregation to sing it is a subtle suggestion that the music and the words make no appeal to their souls. I have yet to come upon a congregation which does not take to the *Ein Keloheinu* quite readily. Text and music seem out of the very life of the Jewish people. Let us re-introduce Jewish congregational singing (for as a matter of fact congregational singing is Jewish in origin and came into Christian worship by way of the synagogue). We can restore it best by teaching our children to respect the responses and the hymns they learn in the school. We need not plan that they, in their turn, may teach these melodies to their parents, for this is an inversion of the natural order which even the sacred cause cannot make either logical or natural. These children will eventually themselves be parents and will hand down the musical and liturgical tradition. Music can do more than anything else to impart piety to the modern home and to hold it there. And it is the opportunity of the Religious School to bring this about.

Singing Should Be Natural and Hearty

There is no absolute need for an organ or a piano. Good singing can be called out of children by any suggestive teacher without elaborate equipment. Nor is a hymn book in the hand of each child an essential requirement. In fact, it is advisable to see to it that the children get the repertoire of Jewish music "by heart." Music comes best out of the soul of the children when they sing freely, without their eyes on their books. It is especially desirable that the children sing their responses in the service spontaneously. This is merely a matter of previous drill and right spirit. But, by all means, the pedantic "beating of time" during worship by the leader must cease. It is a disturbance of the worship and offends its spirit. Let the drill be given in the class room and at other times than during worship. Again, the musical feature of the worship is only a help; it should never become a feature by itself. The solo, for instance, is a precarious embellishment and had best be discouraged. A selected choir is less likely to be a distraction, but it tends to assume the weight of responsibility for good singing and to induce the rest of the school to lapse into listening. The singing must be done by all the pupils, if the worship is to have meaning for all. Each with all and all with each, applies to religious as much as to all social phases of life.

The Responses

It is good to bridge over the music of the school into that of the Synagogue, and to familiarize the children with the main responses and hymns which are sung in the latter. To be sure, this is equivalent to an appeal to the Synagogue to be less pretentious as to classic choral feats by the Synagogue Choir, and to put the chants within the compass of child voices. But in the end this simplification and this considerateness for the young generation will bring a great gain to child piety and to adult worship as well.

Jewish Music in the Home

The School should also provide the Home with religious music; the songs and the school service responses should become household music, as it were. There need be no fear that they would thus become cheapened or lose their sacred character. On the contrary, they would become endeared to parents as well as children, and it is not at all unlikely that they would, in the course of time, become the vehicle of serious thoughts and feelings as these inevitably arise in the experiences of every household. It is a mark of the decadence of modern Jewish family life that it assembles so little, I was going to say almost not at all, for solemn and serious communion, and I have the hope that we may touch the hidden springs of the sentimental kinship in our families by the magic of song. When once parents and children have begun to sing together, they will have entered upon their religious reawakening. It is here that the printed hymn book may be of use. But in order to satisfy this side of the usefulness of the hymn book, it must contain matter that has reference to family life. There should be morning songs, evening songs, and hymns and chants appropriate to significant household events.

The school is one of the agencies of the communal life, and it should bear a direct and forceful influence on the home.

Sources of Selections

Bayer, Jerome H. "The Future of Jewish Music." *The Menorah Journal*, vol. 5, no. 2 (1919): 109–114.
Cohen, Francis L. "Jewish Music." In *Encyclopedia of Religion and Ethics*, ed. John Hastings. New York: Scribner's, 1917. 51–53.
_____. "Synagogal Music." In *Jewish Encyclopedia*, vol. 4. New York: Funk and Wagnalls, 1906. 119–135.
de Sola Pool, David. "The Music of the Synagogue." *The Menorah Journal*, vol. III (1917): 295–300.
Grossmann, Louis. "Music in the Religious School." In *The Aims of Teaching in Jewish Schools: A Handbook for Teachers*. Cincinnati: Teachers' Institute of the Hebrew Union College, 1919. 231–237.
Guttman, Adolph. "The Life of Salomon Sulzer." *Year Book of the Central Conference of American Rabbis*, vol. XIII (1903): 227–236.
Imber, Naphtali Herz. "The Music of the Ghetto." *Music: A Monthly Magazine Devoted to the Art, Science, Technique and Literature of Music*, vol. XIII (1897-98): 697–708.
_____. "The Music of the Psalms." *Music: A Monthly Magazine Devoted to the Art, Science, Technique and Literature of Music*, vol. VI (1894): 568–588.
Isaacs, Lewis M. "Hebrew Music." In *The Encyclopedia Americana*. New York: Encyclopedia Americana, 1919. 57–58.
Jacobson, Sam L. "The Music of the Jews." *Music: A Monthly Magazine Devoted to the Art, Science, Technique and Literature of Music*, vol. XIV (1898): 412–416.
Jassinowsky, Pinchos. "Hazzanim and Hazzanut." *The Jewish Ministers Cantors Association of America* (1920): 5–12.
Karpeles, Gustav. "Music of the Synagogue." In *Jewish Literature and Other Essays*. Philadelphia: Jewish Publication Society, 1895. 369–379.
Peixotto, Benjamin Franklin. "Solomon Sulzer: Reminiscences of Vienna." *The Menorah Journal*, vol. VIII (1890): 260–264.
Reider, Joseph. "A Revival of Jewish Music." *The Menorah Journal*, vol. 5, no. 4 (1919): 218–225.
_____. "A Revival of Jewish Music: Concluded." *The Menorah Journal*, vol. 5, no. 5 (1919): 280–287.
_____. "Secular Currents in Synagogal Chant in America." *The Jewish Forum* (1918): 6–17.
Schindler, Kurt. "The Russian Jewish Folk-Song." *The Menorah Journal*, vol. 3, no. 2 (1917): 146–155.

Silber, Mendel. "Composers and Players." In *Jewish Achievement*. St. Louis: Modern View, 1910. 29–32.
———. "Jewish Singers." In *Jewish Achievement*. St. Louis: Modern View, 1910. 45–49.
Singer, Jacob. "Music of the Synagog." In *Studies on Musical Education History and Aesthetics*. Music Teachers' National Association, 1916. 206–214.

Bibliography

This bibliography lists works cited, as well as additional English language sources valuable for the broader study of Jewish music. Included are works representing several decades of scholarship, and written from varied perspectives and approaches. While this bibliography is limited to books and monographs, those pursuing research in Jewish music should also be aware of the five journals dedicated to the subject: *Musica Judaica* (American Society for Jewish Music, New York), *Journal of Synagogue Music* (Cantors Assembly, New York), *Journal of Jewish Music and Liturgy* (Cantorial Council of America, New York), *Yuval* (Hebrew University of Jerusalem), and *Orbis Musicae* (Tel Aviv University), as well as many articles on Jewish music published in other learned journals.

Adaqi, Yehiel, and Uri Sharvit. *A Treasury of Yemenite Jewish Chants*. Jerusalem: Israeli Institute for Sacred Music, 1981.
Adler, Israel, ed. *Hebrew Writings Concerning Music*. Munich: G. Henle, 1975.
_____. *Musical Life and Traditions of the Portuguese Jewish Community of Amsterdam in the 18th Century* (Yuval Monograph Series 1). Jerusalem: Magnes, 1974.
_____. *The Study of Jewish Music: A Bibliographical Guide*. Jerusalem: Magnes, 1995.
Adler, Israel, Bathja Bayer, and Eliyahu Schliefer, eds. *The Abraham Zvi Idelsohn Memorial Volume* (Yuval Monograph Series 5). Jerusalem: Magnes, 1986.
Armistead, Samuel G., and Joseph H. Silverman. *Folk Literature of the Sephardic Jews, Vol. 2: Judeo-Spanish Ballads from Oral Tradition*. Berkeley: University of California Press, 1986.
_____. *The Judeo-Spanish Ballad Chapbooks of Yacob Abraham Yona*. Berkeley: University of California Press, 1971.
Avenary, Hanoch. *The Askenazic Tradition of Biblical Chant Between 1500 and 1900*. Tel Aviv: Tel Aviv University Press, 1978.
_____. *Encounters of East and West in Music: Selected Writings*. Tel Aviv: Tel Aviv University Press, 1979.
Bahat, Avner, ed. *Jewish Music Listening Center Catalogue*. Ramat Aviv, Israel: Museum of the Jewish Diaspora, 1984.
Bassan, Jacqueline. *From Shul to Cool: The Romantic Jewish Roots of American Popular Music*. New York: Jay Street, 2003.

Bauer, Susan. *From the Khupe to KlezKamp: The Process of Change and Forms of Reinterpretation of Klezmer Music in New York*. Berlin: Piranha, 1999.

Beeber, Steven Lee. *The Heebie-Jeebies at CBGB's: A Secret History of Jewish Punk*. Chicago: Chicago Review Press, 2006.

Bennett, Roger, and Josh Kun. *And You Shall Know Us by the Trail of Our Vinyl: The Jewish Past as Told by the Records We Have Loved and Lost*. New York: Crown, 2008.

Bernard, Andrew. *The Sound of Sacred Time: A Basic Music Theory Textbook to Teach the Jewish Prayer Modes*. Charlotte, NC: Temple Beth El, 2005.

Binder, Abraham W. *Biblical Chant*. New York: Philosophical Library, 1959.

Bohlman, Philip V. *Jewish Music and Modernity*. New York: Oxford University Press, 2008.

———, ed. *Jewish Musical Modernism, Old and New*. Chicago: University of Chicago Press, 2008.

———. *"The Land Where Two Streams Flow": Music in the German-Jewish Community of Israel*. Chicago: University of Illinois Press, 1989.

———. *The World Centre for Jewish Music in Palestine, 1936–1940: Jewish Musical Life on the Eve of World War II*. New York: Oxford University Press, 1992.

Bohlman, Philip V., and Mark Slobin, eds. *Music in the Ethnic Communities of Israel*. Special Issue of *Asian Music* 17/2 (Spring/Summer 1986).

Braun, Joachim. *Music in Ancient Israel/Palestine: Archaeological, Written, and Comparative Sources*. Grand Rapids, MI: Wm. B. Eerdmans, 2002.

———. *On Jewish Music: Past and Present*. New York: Peter Lang, 2006.

Chicural, Steven R. *George Gershwin's Songbook: Influences of Jewish Music, Ragtime, and Jazz*. Lexington: University of Kentucky, 1989.

Cohen, A. Irma. *An Introduction to Jewish Music in Eight Illustrated Lectures*. New York: Bloch, 1923.

Cohen, Judith, ed. *Proceedings of the World Congress of Jewish Music*. Tel Aviv: Institute for the Translation of Hebrew Literature, 1982.

Corenthal, Michael. *Cohen on the Telephone: A History of Jewish Recorded Humor and Popular Music*. Milwaukee: Yesterday's Memories, 1984.

Davidson, Charles. *From Szatmar to the New World: Max Wohlberg, American Cantor*. New York: Jewish Theological Seminary, 2001.

———. *Immunim Be-Nusach Ha-Tefillah: A Study Text and Workbook for the Jewish Prayer Modes*. Elkins Park, PA: Ashbourne Music, 1996.

———. *Immunim Be-Nusach Ha-Tefillah II: Hallel* (A Study Text and Workbook). Elkins Park, PA: Ashbourne Music, 2004.

Edelman, Marsha Bryan. *A Bibliography of Jewish Music*. New York: Hebrew Arts School, 1986.

———. *Discovering Jewish Music*. Philadelphia: Jewish Publication Society, 2003.

Eisenstein, Judith K. *Heritage of Music: The Music of the Jewish People*. Wyncote, PA: Reconstructionist Press, 1981.

Erdman, Harley. *Staging the Jew: The Performance of an American Ethnicity, 1860–1920*. New Brunswick, NJ: Rutgers University Press, 1997.

Feinberg, Sheldon. *Hava Nagila: The Story Behind the Song and Its Composer*. New York: Shapolsky, 1988.

Fenelon, Fania. *The Musicians of Auschwitz*. Trans. Judith Landry. London: Michael Joseph, 1977.

Flam, Gila. *Singing for Survival: Songs of the Lodz Ghetto, 1940–1945*. Urbana: University of Illinois Press, 1992.

Flender, Reinhard. *Hebrew Psalmody: A Structural Investigation* Press (Yuval Monograph Series 9). Jerusalem: Magnes, 1992.

Freed, Isadore. *Harmonizing The Jewish Modes*. New York: Sacred Music, 1958.

Freedman, Jonathan. *Klezmer America: Jewishness, Ethnicity, Modernity*. New York: Columbia University Press, 2007.
Friedmann, Jonathan L., and Brad Stetson, eds. *Jewish Sacred Music and Jewish Identity: Continuity and Fragmentation*. St. Paul, MN: Paragon House, 2008.
Fromm, Herbert. *On Jewish Music: A Composer's View*. New York: Bloch, 1978.
Fruhauf, Tina. *The Organ and Its Music in German-Jewish Culture*. New York: Oxford University Press, 2009.
Gerson-Kiwi, Edith. *Migrations and Mutations of the Music in East and West: Selected Writings*. Tel Aviv: Tel Aviv University Press, 1980.
Gilbert, Shirli. *Music in the Holocaust: Confronting Life in the Nazi Ghettos and Camps*. New York: Oxford University Press, 2007.
Gilbert, Sylvia. *Jewish Music from Bible to Broadway: A Short History of Jewish Music*. Nashville: Winston-Derek, 1995.
Glanz, Jerry, ed. *Leib Glanz: The Man Who Spoke to God*. Tel Aviv: Tel Aviv Institute for Jewish Liturgical Music, 2008.
Glazerson, Matisyahu. *Music and Kabbala*. Jerusalem: Raz-Ot Institute, 1988.
Goldin, Max. *On Musical Connections between Jews and the Neighboring Peoples of Eastern and Western Europe*. Amherst: University of Massachusetts Press, 1989.
Goldschmidt, Ernst Daniel, and Akiva Zimmerman. "Solomon Sulzer." *Encyclopedia Judaica*. 2007. Vol. 19, 308–309.
Gorali, Moshe. *The Old Testament in Music*. Jerusalem: Maron, 1993.
Gradenwitz, Peter. *Music and Musicians in Israel*. 3rd ed. Tel Aviv: Israel Music, 1978.
———. *The Music of Israel: From the Biblical Era to Modern Times*. Portland, OR: Amadeus, 1996.
Grossman, Elayne Robinson, and Ben Steinberg. *One People, One Voice: How to Organize a Jewish Community Chorus and Choral Festival*. New York: Jewish Music Council of the Jewish Welfare Board, 1989.
Harrán, Don. *Salamone Rossi: Jewish Musician in Late Renaissance Mantua*. Oxford, UK: Oxford University Press, 1999.
Heller, Charles. *What to Listen for in Jewish Music*. Toronto: Ecanthus, 2006.
Herzog, Avigdor. *The Psalm Singing of the Jews of San'a*. Tel Aviv: Israel Music Institute, 1968.
Heskes, Irene. *Passport to Jewish Music: Its History, Traditions, and Culture*. New York: Tara, 1994.
———. *The Resource Book of Jewish Music*. Westport, CT: Greenwood, 1985.
———, ed. *Studies in Jewish Music: Collected Writings of A. W. Binder*. New York: Bloch, 1971.
———, and Arthur Wolfson, eds. *The Historic Contribution of Russian Jews to Jewish Music*. New York: Jewish Music Council of the Jewish Welfare Board, 1967.
Hirschberg, Jehoash. *Music In the Jewish Community of Palestine 1880–1948: A Social History*. New York: Oxford University Press, 1996.
Hoffman, Lawrence A. *The Canonization of the Synagogue Service*. Notre Dame, IN: University of Notre Dame Press, 1979.
———, and Janet R. Walton, eds. *Sacred Sound and Social Change: Liturgical Music in Jewish and Christian Experience*. London: University of Notre Dame Press, 1992.
Holde, Arthur. *Jews in Music: From the Age of Enlightenment to the Present*. New York: Philosophical Library, 1959.
Idelsohn, Abraham Z. *Jewish Music: Its Historical Development*. New York: Schocken, 1929.
———. "My Life: A Sketch." *Jewish Music Journal*, vol. 2, no. 2 (1935): 8–11.
———. *Thesaurus of Hebrew Oriental Melodies*. 10 volumes. Leipzig: Friedrich Hofmeister, 1914–1933.

Isaacs, Ronald H. *Jewish Music: Its History, People, and Song.* Northvale, NJ: Jason Aronson, 1997.
Isaacson, Michael. *Jewish Music as Midrash: What Makes Music Jewish?* Los Angeles: Egg Cream Music, 2007.
Jacobson, Joshua R. *Chanting the Hebrew Bible: The Complete Guide to the Art of Cantillation.* Philadelphia: Jewish Publication Society, 2002.
_____. *A Selective Annotated Bibliography of Jewish and Israeli Choral Music.* Newton, MA: HaZamir, 1990.
Kantor, Kenneth Aaron. *Jews on Tin Pan Alley: The Jewish Contribution to American Popular Music, 1830–1940.* Jersey City, NJ: Ktav, 1982.
Karen, Zvi. *Contemporary Israeli Music: Its Sources and Stylistic Development.* Ramat Gan: Bar Ilan University Press, 1980.
Katz, Israel J. *Judeo-Spanish Traditional Ballads from Jerusalem, Vol. 1.* New York: Institute of Medieval Music, 1972.
_____. *Judeo-Spanish Traditional Ballads from Jerusalem, Vol. 2.* New York: Institute of Medieval Music, 1975.
Katz, Jacob. *The Darker Side of Genius: Richard Wagner's Anti-Semitism.* Hanover, NH: University Press of New England, 1986.
Kligman, Mark L. *Maqam and Liturgy: Ritual, Music, and Aesthetics of Syrian Jews in Brooklyn.* Detroit: Wayne State University Press, 2009.
Koskoff, Ellen. *Music in Lubavitcher Life.* Champaign: University of Illinois Press, 2000.
Lachmann, Robert. *Jewish Cantillation and Songs in the Island of Djerba.* Jerusalem: Azriel Press, 1940.
Landman, Leo. *The Cantor: An Historical Perspective.* New York: Yeshiva University, 1972.
Lyman, Darryl. *Great Jews in Music.* Middle Village, NY: Jonathan David, 1986.
Levin, Neil, ed. *Salomon Sulzer.* Bregenz: Land Vorarußerg, 1991.
Levine, Joseph A. *Rise and Be Seated: The Ups and Downs of Jewish Worship.* Northvale, NJ: Jason Aronson, 2000.
_____. *Synagogue Music in America.* Crown Point, IN: White Cliffs, 1989.
Liszt, Franz. *The Gipsy in Music.* Trans. Edwin Evans. London: William Reeves, 1926.
Loeffler, James Benjamin. *A Gilgul Fun a Nigun: Jewish Musicians in New York, 1881–1945.* Cambridge, MA: Harvard University Press, 1997.
Lubin, Abraham. "Salomon Sulzer's *Schir Zion*, Volume One: A Survey of Its Contributors and Its Contents." *Musica Judaica*, vol. 8, no. 1 (1985-86): 23–44.
Mazor, Yaacov, and Andre Hajdu. *The Hasidic Dance-Nigun: A Study Collection and Its Classification Analysis.* Jerusalem: Magnes, 1974.
Mendelsohn, Ezra. *Modern Jews and Their Musical Agendas.* (Studies in Contemporary Jewry, 9.) New York: Oxford University Press, 1993.
Moddel, Philip. *Max Helfman: A Biographical Sketch.* Berkeley, CA: Judah L. Magnes, 1974.
Moricz, Klara. *Jewish Identities: Nationalism, Racism, and Utopianism in Twentieth-Century Music.* Berkeley: University of California Press, 2008.
Newman, Joel, and Fritz Rikko. *A Thematic Index to the Works of Salamon Rossi.* Hackensack, NJ: Boonin, 1972.
Nulman, Macy. *Concepts of Jewish Prayer and Music.* New York: Yeshiva University, 1985.
_____. *Concise Encyclopedia of Jewish Music.* New York: McGraw-Hill, 1975.
_____, ed. *Essays of Jewish Music and Prayer.* New York: Yeshiva University, 2005.
Orenstein, Walter. *The Cantor's Manual of Jewish Law.* Northvale, NJ: Jason Aronson, 1994.
Pasternak, Velvel. *The Jewish Music Companion: Historical Overview, Personalities, Annotated Folksongs.* New York: Tara, 2003.

Portnoy, Marshall, and Josée Wolff. *The Art of Cantillation, Vol. 2 (Haftarah* and *M'gillot).* New York: Union of American Hebrew Congregations, 2001.

———. *The Art of Torah Cantillation.* New York: Union of American Hebrew Congregations, 2000.

Rabinovitch, Israel, and A. M. Klein. *Of Jewish Music: Ancient and Modern.* Montreal: Book Center, 1952.

Regev, Motti, and Edwin Seroussi. *Popular Music and National Culture in Israel.* Berkeley: University of California Press, 2004.

Ringer, Alexander L. *Arnold Schoenberg: The Composer as Jew.* New York: Clarendon, 1990.

Rogovoy, Seth. *The Essential Klezmer: A Music Lover's Guide to Jewish Roots and Soul Music, from the Old World to the Jazz Age to the Downtown Avant-Garde.* Chapel Hill, NC: Algonquin, 2000.

Rosenbaum, Samuel. *A Guide to Haftarah Chanting.* Hoboken, NY: Ktav, 1973.

———. *A Guide to Torah Chanting.* Hoboken, NY: Ktav, 1973.

Rosenfeld, Lulla. *Bright Star of Exile: Jacob Adler and the Yiddish Theater.* New York: Thomas Y. Crowell, 1977.

Rossen, Jane Mink, and Uri Sharvit. *Fusion of Traditions: Liturgical Music in the Copenhagen Synagogue.* Odense, Denmark: Syddansk Universitetsforlag, 2006.

Rothmuller, Aron Marko. *The Music of the Jews: An Historical Appreciation.* Cranbury, NJ: A. S. Barnes, 1967.

Rubin, Emanuel, and John H. Baron. *Music in Jewish History and Culture.* Sterling Heights, MI: Harmonie Park, 2006.

Rubin, Ruth. *Voices of a People: The Story of Yiddish Folksong.* New York: McGraw-Hill, 1963.

Sandrow, Nahma. *Vagabond Stars: A World History of Yiddish Theater.* New York: Limelight, 1986.

Sapoznik, Henry. *Klezmer: Jewish Music from Old World to Our World.* New York: Schirmer, 1999.

Schiller, David M. *Bloch, Schoenberg, and Bernstein: Assimilating Jewish Music.* New York: Oxford University Press, 2003.

Schneider, Gertrude, ed. *Mordechai Gebirtig: His Poetic and Musical Legacy.* Westport, CT: Praeger, 2000.

Sendrey, Alfred, *Bibliography of Jewish Music.* New York: Columbia University Press, 1951.

———. *Music in Ancient Israel.* New York: Philosophical Library, 1969.

———. *Music of the Jews in the Diaspora.* New York: Thomas Yoseloff, 1970.

———, and Milton Norton. *David's Harp: The Story of Music in Biblical Times.* New York: New American Library, 1964.

Sharlin, William. "Congregational Singing Past and Present: Continuity and Fragmentation." *CCAR Journal: A Reform Jewish Quarterly* (Spring 1994): 31–41.

Shelemay, Kay Kaufman. *Let Jasmine Rain Down: Song and Remembrance among Syrian Jews.* Chicago: University of Chicago Press, 1998.

———. *Music, Ritual and Falasha History.* East Lansing, MI: African Studies Center, Michigan State University, 1986.

———. "Mythologies and Realities in the Study of Jewish Music." In *Enchanting Powers: Music in the World's Religions,* ed. Lawrence E. Sullivan, 299–318. Cambridge, MA: Harvard University Press, 1997.

Shiloah, Amnon. *Jewish Musical Traditions.* Detroit: Wayne State University Press, 1995.

———. *Music and Its Virtues in Islamic and Jewish Writings.* Burlington, VT: Ashgate, 2007.

Silverman, Jerry. *The Undying Flame: Ballads and Songs of the Holocaust.* Syracuse, NY: Syracuse University Press, 2002.

Slobin, Mark. *Chosen Voices: The Story of the American Cantorate.* Chicago: University of Illinois Press, 2002.

———. *Fiddler on the Move: Exploring the Klezmer World.* New York: Oxford University Press, 2003.

———. "Learning the Lessons of Studying Jewish Music." *Judaism,* vol. 44, no. 2 (1995): 220–225.

———. *Tenement Songs: The Popular Music of the Jewish Immigrants.* Champaign: University of Illinois Press, 1996.

———, ed. *American Klezmer: Its Roots and Offshoots.* Berkeley: University of California Press, 2002.

———, ed. *Old Jewish Folk Music: The Collections and Writings of Moshe Beregovski.* Syracuse, NY: Syracuse University Press, 2001.

Smoira-Roll, Michal. *Folk Music in Israel: An Analysis Attempted.* Tel Aviv: Israeli Music Institute, 1963.

Solomon, Norman. *Judaism: A Very Short Introduction.* New York: Oxford University Press, 1996.

Soltes, Avraham. *Off the Willows: The Rebirth of Modern Jewish Music.* New York: Bloch, 1970.

Stevens, Lewis. *Composers of Classical Music of Jewish Descent.* London: Vallentine Mitchell, 2005.

Strassberg, Robert. *Ernest Bloch: Voice in the Wilderness.* Los Angeles: California State University Press, 1977.

Strom, Yale. *The Book of Klezmer: The History, the Music, the Folklore.* Chicago: Chicago Review Press, 2002.

Sulzer, Salomon. *Denkschrift.* Vienna, 1876.

Summit, Jeffery A. *The Lord's Song in a Strange Land: Music and Identity in Contemporary Jewish Worship.* New York: Oxford University Press, 2000.

Vigoda, Samuel. *Legendary Voices.* New York: M. P., 1981.

Weiner, Marc A. *Richard Wagner and the Anti-Semitic Imagination.* Lincoln: University of Nebraska Press, 1995.

Weisser, Albert. *The Modern Renaissance of Jewish Music: Events and Figures, Eastern Europe and America.* New York: Bloch, 1954.

Werner, Eric. *From Generation to Generation.* New York: American Conference of Cantors, 1967.

———. "Manuscripts of Jewish Music in the Eduard Birnbaum Collection." *Hebrew Union College Annual* (1944): 397–428.

———. *Mendelssohn: A New Image of the Composer and His Age.* Trans. Dika Newlin. New York: Free Press, 1963.

———. "The Role of Tradition in the Music of the Synagogue." *Judaism,* vol. 13, no. 2 (1964): 156–163.

———. *The Sacred Bridge: The Interdependence of Liturgy and Music in Synagogue and Church During the First Millennium.* New York: Columbia University Press, 1959.

———. *The Sacred Bridge: The Interdependence of Liturgy and Music in Synagogue and Church During the First Millennium, Vol. 2.* New York: Ktav, 1984.

———. *A Voice Still Heard...: The Sacred Songs of Ashkenazi Jews.* University Park: Pennsylvania State University Press, 1976.

———, ed. *Contributions to the Historical Study of Jewish Music.* New York: Ktav, 1972.

Whitfield, Stephen J. *In Search of American Culture.* Hanover, MA: Brandeis University Press, 1999.

Index

"A las Montañas Mi Alma!" 45
Aaron 93
Abimelech 123
Abodah 63
Abraham 85, 88, 122, 123
Adam 88
Addir Hu 68, 181
Adon Olam 160, 161, 182
Adonai Elohim 174
Adonai Melekh 46
Aeolian harp 151
Aeolian mode 63, 163, 176
African music 49, 177
Africane 159
Agrippa 86
Aguilar, Emanuel 165
Ahot Ketannah 45
The Aims of Teaching in Jewish Schools 134
Akdamut 125
Aleppo 69
Alexander the Great 84
Alexandria 92, 93, 149
Algeria 177
Algiers 91
Alhambra 90
Alkalay, Joseph 125
Alska Chasidim 98
Alt-neu Shul, Prague 50
Ambrosian Chant 163
amen 53, 60, 124
American Hebrew 160
Amidah 35, 38, 39, 42
Amsterdam 27, 69
Ancient Melodies of the Spanish and Portuguese Jews 72–73, 157
Anglican Church 160

Anti-Semitism 9
antiphony 35
Arab (Arabic) 14, 31, 38, 44, 82, 88, 92, 166, 171, 177, 180
Arabia 91, 171
Aram-Naharaim 123
Aramaic papyri 133
Archduchess Sophia 137
Archevolti, Samuel 44, 151
Arion 149
Aristotle 93
Armenian Church 36, 55, 63
art music 10, 43
Asaph 83, 85, 88
Asbein mode 180
Ashkenazi music 8, 15, 38, 40, 42, 43, 49, 61, 68, 74, 79, 158
Asia (Asian) 1, 36, 49, 97, 105
Asia Minor 37, 41, 54, 91, 177
asor 67
assimilation 79, 131
Assun 133
Auer, Leopold 110
Auerbach, Berthold 135
Austria 107, 110, 132, 135, 138, 139, 145, 162, 168
Austrian Imperial Gold Medal for Art and Science 137, 143
Austro-Hungarian empire 12
Avinu Malkeinu 13
"Avrahm, Avrahm" 113, 114, 169

Az Yashir (*Oz Yashir*) 68, 72–73, 74, 157

Baal Shem Tov, Israel 96, 97, 98
ba'al tefillah 124
Ba'al Tefillah, oder der Praktische Vorbeter 49
Babylonian exile 54, 60, 88, 91, 122, 143, 149, 168, 174
Babylonian Jews 17, 19, 36, 77
Baer, Abraham 49, 57
Baghdad 50, 55, 63, 68
Balakireff, Mily 113
Balfe, Michael William 160
Baltimore 169
banjo 88
bar Adda, Hiyya 35
Bar Kochba 165
bar mitzvah 139
Il Barbiere di Siviglia 166
Barlaam and Josephat 138
Bartók, Béla 14
Baruch She-Amar 38
Bavaria 16
Bayer, Jerome H. 133
Bayreuth 97
Bedouins 177
Beethoven, Ludwig van 13, 63, 77, 87, 94, 151, 159, 166, 175, 177
bells 11, 32, 102
Belzer, Nissi 126, 127
Belzer Chasidim 98
ben Arsa 53
ben Cherus, Gebuni 86

199

Index

ben David Portaleone, Abraham 151
ben Hananiah, Joshua 34, 53
Berakhah 39
Beril the Blind 95
Berlin 147, 167, 168
Berlin Academy of Fine Arts 132
Berlin Conservatory 167
Berlin Jewish Community 132
Beth, Lola 107
beth hammedrash 97
Binder, Abraham W. 13, 14
Birnbaum, Eduard 17–18, 47
Biscayan 49
Bizet, Georges 109
Blavatsky, Elena 96
Bloch, Ernest 173–175, 177
Bloomfield-Zeissler, Fannie 111
Blumenberg, Louis 110
"Blümlein auf Breiter Heide" 45
Bohemia 110, 162, 167, 168
Bohemian Girl 160
Bonaparte, Napoleon 94
borscht 102
Bourgault-Ducoudray, Louis-Albert 41
Braham, John 107
Brahms, Johannes 175
Brazil 165
Breslau 48
Brodsky, Adolph 110
Brounhoff, Platon 167, 169
Bruch, Max 63, 68, 73, 109
Brunswick 48
Buber, Martin 131
Bukharian Jews 17
Byron, Lord 57
Byzantine Church 36, 55, 63, 163

California 133
cantillation 14, 26, 30, 34, 35, 36, 38, 39, 40, 42, 50, 53–54, 55, 56, 57, 61, 62, 63, 70, 79, 180, 181
cantor 10, 14, 16, 21, 33, 35, 41, 58, 79, 106, 110 132, 139, 140, 142–143, 161, 180, 181, 183, 184; see also *hazzan*

Cantors Association of America 162
Cantus Pere Grinus 154
Carlsruhe 136, 140
castanets 149
Catholic Church 31, 36, 37, 42, 48, 63, 67, 154, 162, 165, 180
cello 110, 145, 172
chalil 61, 88
chazozro 84
cheder 107, 113, 115
Chicago 162
Children's Savings and Aid Society, Vienna 144
China 87
chironomy 53
choir 8, 15, 32, 34, 47–48, 49, 51, 58, 72, 94, 97, 99, 132, 183, 184, 189
Chonow 93
chorale 11, 45, 159
"Chossidl" 117
Christianity (Christian) 3, 7, 11, 20, 21, 31–32, 46, 50, 53, 55, 57, 61, 62, 67, 72, 74, 93, 128, 132, 155, 160, 163, 164, 166, 182, 183, 187, 188
Cincinnati 17, 18, 134
cithara 149
clapper 88
Clarke, Morris 169
clerical gown 11
Cohen, Francis L. 26, 49, 155, 159
Committee on Synagogue Music 26
Congregation B'nai Jeshurun, Cincinnati 134
Congregation B'nai Jeshurun, Lincoln 26
Congregation Gates of Prayer, New Orleans 78
Congregation Shearith Israel, New York 26
congregational singing 15, 32, 187–188
Consolo, S. 49, 58
Copenhagen 136
cymbals 32, 52, 88

Daghestanian Jews 77
Damrosche, Leopold and Walter 111
Daniel Deronda 109
d'Annuzio, Gabriele 173

"Danse Juive" 113, 169
Danube 105
Da Silva, Antonio José 165
David 66, 78, 83, 84, 85, 87, 88, 89, 90, 109, 149, 151, 152
David, Felicien 169
Davidow, Carl 110
Deborah 84
Debussy, Claude 175
Delitzsch, Franz 44
Demuth, Leopold 107
Denmark 107
Descartes, René 14, 64
de Sola, David A. 49, 58, 72, 157
"Dessau Marsch" 171
Deutsch, Moritz 48
Diaspora 1, 17, 19, 39, 53, 174, 178
"Dietrich von Bern" 45
"Di Gilderne Pave" 116
"Di Mesinke" 117
"Doliente Estaba Alessandri" 46
Don Giovanni 166
Don Juan 166
Door, Anton 111
Dorian mode 63, 157, 163
"Doxology" 160
Dropsie College 133
drum 88, 102
Dufay, Guillaume 44
Dvořák, Antonín 133, 172

Eastern Europe 17, 43, 57, 61, 69, 71, 77, 78, 79, 127, 159
Echad Mi Yodea 158
Eduard Birnbaum Collection 17–18
Egypt (Egyptians) 31, 69, 123, 174, 177
Ehrenkranz, Wolf 95
Eil Nora Alila 155
"Eili, Eili" 113, 114, 169
Elephantine 133
Eliezer 123
Elijah 153, 161, 178, 183
Eliot, George 109
Elisha 66
Elizabethan Period 162
Ellman, Mischa 110
Elsace and Lorraine 140
Emancipation 1, 7, 10, 20, 74
Emerson, Ralph Waldo 160

Emperor Ferdinand 143
Ems 138
En Keloheinu 46, 68, 160, 188
"En los Campos di Alvansa" 45
"En Toda La Tramontaña" 45
Encyclopedia Americana 26
Encyclopedia of Religion and Ethics 26
Engel, Carl 156, 171, 172
Engel, Julius 113
England 49, 51, 55, 107, 155, 162
Enlightenment 7; see also *Haskalah*
Episcopal Church 31
Erkel, Ferenc 167
Ernst, Heinrich Wilhelm 110
Essa 'Eni 45
Essai sur li Musique 167
Essenes 96, 98
Esther 62
Esther (oratorio) 153
Ethan 88
Euphrates 92, 123
Europeanization 11
Ezra 124

"Fasi Abassi Silvann" 45
Father Eximeno 166
"Ein feste Burg" 155
"Les Filles de Tarascon" 45
Finkelstein, Jettka 107
Finsbury Park Synagogue 73
Fischhoff, Joseph 10, 13, 141
Florence 58, 69
Florentiner Nächte 174
flute 53, 88, 149
folklore 15
Foster, Stephen 161
Fra Angelico 154
"Fra Diavolo" 46
France 107, 120, 145, 151
Frankl, August 141
Frankl, Ludwig 143
Franz Joseph Order 137, 143

Gabirol, Solomon ibn 157, 187
Gabrilowitsch, Osip 111
Galicia 47, 51, 77, 90, 96, 161, 165

Gallo-Belgic school 44
Gaon, Hai 36
Gaon, Saadia 40
Gaza 44
Genesis 83
Germany (German) 2, 9, 10, 17, 27, 30, 40, 44, 45, 46, 49, 56, 57, 69, 71, 72, 74, 78, 97, 107, 110, 120, 132, 146, 148, 151, 152, 156, 158, 159, 160, 162, 168, 171
Gerona 45
ghetto 1, 2, 7, 10, 52, 61, 72, 78, 97, 98, 103, 105, 108, 127, 133, 141, 151, 172, 175
Gideon, Henry 169
"The Girl I Left Behind Me" 46
gittith 88
"Giulianita" 46
Glazounoff, Alexander 172
Glinka, Mikhail 167
Gloria 31, 154
Gluck, Alma 113, 168
"God Save the Queen" 92, 171
Goethe, Johann Wolfgang von 14
Goldberg, Abraham 106
Goldfaden, Abraham 95, 165
Goldmark, Karl 61, 109
Golus 70; see also Diaspora
Gothenberg 49, 58
Gottheil, Gustav 160
gramophone 55
Great Synagogue, Australia 26
Greece (Greek) 31, 34, 44, 54, 55, 59, 66, 69, 84, 88, 93, 161, 163, 171
Gregorian chant 31, 42, 55, 56, 64, 154, 163
Gregorowitsch, Charles 110
Grieg, Edvard 167
Grisi, Giuditta 106, 107
Grisi, Guilia 106, 107
Grossman, Louis 134
Gruen, Jacob 110
Gruenfeld, Heinrich 110
Gusikow, Michael Joseph 110
Gutman, Elizabeth 113, 169
Guttman, Adolph 132

Gypsies 36, 43, 47, 63, 71, 176, 180–181

Had Gadya 158
The Hague 69
Ha Kalir, Lazar 93
ha-Levi, Jacob Mölln 50
ha-Levi, Judah 44, 157, 187
Halévy, Fromental 49, 109, 120
Hallel 73, 154, 162
Hallelujah 60, 77, 87, 89, 152
Hamburg 69
Handel, George Frideric 71, 74, 151, 153, 160, 161, 178
Hanosri, Sirach 96
Hanslick, Franz 142
Hanukkah 45, 68, 155, 159, 160
harp 32, 48, 53, 88
Harvard University 4
Ha Shirim Asher Li-Shelomo 47
Hasidism (Chasidism) 17, 21, 71, 77, 78, 79, 96–105, 161, 169
Haskalah 9, 68; see also Enlightenment
Hasmoneans 52
Hatikvah 73, 74, 77, 162, 170
Hauser, Mishka 110
Haydn, Joseph 151, 159
hazzan 35, 37, 41, 44, 45, 46, 47, 48, 51, 53, 57, 62, 69, 71, 73, 79, 94, 95, 97, 122–129, 135, 136, 137, 155, 161; see also cantor
Hazzan, Abraham 45
hazzanut 17, 18, 36, 38, 42, 43, 49, 55–56, 63, 79, 122–129, 139, 163
Hebrew Melodies 49, 57
Hebrew Standard 85, 92
Hebrew Teachers Seminary 16
Hebrew Union College 17, 18, 134
"Heil dir im Siegerkranz" 171
Heine, Heinrich 14, 101, 174
Heinefetter, Clara 106, 107
Heinefetter, Eva 107

Index

Heinefetter, Fatime 107
Heinefetter, Kathinka 107
Heinefetter, Sabine 107
Hellenism 92, 149
Heman 83, 88, 89
Henschel, George 107
Herod 52
Herschel, William 97
High Holy Days 15, 63;
  see also Rosh Hashanah;
  Yom Kippur
Higros 147, 148
Hiller, Ferdinand 30
Hindemith, Paul 14
Hirschfeld, Franziska 145
Hodo Al Eretz 15
Hodu L'adonai 158
Hoffman, Joseph 111
Hogras (Hugras) 53, 57, 8 6
Hohenems 136, 138, 139, 140, 145
Hollaender, Gustav 110
Homer 87
"L'Homme Armé" 45
Horace Mann Auditorium 78
Hubermann, Bronislaw 110
Hucbald 164
Hugo, Victor 175
Huguenots 159
Hülfsverein 167
Hungary (Hungarian) 47, 107, 110, 161, 167, 168, 176, 180–181, 183
hymns 11, 12, 14, 30, 44, 45, 46, 56, 57, 62, 63, 125, 132, 134, 157, 181, 186–187, 188
Hymns and Anthems Adapted for Jewish Worship 160
Hypodorian mode 63, 71, 157

ibn Ezra, Abraham 36, 44
ibn Misgah 171
iconoclasm 52
Idelsohn, Abraham Z. 2–3, 4, 8, 9, 11, 15–20, 25, 131–132, 157, 167
Imber, Naphtali Herz 77–78
Imperial Russian Gold Medal for Art and Science 137, 143
India 36, 52, 54, 55

"Innsbruck, I Must leave Thee" 55, 56
Institute for the Blind, Vienna 144
instrumental music 50, 53, 59–60, 67, 85, 149, 159
introit 43
Iraq 171
Irish Melodies 58
Isaac 123
Isaacs, Louis M. 26, 68
Isaak, Heinrich 45
Islam 128
Israel 174
Israel in Egypt 178
Italy (Italian) 27, 40, 44, 47–48, 57, 63, 71, 107, 145, 151, 161, 165, 166, 181

Jacob 148
Jacobson, Israel 11
Jacobson, Sam L. 25–26
Janina 69
Jassinowsky, Pinchos 79, 113, 169
Jedutan 85, 88
Jellinek, Adolph 135, 143, 146
Jericho 67, 86, 149, 151
Jerusalem 12, 15–16, 44, 68, 85, 91, 92, 93, 105, 143, 147, 149, 167
Jesus Christ 92, 101, 154
Jewish Achievement 78
Jewish Encyclopedia 26
Jewish Exponent 96
Jewish Liturgy and Its Development 18
Jewish Music Forum 1
Jewish Music in Its Historical Development 2, 18
Jewish Spirit 4, 9, 16
Joachim, Joseph 110
Job 54, 62, 89, 91, 133
Johannesburg 16
Joseph, Franz 137, 143
"Joshua" 113, 173
Jubal 67
Judah 48
Judas Maccabeus 160, 178
Judea 170
Das Judenthum in der Musik 169

Kabbalah (Cabala) 78, 96, 101
Kaddish 35, 46

Kaiserstadt 135
Kalir, Eliezer 125
Kalisch, Paul 107
Karpeles, Gustav 132–133
Kepler, Johannes 97
Ki Eshmera Shabbat 157–158
Ki Mitziyon 15
Kiddush 137
Kiev 79
Kindler, Hans 172
kinnor 67, 88, 149
klaus 97, 98, 99, 100, 103
klezmer 151, 164
klipos 102
Koenig, Sophie 107
Koenigsberg 17, 18
Kohn, Maier 48
Kol Nidrei 63, 68, 73–74, 155, 178
Kol Rinnah u-Tefillah 49
Korach 83, 88, 89, 147
Koran 38, 63, 82, 97, 180
koreh 53
Krehbiel, Henry Edward 73
Krein, Alexander 172
"Krodos Yar, Yar, Yar" 45
kultus-gemeinde 127

Lamech 83, 148
Lamentations 70
Landau, Leonard 106
Latvia 15, 16
Laub, Ferdinand 110
Ledavid Barch 158
Leeser, Isaac 157, 158
Lefkowitz, Henry 169
Leipzig Academy 16
"Leoni" 63, 155, 178
Levant (Levantine) 45, 51
Levitical choir 47, 53, 66, 78, 84, 85, 86, 122, 126, 150
Lewandowski, Louis 21, 32, 49, 51, 58, 64, 106, 132–133, 147, 159, 165, 186
Lewry Brothers 110
Libro dei Conti d'Israele 49
Liebling, George 111
lieder 10
Liszt, Franz 9, 133, 137, 142, 143, 161, 172
Lithuania 120
"The Little Maid" 45
London 27, 47, 49–50, 57, 69, 125, 158

Lonsano, Menachem 151
Lotto, Isidor 110
Löw, Leopold 164
Lucca, Pauline 107
lute 32
Luther, Martin 45, 152, 155

Maccabean revolt 62
Maccabees 150
Macedonia 149
"Macht der Chossidl" 169
machzor 44, 157
Mahler, Gustav 16, 172
Maimonides, Moses 14, 123–124
Manchester 27, 69
Manizer, Joseph 9
Mannheimer, Isaac Noah 11–12, 14, 136, 140, 141
Mantua 57
Maoz Tzur 45, 46, 68, 158–159, 182
"Mar li Mar Mar Mar" 45
"La Marseillaise" 46
Mascagni, Pietro 161
masoretic accents 54, 70
Mass 56
Maximilian of Bavaria 143
Mayence 43
mazurka 115, 120
Mecca 171
Medjidie Order 137, 143
"Meet Me by the Moonlight Alone" 158
"Meierke, Mein Sun" 113
Meir of Worms 125
Melchisedech 88
melisma 41
melos 13
Mendelssohn, Felix 16, 90, 109, 133, 153, 159, 161, 172, 178
Menorah Journal 26, 133, 135
"Meromi 'al Mah 'Am Rab Homah" 45
meshorerim 47, 84, 164
Messiah 92
Messiah (oratorio) 166
Methodist Church 160
Metropolitan Opera 107
Meyer, Jenny 107
Meyerbeer, Giacomo 49, 90, 95, 109, 137, 159, 172
Michelangelo 154
military band 50
Milner, Moses 113, 172

Milton, John 95
minim 88
minnesinger 43, 56, 63
Miriam 68, 73, 84
Miserere 153
Mishna 54
Mixolydian mode 31, 63, 71
Mizmor Shir 45
Moawiya the First 171
Modena, Leon de 47, 57
modernization 7, 8, 64, 72–73
Modinha 165
Mohammed 82, 102
Mölln, Jacob ben Moses 43
Moniuszko, Stanislaw 166
Montreal 27, 69
Moody-Sankey tunes 160
Moor (Moorish) 27, 36, 49, 51, 61, 71, 90, 91, 156, 157, 170
Moore, Thomas 58
Moriah 149
Morocco 17, 77, 91, 168, 177
Moscato, Judah 151
Moscow 110, 113
Moses 67, 73, 82, 83, 84, 88, 91, 124, 184
mosque 97
Mozarabian Christians 38
Mozart, Wolfgang Amadeus 94, 151, 153, 159, 166, 175, 176
Muehlmann, Adolf 107–108
"Muerame mi Alma ai!" 45
muezzin 19
Muggletonians 155
Munich 48, 136
music education 29–30, 186–189
Music Magazine 26
musicology 3, 4, 8, 17, 18, 20, 21
Muslims 19, 43
Mussorgsky, Modest 112, 173
"My Country" 171
mystics 100–102, 104–105

Nadel, Arno 168
Najara, Israel 44
Napoleonic Wars 64
Nathan, Colestine 107

Nathan, Isaac 49
nationalism 2, 15, 84, 156
Naumbourg, Samuel 32, 49, 58, 64, 106, 186
nebel 67, 88
Nebuchadnezzer 122
neginoth 62
negoh 88
Nehemiah 34, 53
ne'imah 40
neumes 55, 62
New Synagogue, London 50
New York 26, 27, 47, 69, 78, 107, 112, 113, 158, 161, 162, 169, 172, 173
New York Tribune 73
Ney, David 107
niggun 40, 104
Nineveh 47, 57
Nishmat 38
Nissen, Henrietta 107
"Nito kein Mame" 114
Norway 167
Notker Balbulus 39
Le Nozze di Figaro 166
Nuremburg 152
nusach ha-tefillah 12, 13; see also synagogue modes

"O World, I Must Soon Leave Thee" 45
Oberon 166
The Occident 158
Odessa 108
Offenbach, Jacques 77, 87, 95, 109
"Oif'n Pripetshok" 115
Oko, Adolph 18
"Old Black Joe" 161
"Old One Hundred" 160
Olitska, Rosa 107
On the Moldau 166, 170
opera 106–108, 158, 159, 161
oral tradition 19, 56
oratorio 159, 161, 177
Orenstein, Leo 172
organ 8, 14, 32, 50, 149
Orient (Oriental) 2–3, 13, 39, 41, 46, 48, 59, 61, 62, 63, 67, 71, 97, 104, 105, 120, 147, 154, 156, 157, 163, 169, 170, 173, 177
Oriental Sephardic Jews 17
Orpheus 149

Orthodox Judaism 57, 67, 85, 90, 94, 136, 184
"Otavorite vorata" 168

Palestine 16, 17, 74, 93, 120, 122, 164, 167, 170, 177
Palestrina, Giovanni Pierluigi da 64, 71, 165
Paris 49, 58, 69, 106
"Partant pour la Syrie" 158
"Partistas Amiga" 45
Passover 68, 154, 158
Pasta, Giuditta 107
"Pavierweiss" 45
payyetanim 63
Peixotto, Benjamin Franklin 132
pentatonic scale 63
Pentecost 86
"Perdone di amor" 45
"Permetid Bella Amaryllis" 45, 157
Persia 84, 88, 90, 93, 168, 171
Persian Jews 17, 77
Perso-Arabs 36, 39, 43, 55, 62, 63
Pethahiah of Regensberg 50, 55
Pharisees 92
Philadelphia 69
Philistines 66
Phrygian mode 63
pilpul 46, 125
piyyut 35, 42, 157, 161
pizmon 46
plainsong 37, 39, 55
"Plaint of the Women of America" 113, 173
"Un Poggio Tiene la Contessa" 45
Poland (Polish) 41, 47, 49, 51, 64, 72, 90, 91, 92, 94, 97, 100, 107, 110, 115, 117, 120, 136, 161, 167
polka 120
polyphony 48, 72, 175
Pool, David de Sola 26–27, 162
Pope Benedict XVI 25
Popper, David 110
"Porque No Me Hablas" 45
prayer book 30
Priestly Benediction 46
Prophete 159

Protestantism 11, 12, 13, 14, 45, 46, 74, 132, 152, 155
Provence 49
Proverbs 54, 62, 89
Psalms 10, 21, 35, 36, 42, 43, 51, 52, 54, 55, 60, 62, 67, 77–78, 82–95, 101, 103, 137, 151, 152
psaltery 67, 88, 149
Pskoff 112
"Pues Vos Me Feristes" 45
Purim 86, 150
Pyrker, Archbishop 143

rabbis 7, 11, 25, 32, 47, 50, 57, 63, 71, 85, 97, 127, 150, 164
Rabinowitz, Abraham Mordecai 16
Rachmaninoff, Sergei 110, 120
raga 54, 55
"Rakoczi-March" 161
Ramsgate 69
Rashi 125
Ravel, Maurice 113, 168
recitative 13–14, 133
Red Sea 66, 73, 174
Reform Judaism 7, 8, 11, 12, 13, 14, 26, 48, 57, 74, 94, 127, 132, 159, 160, 178
Regensberg 16, 50
Reider, Joseph 133
Renaissance 64, 151, 154, 155
"Ein Retenis" 118
retrenchment 7
Reuchin, Johannes 56, 57
Rhineland 49
Rimsky-Korsakov, Nikolai 113, 121, 172
Robert le Diable 159
Romania 110, 117
Rome (Romans) 62, 86, 93, 122, 143, 153, 165, 173
Rose, Arnold 110
Rosenthal, Moritz 111
Rosh Hashanah (New Year's Day) 32, 46, 94, 98
"Rosinkes mit Mandlin" 114
Rossi, Salomon de 47, 57, 64, 151, 165

Rossini, Gioachino 159, 166
Rosumowsky, Andrej 166
Roth, Philip 110
Rothauser, Therese 107
Rothmuehl, Nicholaus 107
Royal Horse Guards 50
Rubens, Peter Paul 154
Rubin, Ruth 77
Rubinstein, Anton 61, 90, 110, 111, 121, 172
Russia (Russian) 2, 21, 49, 51, 69, 71, 72, 74, 78, 90, 91, 93, 94, 96, 97, 100, 107, 110, 112–121, 127, 156, 161, 165, 166, 167, 168, 170, 172, 173

Sachs, Curt 1
Sadducees 92
Sahud, Isaac 125
St. Cecilie Movement 162
St. Gall 39
St. Paul 161
St. Petersburg 167
Saint-Saens, Camille 169
Salvation Army 33, 96, 155
San Francisco 162
Sanctus 154
Satan 98, 102
Saul 66
Scarlatti, Domenico 71
Schindler, Kurt 78–79, 169
Schir Zion 10, 12, 13, 48, 68, 128, 132, 137, 141, 145
Schlomo 174
Schoenberg, Arnold 16, 173
Schola Cantorum 113, 169
Schubert, Franz 10, 13, 27, 49, 74, 137, 141, 143
Schumann, Robert 143
Scribian, Alexander 175
Seesen, Germany 11
"Sehnsucht" 168
Seitenstettengasse Temple 10, 142
selah 89
selichot 106
Semitic people 2–3, 91, 178
Sendrey, Alfred 18
"Señora" 56
Sephardic music 27, 37, 38, 40, 42, 43, 45, 49,

60, 69, 72, 73, 74, 77, 90, 91, 155, 156, 157, 158, 166
sermon 8, 11, 101
Seyfried, Ignaz von 10, 13, 141, 143
shaarat ha-ari 126
Shabbat (Sabbath) 41, 43, 57, 63, 83, 101–102, 103, 127, 137, 139, 140, 142, 143, 155, 158
Shakespeare, William 87
Shalit, Heinrich 113, 172
Sharlin, William 4, 10, 15
Sharon 170
Shavuot 125
She'eh Ne'esor 46
Shelemay, Kay Kaufman 16
sheliach tzibbur 53, 124
Shem Nora 45, 56
Shema Yisrael 15, 35, 42, 123
shiminith 88
shir 82, 84, 88, 89, 170
Shir ha-Ma'alot (Song of Ascents) 46, 68, 88, 162
Shir Todah 45
Shitomirsky, Alexander 113, 172
Shklyar, Ephraim 113, 172
shofar 32, 52, 60, 61, 67, 84, 88, 178, 184
shokhet 16
Shulamith 165
Shushan 88
"Si alte Kashe" 119
siciliana 161
Sicily 125
Sievers, Eduard 177
Silber, Mendel 78
Simchat Torah 117
Sinai 67, 94, 104, 105
Singer, Jacob 26
Singer, Joseph 31
Sistine Chapel 153
skarbowa 40
Slav 40, 43, 64, 71, 156, 161
Smetana, Bedrich 162, 166, 170
Society for Jewish Folk-Music 113, 168
Society of American Cantors 162
Söderland 167
Sodom 123
"Song of Solomon" 113, 173
Song of Songs 70

Sontheim, Heinrich 107
Soup and Tea Institute, Vienna 144
South Africa 16
Spain (Spanish) 44, 49, 56, 71, 125, 145, 156, 157
Spanish Hidalgos 91
Spanish-Portuguese Jews 26, 68, 120, 168, 170
Spinoza, Baruch 14
Stanford University 4
steiger 40
Stern Conservatory, Berlin 16
Strakosch, Ludwig 107
Strauss, Johann 15
Strauss, Richard 173
Sulz 136, 139
Sulzer, Fannie 136
Sulzer, Joseph (Salomon's father) 136, 139
Sulzer, Joseph (Salomon's son) 110
Sulzer, Salomon 3, 4, 8, 9–15, 17, 20, 26, 32, 48–49, 58, 68, 106, 128, 132, 135–146, 159, 165, 186
sura 82
Susa 47, 57
Svengali 105
Sweden 167
Switzerland 136, 139, 140, 145, 173
synagogue modes 12, 30, 36, 37, 38, 39–40, 41, 54, 61, 64, 79, 126, 133, 180; see also *nusach ha-tefillah*
Syracuse 132
Syria 71, 168

taf 84, 88
Talmud 52, 54, 86, 92–93, 97, 101, 107, 136, 147, 163
tambourine 102
Tannhauser 160
Tarters 71
Tausig, Karl 111
Te Deum 31
tefillah 89
Temple (Jerusalem) 20, 25, 34, 35, 38, 39, 47, 53, 55, 57, 60–61, 66, 78, 79, 84, 85, 86, 90, 92, 106, 109, 122, 126, 149, 150, 163

Temple Emmanuel, New York 160
"Temprano Naces Almendro" 45, 157
Ten Commandments 67
Theosophy 96, 104
Thesaurus of Hebrew Oriental Melodies 2, 15, 16–17, 18, 20
Titus 122
Todah we-Zimrah 49
tonic-dominant system 13
Torah (Pentateuch) 15, 34, 62, 66, 70, 82–83
La Traviata 46
"Tres Colores in Una" 45, 157
Tripoli 177
"Les Trois Rois" 45
troubadour 43, 63
trouvère 43
trumpet 32, 53, 143
Tschaikowsky, Peter Ilyitch 133, 172
Tunis 91
Turkey (Turkish) 44, 45, 49, 71, 90, 137, 151, 173
Twain, Mark 111

ugab 67, 149
Ukraine 120, 166
Ulhand, Ludwig 140
Union Hymnal 160
United States of America 17, 26, 51, 55, 58, 78, 79, 100, 105, 107, 113, 127, 133, 137, 143, 153–162, 168
University of California, Los Angeles 4
University of Michigan 4
University of New Mexico 78
Ur-Tradition 18
Urmelos 19

"El Vaquero de la Morayña" 45
Venice 47
Verdi, Giuseppe 27, 74
Vieniawski, Joseph 111
Vienna 3, 8, 10, 11, 12, 15, 31, 48, 106, 108, 132, 135, 137, 140, 141, 142–143, 144, 146
Vienna Academy of Science 16

Index

Vienna Congregation 136
Vienna Conservatory of Music 144
Vienna Men's Choir 136, 140
Vienna Opera House 145
Vienna Rite 12
violin 88, 109, 149
Virgil 87
Voice of Prayer and Praise 49
Volga 105
Voltaire, François-Marie 169
von Bülow, Hans 175
Voralberg 136, 139
Vorbeterschule 48

Wagner, Richard 27, 74, 77, 87, 94, 97, 103, 160, 169
Die Walküre 78, 87
"Der Wanderer" 10
Warsaw 110
Watts, Isaac 160
Weintraub, Hirsch 17, 48
Werner, Eric 1, 12, 14, 15
Wesley, John 155, 160
West Indies 69
Western music 3, 8, 10, 12, 13, 14, 20, 78, 105, 132
Westmorland, Lord 137
Whittier, John Greenleaf 160
Wise, Isaac Mayer 134
Wissenschaft des Judenthums (Science of Judaism) 8, 16, 131
"World, I Soon Must Leave Thee" 56
World's Exposition, Vienna 132, 135

Ya'alat ha-mor 45
Yaaleh 161
Yasser, Joseph 1
Yemen 91, 92, 95
Yeminite Jews 17, 19, 55, 77, 90, 157, 168
Yeshiva 107, 122
Yigdal 155, 160, 182
Yom Kippur (Day of Atonement) 32, 63, 68, 73, 94, 98, 149, 155, 161, 173

zemirot 46
Zemirot Yisrael 49
zilzal 88
Zimbalist, Ephraim 113, 169
Zimrath Ya Society 169
Zion 12, 35, 47, 86, 90, 91, 93, 104, 143, 147
Zionism 68, 77, 162, 165, 170
Zohar 59, 100
Zunz, Leopold 148

www.ingramcontent.com/pod-product-compliance
Lightning Source LLC
Chambersburg PA
CBHW032058300426
44116CB00007B/792